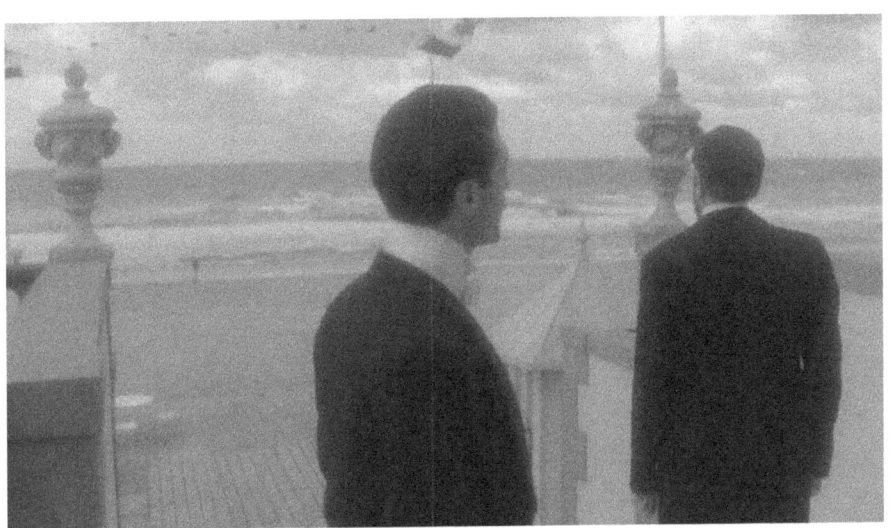

In *Time Regained* (1999), the film made from Marcel Proust's 'In Search of Lost Time', Marcel in middle age looks at Marcel in older age gazing at Marcel as a boy running along the edge of the sea at Balbec in Normandy (see p.146).

FILM PAST, FILM FUTURE:

an enquiry into cinema and the imagination

by Tim Cawkwell

Sforzinda Books

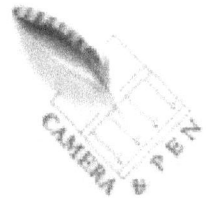

Published by Sforzinda Books

30 Eaton Road

Norwich NR4 6PZ

www.timcawkwell.co.uk

www.cawkwell200.com

First edition in digital format 2011

Second edition as paperback 2019

Copyright © Tim Cawkwell 2011 and 2019

Set in Garamond 10 pt

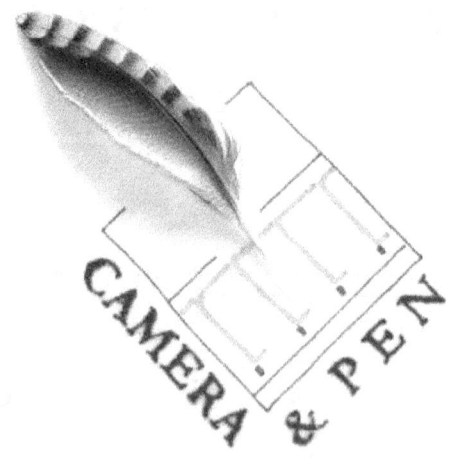

"The work of art on the stage is inexorably bound to synthesize; in the cinema on the other hand the multiplicity of the details assert themselves as ideas unrestrained by any impediment . . . It is a false premise to adopt theatrical methods for an art which is utterly dissimilar . . . On the stage, the picture stays fixed; in the cinema, it is perpetually on the move. One of its remarkable properties is to focus movement, expression and attitudes on the infinite, in pursuit of changing spaces and settings, by the multiplication of scenes and the incessant displacing of the spectator . . . We should discern the eventual difference between the cinema, which is a living, airy creation, and the theatre, whose principle is by contrast the imitation of nature."

André Antoine (1858-1943) writing circa 1920, quoted in Georges Sadoul, Dictionnaire des Cinéastes, *Éditions du Seuil (Paris) 1965*

CONTENTS

INTRODUCTION AND PROSPECT

How true is it that the British value films solely for their theatrical qualities – for their screenplays and for the acting, in effect seeing films only as illustrations of these virtues? While few people in other countries might openly espouse such opinions, the British seem more ready to take this view than others. The Americans like films for themselves: they invented and developed the cinema; it is (they might argue) their greatest contribution so far to culture. The French quickly embraced the cinema in an intellectual way – can you be literate in France without being cine-literate? And in the Far East, the astonishing riches of Japanese and other national cinemas reveal a film culture of great depth that could only have come about through the urgent interest of film directors and producers responding to a public thirst for cinema and in order to project a national presence in the means best suited to the modern age. By contrast the British seem lukewarm, devoted to a theatrical tradition enriched by Shakespeare and the other Elizabethans, by the creation of acting schools from which superlative actors have emerged, and in the twentieth century by an efflorescence of new drama to reinvigorate the tradition. As a result have they been too preoccupied with appreciating and digesting these things to take the cinema as more than a means of diffusing theatrical values? It is only in Britain surely that George Steiner, a noted thinker and academic, would take the view that a film would exhaust its meaning in four or five viewings at best, whereas a great work of literature is inexhaustible [as proposed by him on the BBC Radio 3 programme, 'Private Passions', June 2002].

Facetiously, one can summarise the British contribution to film culture as an oblique one: at Christmas 2002, three film blockbusters were on release. The first, *The Two Towers*, the second part of the *Lord of the Rings* trilogy, was taken from an epically imaginative book by an Englishman, written and structured with exemplary narrative clarity, and informed at every turn by ideas of Englishness; second, *Harry Potter and the Chamber of Secrets* was a story set in a boarding school, that peculiar British institution; and the third, *Die Another Day*, featured James Bond, a product of that boarding-school system, smooth and elegant certainly, something of a superman but also something of a bastard. Although all three films were internationally produced and financed, it was bemusing to realize that all three expressed something inherently British even under the layers of mass global culture: so this was the British contribution to the art of film – Ian McKellen as Gandalf in *The Two Towers*, a bevy of British actors in Harry Potter, Pierce Brosnan (a masquerading Irishman, actually) as the incarnation of James Bond in *Die Another Day*.

In reality, there is a lively film culture in Britain: in Alfred Hitchcock, Britain produced arguably the greatest film director of the twentieth century; British film directors continue to emerge and be taken seriously; study of the cinema has invaded the university; critical writing about films, while it can be stultifying, can be lively as well. I use the situation in Britain as a way of open-ing up a large area of study – how does film engage the imagination? This ques-tion seems especially pertinent here because of the strength of its literary tradi-tion, giving the word a primacy over the visual – and it is in words, this tradition asserts, that the imagination is truly set free. So my initial question is a simple one: if the value of art is to enlarge the imagination, how highly can we value film? Writing, especially poetry, releases its meaning in a process that involves both writer and reader. Can a film ever do something similar, that is, take on an enlarged sense as a result of a process involving both maker and viewer? This idea quickly leads on to another, larger question: what is the 'essence of cine-ma'? What is it that makes it unique as an art form, as good as written fiction, as painting, as opera, but different?

In trying to answer this, we find ourselves on a journey, picaresque in places, as I trawl through a variety of answers. First of all, it seemed to me that what films were particularly good at was suspense, whether understood as 'What will the ending be?' or as 'We know the ending, but how do we reach it?'. Films are not uniquely good, because narrative fiction is full of page-turners, books we can't put down. But the suspense film seen in the cinema can com-mand attention to the point of tyranny and of exhaustion. Secondly, in arguing against the film closing the imagination, I then started to think of ways in which it opened it, allowing us to experience the world in new ways. This followed a path through the thicket of film's seemingly natural home territory of horror, sex and violence, the crude but potent explorations of the sub-conscious in the horror film and its links with the gothic and surrealist imaginations, an idea which leads naturally to the realm of the sexual imagination and to the attraction of violence on screen. And reflecting on violence leads to a consideration of the specific genre of the battle movie, one that the cinema has made its own, as an example of how film-making can imaginatively recreate onscreen the face of battle – and show how it is fought in the mind as much as with the body. This leads into still darker and more difficult territory, for it is the cinema that has done more than any other art form to engage audiences with the nature of Hit-ler's war against the Jews and the resulting Holocaust. Detractors would say that there is a meretricious core to this process, because those who did not ex-perience it cannot understand it, and those who try to recreate it can never truly do so. To counter this my argument is that the attempt has to be made (and not just in the cinema), that the story of film-makers engaging with the Holo-caust has been enormously fruitful, not just in educating people, but in turning the questions of true and false representation into a lively, enriching and neces-sary debate. "We have learnt much but still know very little, yet the less we real-ise we know, the wiser we get."

These are areas of subject matter. Part Two then turns to questions of production, of the way films are made, which for some people is as opaque a process as the composition of music is for me: this does not stop me finding music indispensable, just as people can enjoy films immensely without under-standing the mechanics, but to get an understanding, even partial, of the artifice involved in making films, which often in the case of feature films entails hundreds of creative decisions, is to get some illumination of how a shot or a sequence may have special qualities. I start with humans performing for the camera, which is different to performing on the stage, and ask what is the essence of their performance that makes film acting special. There are two poles in screen presence – at one end is the complexity in expression that audiences used to the theatre expect from actors, and at the other is 'non-performance' amounting to suppression of the ego, which I call 'Bressonian' after its articulate practitioner, the French film director Robert Bresson – so which of these is better? In chapter 5, 'It's in the acting', I weigh the virtues of both, although I confess to a particular bias in favour of suppression of actorly ego even while realizing that this is unrealistic, for the Bressonian style may be an ideal but it is hardly practicable it seems: the aim should therefore be for a middle way, with director and actor collaborating on finding the nuances appropriate to a particular character or narrative in which the inexpressive may play a crucial role.

Discussion of acting then leads to consideration of the role of other collaborators. Is the essence of cinema in its hybridity, i.e. in the way it deploys words, theatrical effects, visual effects, musical reinforcement? Instead of making that an aesthetic stumbling block, does it make it something of special value to the cinema? I turn away from this, because it seems to lead back to the notion that as an art form the cinema is of a second order: it is not just hybrid, but bastard, somehow lacking purity. Of the elements that make up this impure mix, I want to single out the fact that film's essence is in giving motion to still photographs and then in the way images are placed in sequence in order to allow not just words and human expressivity but also time and space to reveal meaning. Even so, I realise I am on questionable ground here, because why should the contribution of actors, of screenwriters, of film composers (for example) be made secondary to that of directors working with their cameramen and their editors? My answer is that acting or writing or composing do not need the cinema in order to flourish, whereas camerawork and editing (or 'montage' to use a word that now feels old-fashioned and precious) are skills proper to the cinema and no other art form. This rather defensive argument then leads into two much more positive areas. The first is the way film narrative can manipulate time in new and interesting ways, giving yet another essence of cinema, something it can do uniquely well. I attempt to categorize the major strategies for deepening narration through the manipulation of cinematic time. Secondly, I honour the French film-maker, Georges Méliès, as the earliest film-maker to recognize the creative possibilities of manipulating film not just in sequencing images but in sequencing frames, and from there focus on Stan Brakhage to make an initial exploration of the way 'underground', 'experimental', 'avant-garde' film has shown how cinema might learn to develop new ways in which we experience our interior world. This leads to a discussion of how film currently depicts interior states and how it might do so more richly. Again I categorize some of the strategies available to do this. In the final chapter I reflect speculatively on a forthcoming golden age for the cinema where its present potential for expressiveness superseding its theatrical origins might be realised. Reference is made to the way we watch films now (cinema, dvd, internet, even the handheld screen) and the way films are breaking out of the two-hour format, getting both (much) shorter and (much) longer. In embarking on the long view, I propose an aesthetic history in triads: pre-classical, classical, post-classical, and explore this in painting and in music. This is at the formal level, and I explore how the triad might be applied to the first 110 years of cinema. At the level of content, I map out a triad applicable to the cinema of prelapsarian (delight in the new toy of cinema, innocence, spectacle), lapsarian (the creation of genre, the rediscovery of realism, innocence questioned and encroached, serious social engagement), and postlapsarian (innocence overwhelmed, postmodern emptiness, the prevalence of musical *ostinato* to accompany emotive states). I then speculate on how we need to invent canons for a classical cinema, and I put the kite-flying question of what would be the conditions in which a Shakespeare of the cinema might emerge, one condition for which is a culture that honours the classical canons of restraint, proportion, seriousness and a creative drive to explore the potential of film language.

*

In trying to reach some conclusions, I give a general overview of film history. Despite the fact that too many films are made each year in too many countries for anything truly all-encompassing to be possible, yet any attempt to show what the possibilities of the cinema might be must try to draw on the riches that are now piled up over twelve decades from every continent. Secondly, the primary purpose of film has been to entertain audiences by the telling of stories, but in any assessment of what the cinema is capable of, other kinds of film should not be overlooked: documentaries, animated film, 'film poems', short narratives and so on.

An obstacle is my own formation in the 1960s and 1970s. While this was fruitful because of the contemporary debates taking place in film appreciation at the time and because of the possibilities being opened up by cinematic experimentation, at the same time it has posed a barrier towards appreciating the decades that came after: preconceptions and prejudices began to get in the way. My first engagement with the cinema in a reflective way – beyond the passionate devouring of films as a teenager – was shaped in two particular ways. Early on, I got a sense, but from reading what particularly I cannot remember, of something very valuable having been lost with the demise of the silent cinema before the advent of sound, as if the cinema could only be defined in terms of images in sequence without any sounds attached. Secondly, I came to cine-literacy as the auteur theory was coming into its own, and the notion of the director of the narrative film as a primary author stuck with me for a long time. When I was led to an appreciation of what countercultural American film-makers were doing, these two ideas – an obsession with the image before the word and the valuing of a single author – seem to me to have been truly embodied in a new generation of non-commercial film-makers. Yet both ideas, if not completely overthrown, now have a dated feel. The first was the subject of an effective polemic in VF Perkins's 'Film as Film' while the auteur theory has had to be considerably modified, not just in recognition of its excesses, but in an enhanced appreciation of the range of contributions that go into making a film. More radically, the contemporary reluctance in some quarters to accept any authorial presence in created works has contributed to this process.

This education in film during the 1960s, when I was most impressionable, happens to have coincided with what has been argued to be the demise of classical cinema. A noted analysis of this, at least with regard to Hollywood, is the subject of 'The Classical Hollywood Cinema: film style and mode of production to 1960' by Bordwell, Staiger and Thompson. Dates are tyrannical things – British history is more than iconic dates such as 1066, 1485, 1688, 1945 and so on – and to select 1960 as the cut-off date for classical cinema is an obfuscation. Yet it reveals as well. Something did happen around then to change the face of the cinema, whether it be the epiphany of New Waves in Europe, the erosion of the studio system in Hollywood, the coming of age for television, or the advent of the radical individual film. It is in the 1960s onwards that the seedlings of a cinema of hyperbole, of a mannerist cinema, began to appear that grew into the spreading oaks of several decades later, for example *The Godfather, Perfect Storm, The Thin Red Line, The Road to Perdition, Public Enemies*. If I evince a nostalgia for classical cinema, it may only be because I admire the generation before mine that shaped my world. But there may be a more objective desire as well, for a means of expression that uses constrained resources imaginatively, that sees the shortage of money or a lack of technical means as an opportunity rather than a difficulty, because creativity is thrown back on what it should always focus on before all else: how is the image framed, and how are images sequenced? Over time, I have come to appreciate the necessity of a return to engaging with narrative cinema, not just because the commercial cinema keeps narrative at the forefront, but because the making and receiving of stories are fundamental human activities, and inevitably engage both one's youth and one's maturity, with the added pleasure of re-engagement as one grows older.

Finally, it may be felt that too much of what I have written here, in striving to achieve a catholicity of taste, is essentially dilettante, that I have not truly shown what are the possibilities of cinema. I concede that such a task is impossible because it entails predicting the future, but in trying to sketch out the essential elements of film, I believe fruitfully creative possibilities may be suggested.

Literature and the power of words have shaped our thoughts and imaginations so deeply that in many cultures the written word is an essential bedrock to how we understand them. This has happened most notably with poetry, which I was taught to consider as 'concentrated sound and sense'. One of the ways I have understood this is to think of poetic phrases, lines and whole poems as containing potential as much as actual energy, a sustained power that reverberates down the decades and centuries, a process in which extended time has been important. In trying to realise the possibilities for the young art of cinema we need, I conclude, to create films of 'concentrated image and meaning' that can then release their own energy over the coming decades and centuries.

Films and topics discussed (films in **bold** receive more extended analysis):

PART ONE

c.1:   THE POTENCY OF SUSPENSE

Lord of the Rings (Jackson, 2001-3)/ *Birth of a Nation* (Griffith, 1914)/ *Napole-on* (Gance, 1926)/ *Ben-Hur* (Niblo, 1926)/ Hitchcock: ***Blackmail*** (1928) and ***Saboteur*** (1942)/ ***Touching the Void*** (MacDonald, 2003) & ***A Man Escaped*** (Bresson, 1956) & ***The Pianist*** (Polanski, 2003)

c.2:   UNLEASHING THE IMAGINATION: HORROR, SEX, VIOLENCE

The intensity of the cinema: Kipling and Primo Levi/ Horror: *Ringu*/*The Ring* (Nakata, 1998)/ *The Blair Witch Project* (Myrick & Sánchez, 1999)/ *Black Sunday* (Mario Bava, 1960)/ *Repulsion* (Polanski, 1965)/ *The Wild Bunch* (Peckinpah, 1969)/ *Faust* (Svankmayer, 1994)/ *Les Yeux sans visage* (Franju, 1959)

Desire: *Casablanca* (Curtiz, 1943)/ ***Build My Gallows High/Out of the Past*** (Tourneur, 1948)/ Roger Scruton on Boucher/ screen goddesses/ ***Summer with Monika*** (Bergman, 1952)/ *Les Amants* (Malle, 1958)/ ***Le Mépris*** (Godard, 1963)/ underground films/ ***Gertrud*** (Dreyer, 1964) & ***Blue Velvet*** (Lynch, 1986)/ *In the Mood for Love* (Wong Kar-Wai, 2000) & ***Three Times*** (Hou Hsiao-Hsien, 2005)/ ***Girl with a pearl earring*** (Webber, 2003)/ ***King Kong*** (1933 and 2005)

Westerns: Anthony Mann: ***The Furies*** (1950)/ ***The Man from Laramie*** (1955)/ *Winchester '73* (1950)/ *Man of the West* (1958)/ John Ford/ Sam Peckin-pah: *The Wild Bunch* (1969) & *Major Dundee* (1964)/ Cormac McCarthy and the US-Mexican border/ *No Country for Old Men* (Coen Bros, 2007)/ *Three Burials of Melquiades Estrada* (Tommy Lee Jones, 2005)

Violence: ***Scarface*** (1932 and 1983)/ *The Godfather*/ Eastwood: ***Mystic River*** (2003)/ ***Unforgiven*** (1992)/ ***Flags of Our Fathers*** & ***Letters from Iwo Jima*** (2006)

c.3:   LIGHTS CAMERA ACTION AND THE POOR BLOODY INFAN-TRY

Shakespeare's 'Henry V'/ *Henry V* (Olivier, 1944)/ World War One: ***All Quiet on the Western Front*** (Milestone, 1930) & ***Westfront 1918*** (Pabst, 1930)/ Vietnam films: war in colour, a history/ ***War and Peace*** (Bondarchuk, 1967)/ ***The Thin Red Line*** (Mallick, 1999) & ***Saving Private Ryan*** (Spielberg, 1998)/ ***Band of Brothers*** (HBO TV, 2001)/ Lewis Milestone: ***Pork Chop Hill*** (1959) & *All Quiet on the Western Front* & ***A Walk in the Sun*** (1945) c.4: IMAGINING THE HOLOCAUST

The Pawnbroker (Lumet, 1964)/ *The Holocaust: the story of the family Weiss* (TV, 1977)/ *Kitty: return to Auschwitz* (TV, 1980)/ **Night and Fog** (Resnais, 1955)/ **Shoah** (Lanzmann, 1985)/ **Schindler's List** (Spielberg, 1993)/ **The Pianist** (Polanski, 2002)

The German perspective: *Germany Year Zero* (Rossellini, 1946)/ *Downfall* (Hirschbiegel, 2004)/ **Heimat** series (Reitz, 1984, 1993 & 2004)

Holocaust and representation: W G Sebald's 'Austerlitz' and Theresienstadt/ *Hitler presents a town to the Jews* (German propaganda film, 1944)

PART TWO

c.5: IT'S IN THE ACTING

Roger Scruton on photography/ *Wild Strawberries* (Bergman, 1955)/ Bresson's theory of models not actors in 'Notes on the cinematographer'/ **A Man for all seasons**: play and film (Zimmermann, 1966)/ Dreyer's **Passion of Joan of Arc** (1928) and Bresson's **Trial of Joan of Arc** (1964)/ By contrast, an actor's director: Mike Leigh/ **Vera Drake** (Leigh, 2004)/ ensemble acting in Bergman, Ford, Altman/ the 'voluntary inexpressive' in *Two-lane Blacktop* (Monte Hellman, 1970), Jean-Pierre Melville, *A Fistful of Dollars* (Leone, 1964), *No Country for Old Men* (Coen Brothers, 2007)/ non-professionals: *Bicycle Thieves* (De Sica, 1948), *Diary of a Country Priest* (Bresson, 1950), *Gospel according to St Matthew* (Pasolini, 1964), *Little Dorrit* (Edzard, 1988), *Pickpocket* (Bresson, 1958)/ celebrity acting: **The Player** (Altman, 1992), Kenneth Anger & Andy Warhol

c.6: IT'S NOT IN THE ACTING

VF Perkins's 'Film as Film'/ Preminger, Ray, Minnelli/ collaboration in film/ seeking a defining essence: grand theory, Deleuze, postmodernism, structuralist film-making/ film's uniqueness/ Mitchell & Kenyon/ *The Prestige* (Christopher Nolan, 2006)/ *Passion of Joan of Arc* (Dreyer, 1928)/ *Ordet* (Dreyer, 1955)/ *On the Black Hill* (Grieve, 1987)/ *Blade Runner* (Scott, 1982)/ *Lord of the Rings* (Jackson, 2001-3)/ *The Dark Knight* (Nolan, 2007)/ *Dog Star Man* (Brakhage, 1964)/ *Central region* (Michael Snow, 1972)/ Warhol films silent and talkie/ *Into Great Silence* (Gröning, 2007)/ Marcel Pagnol/ Eric Rohmer/ the conversation film: *My Dinner with André* (Malle, 1981), *Metropolitan* (Stillman, 1989), *Before Sunrise* & *Before Sunset* (Linklater, 1995 and 2004)/ 'good scenes': **Only Angels Have Wings** (Hawks, 1939)/ screenwriting/ the advent of talkies/ extending the language of films/ 'figures of speech' in the cinema/ **Strike** (Eisenstein, 1924)/ *A Canterbury Tale* (Powell & Pressburger, 1944)/ *Small Back Room* (Powell &

Pressburger, 1948)/ *Gospel according to St Matthew* (Pasolini, 1964)

c.7: TIME'S LABYRINTH

Cross-cutting: Shakespeare's 'Richard II'/ Dickens and Griffith/ *Intolerance* (Griffith, 1916)/ *Leaves from Satan's Book* (Dreyer, 1919-21)/ *Strike* (Eisenstein, 1924)/ *No Country for Old Men* (Coen Brothers, 2007)/ Tarkovsky/ *Citizen Kane* (Welles, 1940)/ *Mirror* (Tarkovsky, 1972)/ *Un Chien Andalou* (Buñuel/ Dali, 1927)/ *Last Year in Marienbad* (Resnais, 1960)/ *Lost Highway* (Lynch, 1996)/ *Double Indemnity* (Wilder, 1945)/ *Meshes of the afternoon* (Deren/Hammid, 1943)

Flashbacks: *Le Jour se lève* (Carné, 1939)/ *Sunset Boulevard* (Wilder, 1950)/ *Life of Oharu* (Mizoguchi, 1952)/ *Letter from an unknown woman* (Ophuls, 1948)/ *Memento* (Nolan, 2000)

Remembering things past: *Time Regained* (Ruiz, 1999)/ *Jalsaghar/The Music Room* (Satyajit Ray, 1958)/ *L'Eclisse* (Antonioni, 1962)

'what if?' narratives: *Terminator 1 and 2* (Cameron, 1984, 1991)/ *Back to the Future* trilogy (Zemeckis, 1985-9)/ *It's a wonderful life* (Capra, 1946)/ *Unfaithfully yours* (Sturges, 1948)/ *Groundhog Day* (Ramis, 1993)/ *The Woman in the Fifth* (Pawlikowski, 2011)

Repeated action: *Rashomon* (Kurosawa, 1951)/ *Run Lola Run* (Tykwer, 1998)/ *Hero* (Zhang Yimou, 2002)/ *Sliding doors* (Howitt, 1997)/ *Blind Chance* (Kieślowski, 1980)

Conclusions: *Short cuts* (Altman, 1993)/ Iñárritu/Arriaga trilogy: *Amores Perros* (2000), *21 Grams* (2003), *Babel* (2006)

c.8: THE MÉLIÈS WAY

Brakhage as manipulator, Warhol as observer/ *Wavelength* (Snow, 1967)/ *Zorns Lemma* (Frampton, 1972)/ Frampton and Brakhage/ *Mothlight* (Brakhage, 1963)/ Brakhage's 'Metaphors on Vision'/ his career/ Francis Bacon and 'painting coming onto the nervous system'

c.9: INTERIORITY

The Road to Perdition (Mendes, 2002) and *The Return* (Zvyagintsev, 2003) compared/ articulating private thought: Shakespeare and Verdi/ Eugene Onegin: poem, opera and *Onegin* (Martha Fiennes, 1999)/ *A Canterbury Tale* (Powell & Pressburger, 1944)/ *Psycho* (Hitchcock, 1959)

Voice-over: *Le Petit Soldat* (Godard, 1960)/ *Thin Red Line* (Malick, 1999)

Inner emotion: *Passion of Joan of Arc* (Dreyer, 1928)

Music as expressive of character: *Nashville* (Altman, 1978)/ *L'Argent* (Bresson, 1982)/ *The Pianist* (Polanski, 2003)

Space: *Shock Corridor* (Fuller, 1963)/ *Lost Highway* (Lynch, 1996)/ Antonioni: *Cronaca di un amore* (1950), *L'Eclisse* (1962), *Red Desert* (1964)

Close-ups: *Blackmail* (Hitchcock, 1928)

Dreams: *Los Olvidados* (Bunuel, 1950)/ *Spellbound* (Hitchcock, 1945)/ *Small Back Room* (P & P, 1949)/ *Possessed* (Bernhardt, 1947)/ *A Serious Man* (Coen Brothers, 2009)

Visualizing thought: *La Guerre est finie* (Resnais, 1969)/ *The Passionate Friends* (Lean, 1949)

c.10:   IMAGINING THE POSSIBILITIES

Les Vampires (Feuillade, 1917) & *The Dark Knight* (Nolan, 2008)/ erosion of the feature-length norm: *Little Dorrit* (1988), the *Heimat* series (1983-2004), *The Wire* (HBO TV, 2008)/ makers of short films: Brakhage, McLaren, Tait, Svankmayer, Breer/ the dvd/ YouTube & *On the Waterfront* (Kazan, 1951)/ history in triads: pre-classical, classical, post-classical for painting, music, film/ prelapsarian, lapsarian, postlapsarian/ A Shakespeare for the cinema?/ industry structures/ candidates considered: Rossellini, Ford, Dreyer, Renoir, Ozu, Coen Brothers, Hitchcock/ the need for the longer view.

PART ONE

1 THE POTENCY OF SUSPENSE

Should the cinema have been invented? This is a clever technology, allied in origins to the facile art of the photograph, and attracting showmen, self-promoters, hucksters, barkers, artistic climbers, resulting at first sight in the meretricious. In the middle of the last century, CS Lewis wrote, "Nothing can be more disastrous than the view that the cinema can and should replace popular fiction. . . There is death in the camera." [CS Lewis pp.40-41.] What frightened Lewis was the risk that the capacity of literature to pierce to the reader's deeper imagination would be lost to a cinematic imagination that simplified, cut off and thus reduced the activities of the mind.

Lewis was right to regard the imagination as precious, as it makes the person using it, whether as reader, viewer or listener a participant in the process of creating. Look at the way the night sky has been imagined: a myriad of stars, but then in time a pattern emerges. Human beings gave these patterns names to aid them in their work, by land and sea. Then the poets learn them too, for example Hesiod as early as the seventh century BC, and these names pass both into science and into the collective imagination of the human race: Orion, the Great Bear, the Plough. The night sky that lay before us is thus reimagined as live shapes: it has pierced to our deepest imagination.

Lewis was a professor of literature. He was a friend too of JRR Tolkien, and it is possible to imagine them in an Oxford pub finding common ground in seeing the cinema as a ghastly intrusion on the world of popular fiction. What would Lewis have made of the Narnia franchise that was to come, and what would Tolkien have made of the film *Lord of the Rings*? The treatment of the Balrog in the first part, *The Fellowship of the Ring*, illustrates the point: in the book, as Gandalf and his party travel through the Mines of Moria, they disturb orcs, trolls and bigger creatures and become the pursued. They are making for the bridge to safety when their pursuers catch up with them and they turn to face them. But terror paralyses them: "Something was coming up behind. . . What it was could not be seen: it was like a great shadow, in the middle of which was a dark form, of man-shape maybe, yet greater; and the power and terror seemed to be in it and go before it." [JRR Tolkien, 'The Fellowship of the Ring' Bk 2, c.5, 'The Bridge of Khazad-dûm'.] It turns out to be a Balrog, but who or what is a Balrog? It is like a cloud obscuring fire, then flames wreath about it, making a black smoke. It has a streaming mane. Its right hand carries a blade like a tongue of fire, its left hand a whip. It must be serious because it makes Legolas and Gimli quail; to Gandalf it is an "evil fortune". The next description is of a "dark figure streaming with fire" racing towards them. At the bridge, Gandalf faces the Balrog which halts and shows two vast wings. It breathes fire from its nostrils and cracks its whip. It dwarfs Gandalf before its red sword fights with Gandalf's white. Then Gandalf's staff strikes the bridge so that it cracks and the Balrog crashes into the chasm. As he does so, the thongs of the whip whisk Gandalf with him into the abyss.

The book is exciting enough, so how is one to make it more so in the cinema? The film of 'Lord of the Rings' takes what visual clues it can to make a creature of darkness and of flame – but adds a head with a mouth of fire, legs and arms wreathed in smoke (not in Tolkien, although the legs and arms are implied by the Balrog's pursuit and the wielding of the sword and a whip). Is there a tail? The visual clue of Gandalf being caught by a thong of the whip and dragged down is done in brilliant style: the long tongue twists and whirls in the blackness to finally catch Gandalf round the legs and pull him down.

Tolkien's monster is as much a presence as anything of definite form. Its balefulness is as much conjured up by Gimli's exclamation on seeing it, 'Durin's Bane!', and by the terror it inspires, even among the orcs, as from the clues we are given of what it looks like. Should the film have done the same, giving clues to its presence, giving a part for the whole, rather than a full frontal view? This inevitably in the encounter on the bridge it must do, must convey its immensity against the wizard's "wizened tree before the onset of a storm". In making this simile, Tolkien's words employ one of writing's most potent devices for stimulating the reader's imagination, recalling Vergil's use of the same simile in a different set of circumstances to describe Aeneas deaf to Dido's pleas for him to stay at Carthage, like a strong oak "toughened by the years when northern winds from the Alps vie together to tear it from the soil . . . yet still the tree grips among the rocks below . . ."[Vergil, 'Aeneid' 4.441-9.] Literary metaphor seems to cut film adrift, leave it trailing in its wake, because so far the grammar of film has not developed an accepted way of making visual analogies to the same effect.

Balrogs are comparatively easy beside ents, the slow-thinking and slow-speaking trees, capable of a surprising violence when roused. Creating them in words poses a specific challenge to both the writer's and the reader's imagination, because while with monsters there are other referents such as dragons, ents are *sui generis*, their *genus* being radically unlike any other. Again words are an advantage, because they can suggest without having to explain everything. Tolkien omits to trouble the reader with an explanation of how the ent speaks, concentrating on the eyes instead, so we are spared having to imagine its mouth parts. For the film, the question needs answering. A serviceable answer is found, to the credit of the creators. However, devising a way of speaking for them puts the film on a collision course: on the one hand, the need for long rumination before utterance, and then speaking in slow motion as it were, to convey their emphatically unhurried nature, and on the other, the impatience of an audience chewing its popcorn and wanting action. The ents in the film are far too hasty to honour Tolkien's literary creations. And when they destroy Isengard, is there not, even among the enormous technical achievement of creating this onscreen, a failure of cinematic imagination? ['The Two Towers', Bk 3, c.4, 'Treebeard' and c.8, 'The Road to Isengard'.] The scene is one of generalized battle with the ents looking like giant Giacometti stick men wading violently into the puny enemy, and turning the battle to their favour by undamming a river so that the fortress is brought to destruction by rushing water, whose flows the tall trees rise above. The battle between Gandalf and the Balrog is marked by reaction shots from Frodo and others, by vivid close-ups of Gandalf, and an aerial shot of the party racing across the bridge, driving the narrative forward both on screen and in the offscreen music so that the audience is sucked into the story. At Isengard by contrast we only remain spectators abstracted from what is happening; there are no close-ups, no movements accelerated or decelerated to create a filmic rhythm. Both Tolkien and the makers of the film in fact are too squeamish to detail the consequences of entish violence, in terms at least of suffering – because the enemy in *Lord of the Rings* does not suffer.

However, with the Black Riders of Book 1, Tolkien and the film-makers are on more even ground. In the book, Gandalf refers to them briefly when very near the beginning he recites the Ring's spell to Frodo (to which we have already been introduced on the title page): "Nine [rings] for mortal men doomed to die." Gandalf explains that the Enemy gave nine rings to nine men so that they fell under his dominion and became Ringwraiths. He pricks our sense of fear by adding, ". . . they too may walk again." And so they do, when they are sent to search for the hobbits now journeying east to Mordor. Frodo has a first encounter with a large man (and therefore menacing to hobbits) crouching in the saddle of his horse, wrapped in cloak and hood: "his face was shadowed and invisible." The fear increases when Merry glimpses them in Bree, "a sort of deeper shade among the shadows", and then succumbs to the Black Breath. The audience is then privileged to learn (because Frodo is ignorant) that the Black Riders have attacked and ransacked Frodo's house in the Shire with the result that their menace is increased for us. Frodo then has a second encounter when he is attacked and, slipping the Ring on his finger to make himself invisible, sees five of them. They appear to him no longer as invisible, but with white faces, and "keen and merciless eyes" (for once words fail Tolkien – "keen and merciless eyes" cannot be visualised and the description is trite), wearing long grey robes under their black mantles, silver helmets, and carrying swords ['Fellowship of the Ring', Bk 1, c.11, 'A Knife in the Dark']. One carries a knife and in defending himself, Frodo is wounded. Finally, in the third encounter, of the closest kind, all nine pursue Frodo to the river where he crosses successfully but the riders are swept away in a magic flood, three riders being swiftly overwhelmed while the other six maddened by some magic force are born into the torrent.

Against this superlative narrative, the film holds its own, aided by two aspects that are essentially visual. The first is flight on horseback, the second is the sight of the face made invisible by the black hood, and therefore much more sinister than if the eyes are seen, even "keen and merciless" ones. Both have cinematic antecedents such as the invisible presence in the horror film, or the chase in the Western and the samurai film. From the beginning the silent cinema had learnt to revel in speed: the ride of the Ku Klux Klan in Griffith's *Birth of a Nation*, the race to the sea and freedom between Napoleon and his pursuers in Gance's *Napoleon*, the chariot race in Fred Niblo's *Ben-Hur* and throughout the period, the frantic chases of the Keystone Cops, Buster Keaton, Harold Lloyd and others. So, when Frodo has his first encounter, all the menace of Tolkien's narrative is conveyed in the black figure on a black horse sniffing the air, and in the second and third encounters, the pace is quickened and their manifestation as armed spectres of white and grey is properly realised. When the river flood finally sweeps them away, the digital imagery is clear and swift enough to convey what by now in Tolkien is an essentially visual drama. Both book and film work because they share a common device that allows the static first encounter between Frodo and Rider to become a dynamic one that motivates the narrative, which must be resolved in one way or the other, but this resolution is preceded by a crescendo which draws the spectator in and cannot be turned away from: we have to know the outcome. The device is suspense and while centuries of literature show writers appreciating its virtues as a tool of narrative, it is the cinema in the twentieth century that has proved particularly adept at using it. Why?

It is not clear when Alfred Hitchcock was exactly first described as 'the master of suspense', although when he signed for Gaumont-British in 1933, the link between his name and the idea that the audience's emotions could be conducted as by a maestro was irrevocably established by the films of the next five years: *The Man Who Knew Too Much, The 39 Steps, Secret Agent, Sabotage, Young and Innocent, The Lady Vanishes.* Yet even in his silent films he understood that once the audience had identified with the character, they also identified closely with his or her desires and fears: in an early film, *Blackmail*, the heroine murders her attacker with a vicious-looking knife. The sequence is full of ambiguous moral overtones: Crewe has lured Alice into his studio and now uses force to rape her. Alice seems both innocent and foolish and, her assailant may think, is asking for it. Is his murder justified on grounds of self-defence? But these considerations are swamped by Hitchcock's construction of the scene as a desperate, turbulent moment, forcing us to watch not think. Alice is forced onto the bed behind the curtains, so our view is cut off. All we see is her hand flailing out and then falling on a knife lying on the bedside table. In our excitement and horror at this scene of rape, we are forced to project in our imagination an answer to the question, will she succeed or not? Except, does imagination play any part? The scene is too critical, too desperate for such mental detachment. We are not passive observers, but we are actively sucked into the situation, willy nilly: we experience briefly the fiercest emotional attachment to the outcome.

Or take the final scene in a film from his middle period, *Saboteur.* At the end, hero and villain are at the top of the Statue of Liberty, and Hitchcock switches our power of identification to the villain. When the hero finds him clinging to the face of the statue's hand, he is moved to save him, Hitchcock sensing an exquisite moment of suspense: why should we care whether the villain plunges to his death or not? Wickedness should be punished with oblivion. But instead we are hypnotised, our fascination aroused by the circumstances of the hero choosing to rescue one of those who have been pursuing him throughout the film. In passing, one might comment that a written narration of this sequence would feel pale by comparison. It would require a careful description of the jacket's deconstruction and how its preservation was crucial to the man's survival. Hitchcock dismisses such detail as he knows that all he has to do is to give a single shot of the stitches breaking one by one for the audience to gasp without reflection and to foresee in their mind the plunge of a man hundreds of feet from the top of the statue to the ground below.

In order to convey cinema's natural affinity to suspenseful narration, it is worth looking at this sequence in detail since Hitchcock achieves a particular purity of expression. After all the ins and outs of *Saboteur*, the wildly differing locales, and essentially the final resolution of the film, Hitchcock steers the film to the top of the Statue of Liberty: Fry, a man with a suspect look, clearly not all -American, is confronted by a gun in the hands of Barry Kane, who is all-American. Fry panics, falls over the railing and is left clinging for his life on the curve of Liberty's colossal hand, between thumb and forefinger. Kane climbs over to rescue him.

He doesn't wait to do the sensible thing, namely to get a rope, but his instinct – and ours – is to save this villain. Clambering down, he grasps Fry's sleeve in order to pull him to safety. In cutting back and forth between Kane and Fry, the film sucks the spectator into the drama. Fry strains to save himself: "I'll cling. I swear I will." At this point, Hitchcock cuts from Fry's contorted

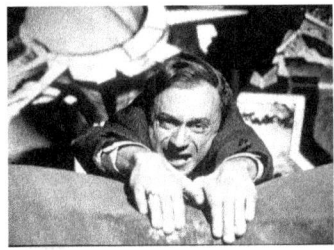

face in his agony, filmed from above so we glimpse the abyss awaiting him if he falls, to an extreme close-up of Fry's suit, the joint between the body of the jacket and the sleeve. We watch as one of the stitches breaks, and then another: Fry's fate in the balance looks as if it will fall the wrong way. To mark the intensity of this climax, Hitchcock cross-cuts between sleeve and Liberty for sev-

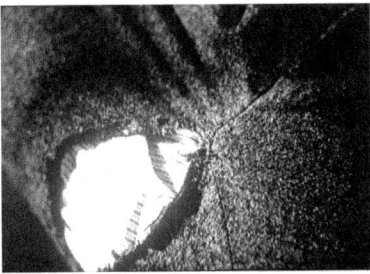

en shots, four of the sleeve as the stitches snap one by one so that in shot seven, the shirt is fully showing, and three of Liberty from three different angles, with Kane and Fry in extreme long shot, dwarfed by the colossus standing against sea and sky. A sinister dimension to the sequence is lent by Liberty's wide open but expressionless eyes, unmoved by the puny mortal struggle taking place in the crook of her hand, an idea developed by Hitchcock from his earlier *Blackmail* when the blackmailer is chased through the British Museum and clam-

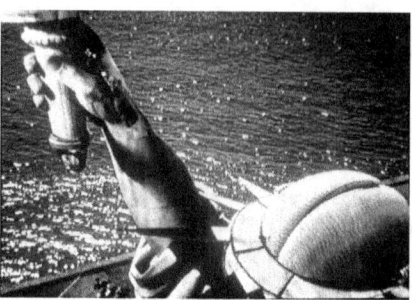

bers down a rope adjacent to an enormous sculpted head with large blank eyes. The soundtrack is not silence, but a virtual soundlessness – the ambient sound of sea and sky with horns echoing distantly from the bay below. In all, the seven shots make 22 seconds of screen time, no time to contemplate the horror of the situation intellectually, but enough for it to register mentally.

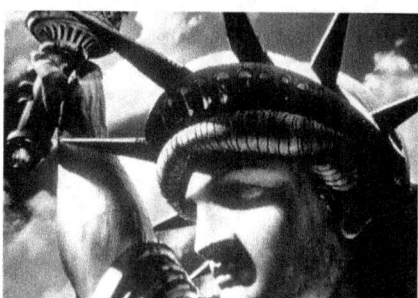

Fry is a goner, and the spell is broken when he too realises that the sleeve Kane holds is coming away. "The sleeve!" he manages to squeeze out desperately, his eyes screwed up with the tension. We see Kane's reaction in close-up, biting his lip. When Fry does fall it is in a vertiginous view, his body streaming away from us getting smaller and smaller, accompanied by his dying scream. Cut to Kane's face again, wearing the blank expression of his failure – when we had willed him to succeed. When the details of *Saboteur* are forgotten, this intense

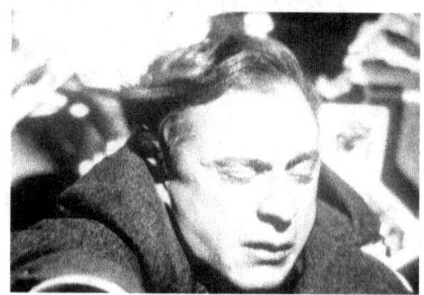

sequence is imprinted on our brain, forcing its way into our imagination.

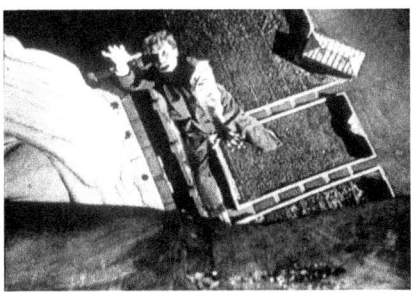

'Will it? Won't it?' is an essential ingredient of cinematic suspense, and it may appear that if we know the outcome, we cease to be interested. But that is far from the case. There are notable examples of stories where we know the outcome but are baffled as to how it could have come about. The circumstances need to be extreme ones: we shall examine later, in a section on imagining the annihilation camps set up by the German Third Reich, how *The Pianist* works as a drama and not as a mere recital of facts, how one man survived in this hell and lived to tell of it. My point here is how enthralling films can be when we know in advance what happens at the end, in other words the suspense is not in what happens but how it happens.

First of all, take a recent remarkable case. The British mountaineer Joe Simpson climbed the west face of the Andean peak of Siula Grande in 1985 with a fellow mountaineer, Simon Yates, leaving Richard Hawking at the base camp. In the descent Simpson falls and breaks his leg; Yates and Simpson continue with Yates letting Simpson out on a rope for 300 meters, then descending to join him and so on, but when Simpson goes over an overhang which allows him no way of climbing back up, Yates has to take a split-second decision to cut the rope in order to save himself; otherwise both are doomed. In fact Simpson falls into a crevasse, surviving the fall and hitting a ledge, while Yates, unable to rescue him, has to leave Simpson for dead and return to base camp. By an extraordinary act of will, allied to mountaineering skill, and a touch of good fortune, Simpson gets himself out of the crevasse and back to the safety of camp. In 1989 he published a narrative in a bare and detailed account, poetically entitled 'Touching the Void'. It quickly became a classic of mountaineering literature, but began to break out of that compartment as non-mountaineering readers discovered what a compulsive story it made. In 2003 it was made into a film by Kevin McDonald, not a fiction film in the classic sense but a documentary version of the events combining a recreation of the climb (shot at Chamonix in the Haute Savoie and on the Grindelwald in Kanton Bern, Switzerland, as well as on Siula Grande itself) with a commentary on the sequence of events by the three mountaineers involved.

Simpson's and Yates's account is matter of fact: we want to understand how Yates made the decision not to undertake Simpson's rescue, and how Simp-

28

son plans and executes his escape: what options he might have in such desperate circumstances: in a crevasse with a broken leg, and so unable to climb out. He has to take a chance that by going to the bottom of the crevasse he can make a hole through to the outside. What are the chances? 50 – 50? Or less than that? Completely incalculable? Once he has lowered himself to the bottom (and therefore unable to make the return to his previous position) and if he cannot dig himself out onto the face of the mountain, then he is dead. All along, he has to set himself a sequence of small goals in order to get to the end.

In many respects, the story is a remarkable echo of the one Robert Bresson used to make *Un Condamné à mort s'est échappé* / *A Man Escaped* (strictly *A Man under condemnation of death has escaped*): André Devigny, imprisoned by the Gestapo in Montluc gaol, and condemned to death, executes an escape with a

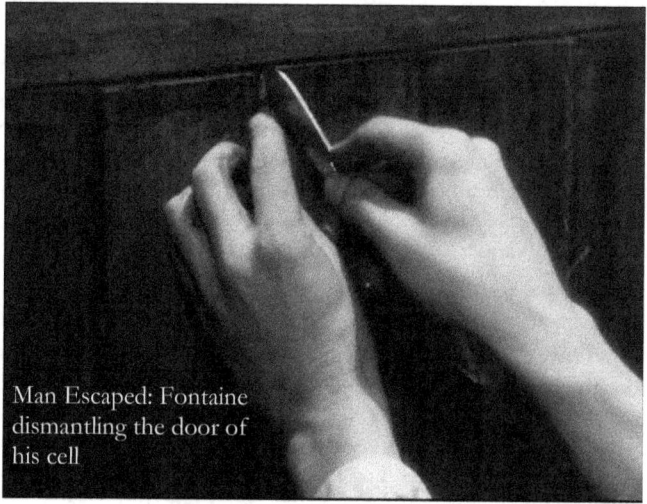

Man Escaped: Fontaine dismantling the door of his cell

fellow prisoner from his cell, over the roofs to the outside wall and thence to freedom, where he is captured again on the outskirts of Lyon and escapes again. Bresson's film confined itself to the prison escape and recreates how Devigny, renamed Fontaine, pieced together the means of escape, step by step. Like Simpson, he is sustained by a burning ambition to survive, and extraordinary inventiveness in making use of the tiny resources at his disposal: a spoon, a wire bed frame, a metal lantern frame.

Like the makers of the film of *Touching the Void*, Bresson professes to be telling the story 'without ornaments'. This should not be taken at face value, since, as the title of the film indicates, he turns it into a Christian parable that draws on Pascal's idea about grace and salvation, and in doing so makes more coherent the religious references in Devigny's account, and fashions a universal statement about the human response to suffering, about chance, and about grace conferred by God. *Touching the Void* explicitly excludes such a metaphysical dimension: Simpson tells us in the film that he was brought up a devout

Catholic, but in his extremity feels no prompting to say a quantity of Hail Maries, and realises that the concept of God means nothing to him – hence the title of his book. At the end, no comment is made on his salvation, nor any reflection recorded of gratitude, either to God or in congratulating himself on what he has achieved. He is the matter-of-fact Englishman, rigorously refusing to imagine that his story illumines a larger pattern in the universe.

This is in many ways admirable, but it may be that it leaves the human imagination starved. As a film, *Touching the Void* is remarkably assembled, and its story will remain a classic of mountaineering literature and cinema, but it is a special attraction of Bresson's film that he articulates a spiritual dimension to this very physical story, that it can be viewed and appreciated both plainly but also as a revelation of divine grace. Another kind of specialness attaches to Polanski's film of *The Pianist* (see further below in chapter 4): as well as being an extraordinary story, it is a parable of the good fortune bestowed on Wladek Szpilman, the pianist – and of the bad fortune, which could be interpreted even as the denial of divine grace, bestowed on his family and his fellow Jews in the Warsaw ghetto.

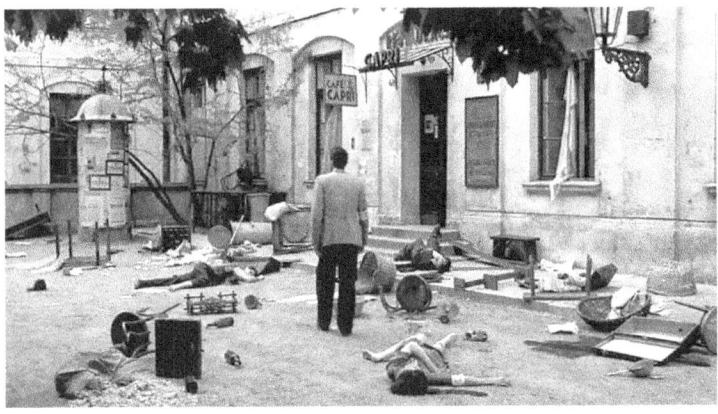

These three stories work so marvellously as films because the resources of the cinema allowed two things in particular to happen. Firstly they can thread the events together in a way that allows concentration of attention. The lengths of the three are: 107 minutes (*Touching the Void*), 95 minutes (*A Man Escaped*) and 146 minutes (*The Pianist*), all of a suitable length to be taken in at one sitting, thus gaining in dramatic concentration. Secondly film is very good at the physicality of things. It can show action not just precisely but realistically, conveying the details of what happened in a way that prevents the viewer from thinking it impossible. Dismantling the prison door without proper tools in *A Man Escaped* seems an impossibility, but Bresson conveys it in the film. We do not just take Devigny's account on trust, but we see it for ourselves: seeing reinforces believing. All three films work too in posing large questions about human behaviour that fascinate us well beyond the experience of the film itself: would we have cut the rope? Is the escape from Montluc really the result of divine grace? Is Szpilman's survival truly a blessing, or a curse – when he has lost his family and his fellow Jews?

However, there is a drawback to these film narratives since the protagonists' internal struggle is largely conveyed through the externalities of mountain, prison or ghetto. *Touching the Void*, in intercutting the story with comments from those involved after the event, does allow some reflection on the dilemmas each mountaineer faced, and in *A Man Escaped*, Bresson makes use of voice-over and whispered snatches of dialogue, pared to essentials, to convey the metaphysical dimensions of Fontaine's desperate position and his response to it. On the other hand the syntax of film has to be developed a good deal before it can achieve a sophisticated level of interiority that might enrich these kinds of narrative still further.

2   UNLEASHING THE IMAGINATION: HORROR, SEX, VIOLENCE

Because the cinema is even better than staged drama at concentrating a story in time, and because as I argue it can reveal physical details so intimately and so realistically, it is good at creating suspense, not just making the spectator curious, but so drawing them to the story that they cannot tear themselves away. But the telling of stories in any medium has always understood the value of suspense: the listener or reader wants to know how the tale will end, both what happens and how it happens. But in the long history of human beings as creative individuals, using their imaginative capacities to reveal themselves to each other, the cinema makes a new milestone in expanding the range of expression beyond what the written word has been able to do on its own. And that expansion and intensity has come about not only from the availability of a new medium, but from the particular social form the cinema required: a place where lots of people assembled to watch a story collectively in the dark. A very early account of the way films could fascinate an audience can be found in Rudyard Kipling's story 'Mrs Bathurst', included in 'Traffics and Discoveries' published in 1904. The story concerns the relationship between Vickery and Mrs Bathurst, and central to it is Vickery mesmerised by the unexpected appearance of Mrs Bathurst in a documentary film of a train coming into Paddington station, probably inspired by the Lumière Brothers' *Arrival of a train at La Ciotat* (1895). Kipling uses a brilliant simile to explain the sight of Mrs B. coming towards the camera and walking out of the frame, both real 'taken from the very thing in itself', and mysterious 'like a shadow jumping over a candle'. [See Montefiore pp. 135-8.]   Watching in the dark is true of the theatre as well, but less intensely: the cinema enforced a new personality on the spectator, not a polite posture absorbing the spoken thoughts and dramas on the stage, but a lying back in the seat mesmerised by the flickering screen, the parade of images that brooked no denial, the sequence of images that enlarged the world we inhabit. The collective experience that the cinema can create is wonderfully captured in the account by Primo Levi in 'The Truce' of the travelling cinema put on by a Soviet military film truck at Starye Dorogi ('Old Roads'), a transit camp for a mainly Italian contingent, including prisoners from Auschwitz, in the Pripet Marshes, *le bout du monde* lit up by flickering pictures.   The incident well illustrates how film, especially as it is made in Hollywood, is able to tap into global imaginations. The audience comprised the Italians and the Russian soldiers accompanying them who, on the third evening, were treated to a showing of *The Hurricane* (1938), set on a South Sea island, the climax of which is a *deus ex machina* in the form of a hurricane that overwhelms the island, resolves the conflict, and indeed in blowing itself out extinguishes all the human passions too. The film wallows in melodrama, with caricatures of both hero and villain, and in sentiment, yet the star attraction is definitely the hurricane created in the studio by what must have been fearsome wind and water machines. For the Italians in limbo between the inferno of Auschwitz and the paradise of going home, and for the Russian soldiers attending, the film unleashed a riot: the sight on a poster for the film of Dorothy Lamour in a sarong had already ignited passions; at the screening itself the story of a Polynesian sailor who has been unjustly imprisoned and who then escapes, and finally in the hurricane itself saves his girl, was watched with vociferous partisanship: "The sailor was acclaimed at every exploit, greeted by noisy cheers and sten-guns brandished perilously over their heads. The policeman and jailers were insulted with bloodthirsty cries, greeted with shouts of 'leave him alone', 'go away', 'I'll get you', 'kill them all'. . . . Stones, lumps of earth, splinters from the demolished doors, even a regulation boot flew against the screen, hurled with furious precision at the odious face of the great enemy, which shone forth oversize in the foreground." [Levi, 'The Truce' pp. 403 sq.]

Now that films are so easily available on television and on DVD, the collective experience of a film watched in a crowded cinema is less common, unless one thinks of their reception being enlarged by the internet in which films, because of their global reach, are discussed, commented on, reacted against or extravagantly praised on message boards which form a contemporary version of the collective conscious. Yet a collective response has been an essential part of the cinema's popularity: it was the mass consumption, whether in a massive big-city Odeon or a ramshackle fleapit in the slums, on a Soviet travelling train or on a desert plain in the open air, that created the wealth which once reinvested produced larger and larger dreams. This is true in its purest form of the horror film. Horror films are usually made on the cheap, for example the niche films Universal Studios made in the 1930s (*Frankenstein, Dracula, The Mummy*), the formula films or *filone* made by Mario Bava between 1960 and 1978 and the Edgar Allen Poe adaptations made by Roger Corman and Richard Matheson in the early 1960s for American International Pictures. This tradition of large effect from minimal resources was continued by the Japanese film *Ringu/The Ring* (1998) which grossed 15.9bn yen, and *The Blair Witch Project*, which grossed $248m worldwide from an initial investment of $35,000 (compared to the $25m spent on marketing the film). Nor do horror films win prestigious prizes such as Palmes d'Or, Golden Bears etc. The Oscar awarded in 1999 to *The Silence of the Lambs* is the nearest a horror film has got.

In his essay 'The Uncanny' of 1919, Freud articulated the idea that "the 'uncanny' is that class of the terrifying which leads back to something long known to us, once very familiar." If so, it is no wonder that the horror film has proved so commercially successful, because it has used cinema's global reach to tap into a global subconscious, crossing national and cultural boundaries. But other factors are in play such as the deep cultural roots of folk-tales dealing with the supernatural, asserting their power in the face of Western rationality, the undead returning to spook the Enlightenment. The Romantic movement in the nineteenth-century sees a flourishing of literature treating supernatural themes: the Gothic novel, the tales of ETA Hoffman, French literature of the time (Nodier, Gautier, Merimée, Nerval, Lautréamont, Villiers de l'Isle-Adam, even Balzac), short story writers in English such as RL Stevenson, WW Jacobs, Edgar Allen Poe and Sheridan Le Fanu. The stories multiply in the twentieth century, but one can single out MR James in particular, of whose stories PJ Stead wrote: "His characters. . . assist in disarming the reader's scepticism, being sedate, academic persons, with comfortable churchy backgrounds – the last people in the world to be mixed up in anything irregular." After disarming their scepticism, James then reveals the physically gruesome ['Cassell's Encyclopaedia of World Literature' s.v. 'Supernatural story']. To this list can be added the strong literary tradition of ghost stories in Japan, and the emergence of a contemporary master of horror fiction achieving huge book sales in the person of Stephen King.

Tales of the supernatural were therefore an established form in many countries, on which the cinema could draw. This posed a challenge too: if ghosts are not of this world, especially if their presence is malevolent, what artistic risks are there in the cinema turning them into flesh and blood to trouble our dreams and even days: is this a case of the cinema foolishly rushing in where angels and even the undead fear to tread? The ghost in literature must be incorporeal to the point of invisibility, the very antithesis of the cinema's drive to reveal, to <u>make</u> visible.

And yet perhaps more than in any other kind of film narrative, it is the horror film that connects most powerfully with the imagination, whether it is the detailed realisation of the zombies in films like George Romero's or the way a film like *The Blair Witch Project* conjures up a feeling of horror from ropey video footage in which nothing monstrous appears but is suggested by the reactions of Heather, Josh and Mike lost in the woods. It turns out that filming premature burial, cannibalism, empty rooms, the drinking of blood, grafting one face on to another, rampaging chain saws objectify these things for us but in doing so, do not diminish their horror. Paradoxically, their cheap origins in low budgets and strict shooting schedules in a way enhance their imaginative power, reinforcing the idea that nightmares can emerge out of nothing, that it is all part of their inexplicability. The challenge to film-makers was to use their imagination to create new nightmares, for example the opening of Mario Bava's *Black Sunday / La Maschera del demonio* (1960): Princess Asa is punished for an illicit affair with Prince Javutich by an exquisitely cruel execution – a mask with spikes on the inside is hammered over her face.

It is in images like this that the cinema makes common cause with Surrealism, that extravagant flowering of the romantic imagination. With the colonisation of image-making by photography, the painters of the twentieth century at first sought new countries of the mind, out of reach of photography's upstart power. The Surrealists found it in painting, only for the cinema to chase after them, and invent a cinematic version, manipulating photographed images to create the rich and strange. However, if surrealism is the chance encounter of an umbrella and a sewing machine on a dissecting table, and you extend this bland definition to more disturbing adjacencies – pipe and "this is not a pipe" (Magritte), a hand covered in ants (Dali), the Virgin chastising the infant Jesus (Max Ernst) – then their location in narrative films poses a risk: the key to the surrealist image is irrationality, and yet film deals with narrative over time, in which a measure of rationality must surely be maintained if the story is to retain our interest. While the short surrealist film, Buñuel and Dali's *Un Chien Andalou*, derives its power from the way it destroys time and space, collapsing them into total disorder, as much as from the suggestion of desire thwarted and from the force of its images, especially the slicing of an eyeball by a cutthroat razor, in mainstream feature-length narrative the potency of surrealism is best realized in the way it periodically erupts: the hands shooting out from the corridor to clutch Cathé

rine Deneuve in *Repulsion*, the scorpion overwhelmed by ants gleefully observed by children in the opening of *The Wild Bunch*, the nightmare version of *Faust* by Jan Svankmayer, the pleading of the girl with a disfigured face hidden behind a plastic mask in *Les Yeux sans visage*.

Possession and desire unfulfilled bring us to the realm of the sexual imagination. To be a screen goddess requires an aura which must not be penetrated. Character is written in the face not the body so that a sex scene with Ingrid Bergman would have destroyed her beauty as we perceive it, made it coarse, ordinary, of the crowd like us and so vulgar. Consider her role as Ilsa in *Casablanca* as Rick, her former lover, sees her, a woman of beauty and desire whom he is longing to forget, and who turns up in the remote corner of the universe that is Casablanca, flesh and blood, and yet (in the film) not flesh and blood but a screen phantom. Within five years of *Casablanca* (1942), RKO made *Build My Gallows High*, which being a B-movie is better able to creep under the censorship radar. Jeff Bailey has fallen for Kathy Moffat in Mexico. She says, 'Let's go to my place.' How can the film show their sexual passion without a bedroom scene? The solution is to catch them in a tropical storm (shades of Vergil's Dido and Aeneas), although opposite in tone to Fred Astaire serenading Ginger Rogers in *Top Hat*: 'Isn't this a lovely day to get caught in the rain?' Jeff and Kathy reach the house soaked. She dries his hair, he dries hers, kisses her neck, then throws the towel so that it knocks the lamp over, while at the same time the wind blows the door open (shades of Wagner's 'Die Walküre' Act 1). Their passion is therefore made into metaphor – of intense rubbing, of storm, of a door swinging open. Not all is bliss, for the cameraman, Nicholas Musuraca, lights the room to create horizontal shadows, investing the shining moment with a strong chiaroscuro, a foreshadowing of the darkness of their subsequent relationship.

In a lecture given by Roger Scruton about the paintings of François Boucher (1703-1770) he invokes Coleridge's distinction between fantasy and imagination: fancy is an 'errant abstraction from realities', in effect giving rise to a fantasy interest in the body, which is pornography, whereas 'imagination' is a way of perceiving and understanding realities, of a man seeing a woman as a creature with a desire of her own. The latter is the realm of painting, 'a presentation of realities', whereas the former is the realm of photographs and in particular of pornographic films, in which the depiction of sexual organs eclipses the subject: hence photography and film are a 'representation of fictions'.

We shall encounter Scruton's downgrading of photography and film again in chapter 5, but here his discussion of the painted nude (Titian, Velazquez, Manet, as well as Boucher – Francis Bacon and Lucien Freud, the twentieth-century masters of flesh, are excluded from this august company) produces fruitful observations on the values of decency, decorum and modesty, the absence of the obscene in these painters, and the essence of a genuinely erotic art that displays the human being as both subject and object of desire, but also as 'a free individual whose desire is a favour consciously bestowed'.

Where does the screen goddess of old – Garbo, Harlow, Dietrich, Lamarr, Crawford, Arletty, many others – fit into this picture? Her individuality is in her face, and we worship her principally for her face. Within the parameters of what censorship allowed, we can see her arms, her neck, her legs, her thighs, but not her naked behind nor her naked torso. After the war, film-makers begin to assault these conventions, particularly in Europe. The screen goddess became a sex symbol, exactly that objectification of the female body as an object of concupiscence which Scruton deplores. But a film-maker like Ingmar Bergman manages both to strip his actresses of their clothes and to preserve their humanity. Take a film made shortly after his apprenticeship may be said to have ended and from the beginning of his highly productive career in the 1950s, *Summer with Monika*. Harry and Monika spend summer by the sea, falling in love (and out of love). Bergman makes us voyeurs of limited vision. Over Harry's shoulder we see Monika standing naked before him, but a view of her breasts is blocked by Harry's shoulder, and one third of the screen is taken up with the landscape behind her. Harry strokes her neck and chest, then his hand strays down to her breasts, and she grasps it. We then cut to a view of Harry over Monika's shoulder. Harry is clothed, and his face lit up with light reflected from the sun on the sea, and he puts his hand on Monika's cheek. Cut again to Monika running away from camera, as though she was only teasing Harry (and us). As Monika, Harriet Anderson is a seductive screen presence, but in this story she is blood as well as flesh, an individual on whose illuminated, dishevelled, pouting, crumpled face we can read vulnerability and the pain of her own suffering. She may be dubbed a sex symbol, but she is, in Scruton's phrase, 'a creature with a desire of her own'. Nor is Harry a simple voyeur. The young man is mesmerised by the sight of Monika's naked body, but his behaviour is characterised by hesitancy, which allows Monika to tease him by running away before he can embrace her.

How does Jeanne Moreau compare in Louis Malle's *Les Amants*, made at the end of the 1950s, when the fashion for the sex symbol was still raging? In succumbing to the young student who visits her house and family, Moreau is shown wandering round the garden in a nightdress and then being made love to in the bedroom, not explicitly, but through our imaginations. Moreau is naked in the bed, and we see her hand opening and closing while the young man ca-

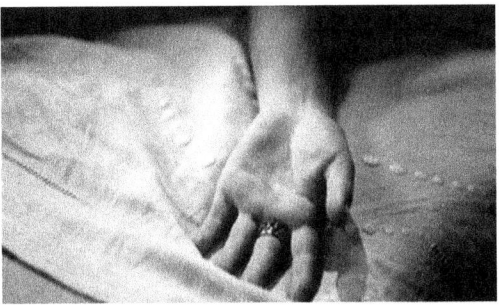

resses her body off-screen. This feels like the nude as object but Louis Malle, the director, uses the scene to emphasise how this sexual passion eclipses the conventional and hypocritical family life around Moreau. The hand opening and closing is a more natural human response of one person to another than has happened in all the rest of the film.

In both Bergman and Malle, there is a pursuit of the genuinely erotic, depicting free individuals 'whose desire is a favour consciously bestowed', in Scruton's description. This erotic showing and not showing can be compared with the chastity of Godard in *Le Mépris,* the background for which is the making of a film at Cinecittà in Rome. His star is none other than the symbol of all sex symbols, Brigitte Bardot, that blatant object of desire. But Godard throws us quite offguard: the film opens with a 3-minute love scene – the precedent for which is Hitchcock's *Psycho* which had opened with a frigid bedroom scene as a way of introducing Marian Crane – in which Camille (Bardot) lies naked on a bed with her husband Paul. The CinemaScope format, described by Fritz Lang in the film as only good for funerals and snakes, is used to good effect in giving us a view of Bardot's horizontal but rearside body, chaste in her mysterious flesh like Velazquez' Rokeby Venus and yet matter-of-fact like Manet's Olympia. Is her body objectified for all to see? It seems to be but Godard shoots the scene with filters, in red for two minutes, then without for 30 seconds, then with a blue filter for the remaining 30 seconds, an original version of chiaroscuro proper to the colour film: we see and yet do not see. So, to compensate, do we see her and Paul making love? We do not and yet we do, because she puts a series of questions to Paul asking whether he likes the parts of her body, starting with her feet, and going on to thighs, buttocks, face and breasts. To each of these Paul gives his assent, culminating in a characteristically Godardian assent that he loves her "totally, tenderly, tragically", a sentiment we applaud but cannot quite appreciate as true. The sequence manages to be verbally explicit and pictorially chaste, and is invested with an extraordinary aura by Georges Delerue's wistful music. One is reminded too of Godard's strapline for the prostitute in *Vivre sa vie*: 'She loses her body, but saves her soul.'

At the same time as these films were appearing, the American underground was being influential in respect of showing the possibilities of what in the arena of sex could be depicted on screen: Brakhage's scenes of love-making involving himself and Jane, Warhol's films of heterosexual, gay and lesbian relationships with a lot of nudity, not to mention films such as *The Kodak Ghost Poems, Echoes of Silence, Fuses, Chant d'amour.* In themselves, these films celebrate the act of love-making in a way that reinforces our conception of humanity and celebrates its value. But in the mainstream cinema, they had a destabilising effect: the explicit became commonplace, with a consequent loss of decorum. Measure the gap between Dreyer's *Gertrud* (1964) and David Lynch's *Blue Velvet* (1986): in Dreyer's film, to emphasize the carnal attraction between its heroine and the anaemic young poet, we are shown Gertrude removing her blouse in silhouette, a delicate visual hint of Gertrude's adultery which preserves her poise and beauty in a way that the flagrant depiction of her fleshy embrace of the young man would corrupt or distort.

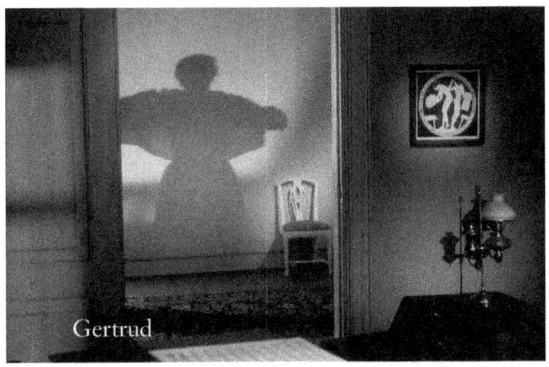

Gertrud

Blue Velvet, seeking to shock us powerfully, has Isabella Rossellini playing Dorothy Vallens, who turns out to be both victim and predator. Adopting the viewpoint of Geoffrey, the innocent hero, we watch through her louvred door, our vision partially obscured, her rape by Frank. The sound of what is happening and the voyeuristic view of what is happening add to the sense of wanting to know and being repelled by the knowledge. The way the director, David Lynch, shoots the scene brings these contradictory imaginings into play. But later in the film Dorothy openly forces Geoffrey to consummate his desire, despite himself. The film is about the depths behind surfaces, the swirling troubling monsters that lurk within ourselves and within society, animal and predatory. Dorothy the victim is herself a monster: beneath the 'blue velvet' eye make-up, cherry red lips, pastel skin, she is a sexual masochist, and Geoffrey has to be the sadist to gratify her. (In passing, one wonders what Isabella's parents, Ingrid Bergman and Roberto Rossellini, would have made of the film.)

To favour the erotic in the cinema is to look askance at grossness, and to celebrate the fact that there are still screen goddesses like Cathérine Deneuve, with that mysterious quality of being and of, where necessary, not showing. It may be too that the art of the erotic has travelled to the Orient, where the drama of Wong Kar-Wai's *In the Mood for Love* rests on the tension between Maggie Cheung's beauty, clothed in tight-fitting silk, and the dramatic necessity for restraint: her mood for love is never consecrated. This idea of restraint is intelligently and indeed exquisitely explored in Hou Hsiao-Hsien's *Three Times*, which sets three love stories in 1966, 1911 and 2005, each about 40 minutes long. The 1960s seems happiest when the advent of songs from America brightened up snooker halls in Taiwan, and the snooker table and its associated rituals became a place of courtship: proprieties are necessary, but relationships are allowed. Compare to this the repressed love of Ah Mei in 1911 for the progressive political reformer – proprieties prevent relationships – and the episode set in 2005, characterised by physical contact rather than feelings – the relationship is overwhelmed by there being no proprieties. It is the first episode that is the most erotic because beside the rituals of snooker, the wooing of her by him is given feeling by the two songs that keep being played, 'Rain and Tears' by Aphrodite's Child and 'Smoke Gets in Your Eyes' by The Platters, as if their repeated surfacing was a substitute for love-making, as if the physicality was being signposted without being shown.

Finally, Scruton's polemical preference for painting over photographs and film is slyly explored in *The Girl with a Pearl Earring*, which revels in the re-creation of seventeenth-century Dutch painting on film. Its central character is Griet, servant girl to the family of the painter Vermeer. The fiction is created that the portrait Vermeer paints of the girl with a pearl earring is of Griet, and is done as a commission to satisfy a patron who lusts after her. The core of the film is in showing how she assists in mixing the paint and becomes his assistant, a collaborator in a way in his painting. This communion is consummated not in an act of love, but in the act of painting, so that Vermeer's attraction towards her is sublimated in capturing her on canvas. In the final shot, we see Scarlett Johansson photographed as Griet in the portrait pose, wearing the pearl earring, gradually dissolve into a close-up of the original painting in an astonishingly natural way. Vermeer's cool portrait is suddenly invested with the feelings derived from the story, enlarging not eroding the mysteriousness of the painted portrait.

All these films have been made by males in homage to the female sex, and I write as a male spectator. How close the cinema can come to porno-graphic fantasy is illustrated in *King Kong*, whether in its original 1933 version of 100 minutes, or in the blockbuster remake from 2005 of 188 minutes (in the version released in cinemas). The film has attained a central status in cinema history for its representation of male desire in an extravagant way: the heroine tied to two posts as a sacrifice to King Kong, the symbol of virile force that will abduct and 'consummate' her. She appears to be an archetype of the personali-ty that is eclipsed by the body and subjected to male desire, in a scene of tre-mendous potency despite the special effects – or because of them inasmuch as they create a distancing effect that increases imaginative curiosity. But unlike a pornographic photograph, the film has a narrative dynamic such that a relation-ship between beast and beauty can materialise and personality can develop, so that in the end beauty has a sympathy with the beast. As a consequence when he is attacked, we feel his pain. This basic folktale was the brainchild of Merian C. Cooper who pours into the film his own experience as an action adventurer: he had taken part in Pershing's Mexican war with Pancho Villa, and had flown both in World War One and against the Bolsheviks during the civil war follow-ing the Russian Revolution. He had then made a pair of documentaries in Tur-key and Siam (now Thailand). *King Kong* became a vehicle for his experience as a larger-than-life adventurer, for his taste for the exotic, for the mythopoeic quality of the beauty and the beast story that overwhelms the fantasy. Its crudeness is unimportant. Rather the story is ripped from popular conscious-ness, not filtered through an educated literary and linguistic screen, and counts as an unadulterated myth appropriate not for words but images, a realisation of the unmediated cinematic imagination. Even in the recent version made by Peter Jackson, a good example of the cinema of hyperbole, the resources of digital cinema are marvellously deployed in the sequence in New York where the Beast has escaped and enjoys an idyll with Beauty, the city at night glisten-ing in the ice and snow. *King Kong* offers us the fantastic: a place of fantasy that we would not have dreamt – literally. In this respect alone, the cinema has enlarged the human imagination, taking us to places which it had not imagined visiting. *King Kong* is no different to 'The Lion the Witch and the Wardrobe', since both come out of the imagination. C. S. Lewis's is educated and literate; Merian Cooper is less literate but more experienced.

The realm of the fantastic is the realm of imagination: heroes and heroines stand in for us, embody our dreams. The list is huge: Ingrid Bergman as the exiled Ilsa in *Casablanca*, Charlie Chaplin as the little man who keeps bouncing back, Sylvester Stallone as Rambo single-handedly turning the historical defeat of the Vietnam War into the fantasy of victory, Masatoshi Nagase as the samurai Katagiri in *The Hidden Blade*, assassinating his tyrannical and sadistic overseer in a swift imperceptible movement of the knife without his victim realising what has happened, Alain Delon as the pseudo-samurai in the Parisian underworld adjusting the brim of his hat before his next job, the stellar Zarah Leander taking the German middle class on a flight from the realities of Nazi Germany, Clint Eastwood bent on revenge without compromise, apocalyptic even, Humphrey Bogart as Marlow in *The Big Sleep*, Bogart and Bacall in *To Have and Have Not* – who is the seducer and who the seduced? – and a whole series of actresses – Falconetti, Ingrid Bergman, Jean Seberg, Florence Carrez, Sandrine Bonnaire, to mention only a few – playing the martyr Joan of Arc, and outfacing their male accusers: the only woman in the movie, but what a woman!

Literature, painting, sculpture have always embodied our imaginings: did not teenagers watch 'Romeo and Juliet' in the centuries before movies thinking that this was them? Did males not look at the classical sculpture of a gladiator as a contemporary samurai in a role to aspire to? Indeed is not the classical nude, male and female, an idealisation of ourselves, how we would like to see ourselves, and others to see us?

Yet the movies have enlarged the possibilities enormously. Being Luke Skywalker in *Star Wars* is a conventional fantasy in an invented world. Being Randolph Scott in the desert places of Boetticher's Ranown Westerns plays the fantasy in an unfamiliar but semi-real world: men dressed up in the rocky, burning wilderness. Or Jean-Paul Belmondo playing at being the petty gangster,

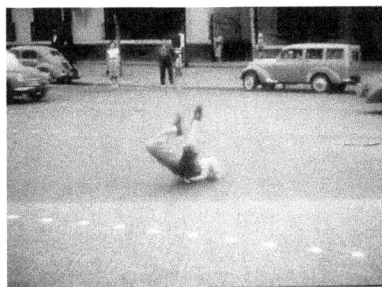 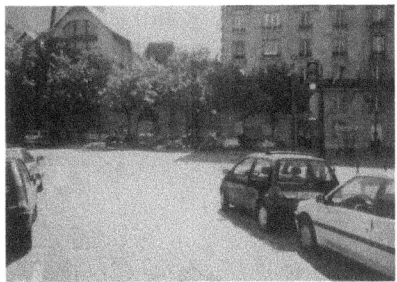

Michel Poiccard, in *A Bout de souffle*, grounds the fantasy in the big city for natives and tourists alike, for you can visit the Rue Campagne-Premiere in the 14e

arrondissement (right-hand image) and see the spot where Poiccard finally falls and dies (left).

*

Without the imagination of film-makers, the Western and the samurai film would not exist, and thus their imagination becomes our imagination. Trying to envisage these places and these characters on our own is beyond us. And although these worlds may exist in written stories first, it is the cinema that has made them a global commodity, consumable beyond national barriers. Above all they have to be realised pictorially: it is the desert landscapes, the Japanese palaces, the cowboy's outfit, the samurai's robes that need to be seen to be understood: we would have no frame of reference otherwise. Above all, we have no understanding of gunplay and swordplay without seeing them happen.

Crime films, whether encompassing the glamorous gangster or the petty hoodlum, are related but different since they locate their values to the contemporary world, the gangster film in America and the yakuza film in Japan. Common to all three genres – Western, samurai, crime film – are protagonists who make the law by their power and the exercise of violence. Indeed, physical conflict is their essence, for without it the entertainment value of these films would shrink markedly. On the other hand, unvarying repetition can reduce their attraction, and the three genres have flourished by ensuring that their stories are continually reinvented. If the 1950s are seen as a golden age of the Western, at least in terms of popularity and in the numbers made, it is because the genre rapidly matures in that decade from the run-of-the-mill B Westerns of the 1930s and learns from John Ford's serious engagement with the form in the 1940s.

No film-maker embodies this maturity better than Anthony Mann, who took the genre characters and finds a cosmic plane for them rooted in Greek tragedy. The masterpieces of the theatre (for example 'Hamlet', 'King Lear', 'Ghosts', 'Dance of Death', 'Long Day's Journey Into Night', 'Who's Afraid of Virginia Woolf?', 'The Birthday Party') dramatize the emotional tensions that membership of a family can create, where blood or marital relationships are much deeper than friendships, where they cannot be jettisoned if things go bad. Nowhere was this emphasis on the family more powerfully focused than in classical Greek tragedy, reflecting the importance of kinship networks that shaped power in ancient societies. Hence Aeschylus' 'Oresteia' trilogy (a story that was also treated by the other two great Greek tragedians); hence Sophocles' 'Oedipous Tyrannos/ Oedipus Rex' and 'Antigone', hence Euripides' 'Hippolytus' and 'Iphigeneia in Aulis'.

Anthony Mann, trained in the New York theatre in the 1920s and 1930s, first as an actor, then as a director for the Theater Guild in 1933 and for the Federal Theater Project from 1936 to 1938, had first-hand experience of the classical American theatre, including Greek tragedy. One of his early Westerns, *The Furies*, about a father-daughter relationship, has elements drawn from the Clytemnestra-Orestes story. By naming the cattle baron's ranch 'The Furies', the script and the title refer to the Erinyes, the Greek demonesses of 'retribution for wrongs and blood-guilt especially in the family' ['Oxford Classical Dictionary' s.v. 'Erinyes'], and the story recounts the fractured relationship between TC Jeffords and his daughter Vance, he trying to dispossess her, she scheming to destroy him. Thus, TC Jeffords is Clytemnestra, Vance Jeffords is Orestes, and TC's proposed bride is Aegisthus.

Reactions to the film generally focus on the energy of the performances by Walter Huston and Barbara Stanwyck as TC and Vance Jeffords, on the Freudianism that nails the film to its time, and an undeveloped quality in the film, "the characters obstinately refusing to come to life amid the studio sets and gloomy lighting" [Buscombe in 'Companion to the Western' s.v. 'The Furies']. The melodramatic and hysterical nature of the film is strongly present in the Greek originals but ritualized by the forms and conventions of the theatre (which were religious festivals). Mann made three Westerns in 1950, and it feels as if only the last of these, *Winchester '73*, following *Devil's Doorway* and *The Furies*, is the one that finally finds him at home in the genre. While *The Furies* has stronger links with the dark chiaroscuro films he made for RKO and Republic between 1947 and 1950, to which John Alton's camerawork made an important contribution, it is *Winchester '73* that opens the way for his engagement with the landscape of the American West, where one could say that the noir elements of his late 40s work is counterpointed – as a positive to a negative – in the bleaching light that informs the outdoor westerns: film noir becomes film noir et blanc. It is in these settings that Mann most powerfully expresses the family fractures of tragedy. For example in *The Man from Laramie* he draws on a subplot in 'King Lear', that of Gloucester and his two sons, Edmund and Edgar: the rancher Alec Waggoman has married long ago for money and power rather than love and precipitated the corrupt relationships of the family. Initially Mann wanted the hero Will Lockhart to be a brother to Alec's actual son, Dave, and the foster son, Vic – a trio of good and bad at either end and the adopted son in the middle, 'basically decent but corrupted by ambition' [Buscombe in 'Companion to the Western' s.v. 'The Man from Laramie'] but the producers would not allow this [Kitses 'Horizons West' p.158]. This original pattern of father and three 'sons' echoes King Lear and his daughters yet more closely than the subplot concerning Gloucester's family, *Lear* being the drama of Shakespeare that has the greatest resonance with the dynastic struggles of Greek tragedy. The story fascinated Mann, for when he died in 1967, he was thinking about a Western that reworked the Lear story. It is surely Mann's apprenticeship in the theatre allowing him to master structure and the crafting of dramatic conflict that enabled him to express an appropriate intensity in his 1950s Westerns. Screen violence has long been a staple of the American cinema, from fisticuffs to gunplay to war movies. What is so striking about Mann's films is the way they match the externals of the violence with a sense of an internal struggle in all the characters. He uses the landscape of the West, magnificent but harsh and untamed, alongside the 'landscape' of faces, seething with hatred, jealousy, or resentment – in effect harsh and untamed. In a number of films, the two antagonists engage in physical struggle which involves using the hand to 'go for the jugular', to harm the neck and face [Boxwell in 'Senses of Cinema']. His originality comes through also in the way that the rifle duel between the two brothers in *Winchester '73* relocates the genre convention of the fast draw in the main street to the mountains in order to provide a backdrop of suitable cosmic grandeur to the two brothers' hatred of each other, a hatred that must end in the death of one of them. Mann moves that conflict into even more imaginative territory in *Man of the West* where the hero, Link Jones, fights Coaley bare-handed without weapons, the intensity of their hatred made naked. On the other hand Mann understands equally that the act of violence conducted at one remove from the spectator can work the imagination in powerful ways. In a striking parallel to the love scene in *Les Amants*, where Moreau's hand is the provocative index of the act of love being performed on her naked body, it is Lockhart'sface in *The Man from Laramie* that we watch as a bullet is fired through his hand, a face whose features crumpling as the shot is fired register pain in a way that increases our identification with it, rather than shock us with the superficial horror of seeing the bullet go through the hand.

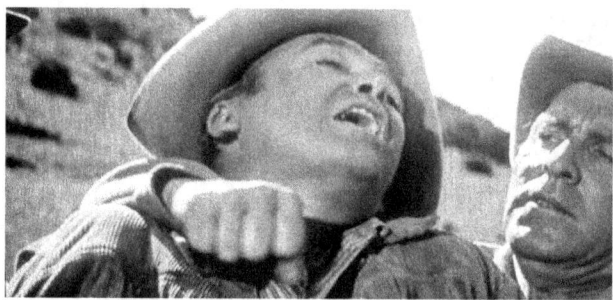

Mann's Westerns contribute to the definition of the twentieth century as the century of violence, the uncovering of subconscious desire and aggression, the overwhelming imperative of evolutionary struggle, and form an interesting bridge between Ford's 'enchanted' communities of *My Darling Clementine*, of his cavalry trilogy and of his rugged pastoral, *Wagonmaster*, and the 'disenchantments' of his late period, such as *The Searchers*, *Sergeant Rutledge* and *The Man Who Shot Liberty Valance*. It might be said that Ford is finally weaned off the Victorian sentimentalism he grew up with by the violence in Westerns such as Mann's.

That disenchantment, an occasional ingredient in the cinema of excess when it is not heart-on-sleeve emotionalism, then becomes the theme of Peckinpah's Westerns, who like Ford uses the genre to undergo a journey, from the elegiac quality of *Ride the High Country* (1961) to the unrestrained brutality of *The Wild Bunch* (1969), a parade of violent action, of masculine sexual domination, and a parody of Fordian conceptions of community – ill-mannered and self-conscious in a way that was fashionable to its time. It is an intriguing hypothesis that it requires action to be located in the US-Mexico border for Western cruelty to achieve its most naked expression: Peckinpah's *Major Dundee* (1964), a story about the US cavalry operating over the border into Mexico, was mutilated in the editing room, one casualty of which (and delicate sensibilities might be grateful for this) was the film's depiction of the Apaches massacring a cavalry troup and white settlers at their ranch. However, Peckinpah made up for this omission by the bloodbath, courtesy of the machine gun's blowing away of the rifle and pistol, in *The Wild Bunch*: the film is set in 1913 when the West had been won for civilization, except for the Texas-Mexico border, still a place for bounty hunters rather than the law, and for a corrupt Mexican warlord rather than state government. If we turn away from the cinema for a moment, this sanguinary history results in a literary masterpiece that holds an honourable place in the depiction of this border warfare, Cormac McCarthy's 'Blood Meridian' (1985). McCarthy then bridges this historical world with the modern one of drugs war on the border. His thrilling 'No Country for Old Men' (2005) is memorable for the creation of an apocalyptic daemon in the person of Chigurh as an agent of lethal violence, a violence which in its turn feeds back into the film of the novel made by the Coen Brothers, and wider still: this new 'McCarthyism' informs *The Three Burials of Melquiades Estrada* (2005).

The American crime film always wallowed in disenchantment. The period book-ended by the Hawks/Hecht 1932 version of *Scarface* and the DePalma/Stone version of 1983 revelled in gangster mythology, characterised by an orgy of violence (as opposed to the private eye film characterised by more intimate scenes of violence-making). The first *Scarface* was influential in setting a pattern, portraying the rise to power of its central character who is audacious in exceeding the ambitions of his deputies, his rivals and the boss who gives him a leg-up on the ladder of power, ruthless and explosive in exercising the violence necessary to his ambitions, and once power is achieved, corrupted by it so that his final destruction is really only self-destruction. The first *Scarface* was lifted from the level of the vulgar by Hawks's intention to portray in American terms the world of the Borgias, from which he drew the suppressed theme of incest between Camonte/Scarface and his sister. But its virtues are much more than this; crisp dialogue, bravura lighting and camera work, exploiting the confines of the studio to suggest the big city, and especially, speed, plus Hawks's trade-

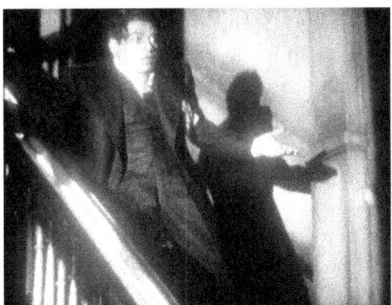

mark of 'good scenes' [Breivold p.41], all these elements are a necessary counterbalance to the rising hysteria of Paul Muni's performance as Camonte. Fifty years later, only the hysteria of Muni's performance as Camonte survives in Al Pacino's extravagance in DePalma's version. Hawks's taut 90 minutes has been turned into a ponderous 160 minutes, doubling the length while halving the interest for the spectator. Curiously too, the film makes an unexpected argument for censorship: Hawks (and his producer Howard Hughes) were obliged to be wily in circumventing the newly imposed production code in Hollywood. Because no such constraints were on DePalma and Stone, the dialogue sinks in a welter of swear words, reducing the one dimension to half a dimension. Violence-wise, the film starts with a shocker, a drug deal going wrong in a hotel with not just machine guns but a chainsaw as well. There is enough spattered blood to ward off torpor, but blood cannot save from indifference the ending, when Montana and his mansion are sprayed with bullets. The lifeblood has been drained from the affair, revealing it to be red paint.

The two *Scarfaces* neatly exemplify the shift from Classicism to the Mannerist during twentieth-century film-making. Although the Mannerist in DePalma's film has a dash of postmodernism in its references to previous gangster films such as the shot of the corpses from overhead from *The Rise and Fall of Legs Diamond* (1960) while the throwing of her drink in Montana's face by his courtesanly wife inverts the thrusting of a grapefruit into the face of his moll by the gangster in *Public Enemy* (1931), yet they fail to add depth. Indeed the period of the classic gangster film is better brought to a close by *The Godfather* (1971) and *The Godfather Part Two* (1974). While as excessive in length as the second *Scarface* – respectively 175 and 200 minutes – the family setting, the dynastic ramifications, the catholic and historical context, and above all the intrigues and plots all make the second *Scarface* look inferior. Whether consciously or not, the *Godfather* films make much better acknowledgement of Hawks's contention that the struggle between and within the gangster families only repeat in an unexpected context the tensions between Italian princedoms in the sixteenth century.

In general, the gangster myth is a descent into the underbelly of America not just by newspapermen and photographers looking for the facts and a good story, but by cinema's myth-makers espousing and exposing the glamour and despair of the criminal life. And yet even in this brutal will-to-power world, 're-enchantment' is possible that allows the spectator of the crime film to engage with a moral and psychological dimension beside that of providing entertainment, and when it engages with it successfully, it can create something universal. Take *Mystic River*. This is a crime film set in Boston, essentially a 'police procedural' film, directed by Clint Eastwood from a novel by Dennis Lehane. The story is finely plotted and exercises its own pull on the imagination: we need to know what happened. But what gives the film an unsuspected depth is its Catholic dimension, something we have to imagine because the film barely sketches it out: in other words it works at a story level in a highly satisfactory way, but it needs to be appreciated at another, which enlarges it in the mind, gives it an intriguing meaning.

There is hardly a church or priest visible: the nearest we get is at the first communion of Jimmy's daughter, Nadine, when we find ourselves inside the church, and a priest is visible in long shot at the altar. This is ceremonial in which Jimmy participates as a good Catholic from Boston should. But part of the film's power is the way that confession, a key practice in Catholicism, is not used in any way to exorcize the drama experienced by the three boys at the beginning of the film, when Dave Boyle is abducted and abused by two men posing as policemen. The dramatic force of the film stems from this knowledge which is bottled up by the three men and by the community. It is a story of crime and punishment, but the desolation is in the removal of any redemption, for the wrong man is killed in revenge for the murder of Jimmy's daughter. We know that death is one sort of release for Dave Boyle but the film ends ambiguously: some of the protagonists know that the wrong man was killed and the trauma is therefore renewed in a new way for different people.

Also, Jimmy is a 'Catholic criminal': just as *The Godfather* is permeated with Italian-American Catholicism, at the end Jimmy Marcus sits on the steps with his family watching the parade (as Corleone does after he has carried out out the assassination of the Black Hand, Don Fanuccio), and side-by-side with his rage for vengeance sit compassionate motives, for he has killed Brendan's father but he still ensures Brendan receives (anonymously) $500 a month. He employs as his enforcers, the Savage brothers, who have an ingrained, natural brutality – to whom violent solutions are the only way of redressing disagreements and displeasures. *Mystic River* thus depicts a whole world, well beyond the immediate intricacies of the crime, the murder of Jimmy's daughter that provides the dramatic hinge of the story. This other dimension is offered in glimpses, not in explicit sequences or explanations – but this light, almost invisible sketching is the more compelling for the way it is veiled by the story. It relies on the spectator to carefully pull it back and reveal what is going on.

A discussion of violence in the cinema, at least American cinema, comes to rest appropriately enough on Clint Eastwood, born an age ago in 1930 and steeped in moviemaking ever since he starred in the TV series, *Rawhide*, in the 1950s. Jim Kitses has described his cowboy persona as a 'redemptive force despite himself' [Kitses, 'Horizons West' (London: BFI Publishing 2004), p.286] whose agency of redemption is the gun that achieves not taming of the wilderness as in Ford, but a satisfaction for the evil violence of the world. The idea culminates in his most powerful Western, *Unforgiven* (1992), where Will Munny, sucked back into his violent past like Link Jones in *Man of the West*, can only exchange that past for oblivion by apocalyptic violence. *Unforgiven* starts as a sordid little story about Will seeking the monetary reward for two wanted men, one of whom had disfigured a whore, but this plotline swings aside to ensnare him in a battle against evil expressed in the sadism of the Sheriff of Big Whiskey, Little Bill Daggett. In order to return the scales of good violence and bad violence to equilibrium, by the death of Little Bill, Will must himself undergo brutal treatment at his hands before he can carry out the retribution necessary to the drama. The power of this end sequence derives from the story's focus on the barbarism of death in the West – no ethics, annihilation of the body, killing in a drunken stupor: in effect a consciousness, and conscience, suppressed. Will has a personal motive for exacting retribution because of the killing of Ned for a murder he did not commit, and for the sight of him in his coffin flanked by burning torches, 'decorating the saloon' where Little Bill and his cronies are gathered. It is night, the rain pours down, the gloomily lit mainstreet is a river of mud – a noir version of the Western town from which the sunlight has vanished. Will enters the saloon and the massacre he performs is punctuated by the thunderstorm outside and dialogue, so that the spectator switches between the fascination of watching and the fascination of listening, sound and image converged. The dialogue is used to reflect on violence in the West, to 'demystify' it, to remove its legendary gloss in favour of the brutality of fact – only to put it back on its pedestal as a means of catharsis: we are awed by Will Munny's mastery of the gun. When he says to the dime novelist, "I've always been lucky when it comes to killing folks," we should believe him but cannot.

The name of Clint Eastwood, despite a list of over two dozen features to his credit as a director, only four of which are Westerns, is closely linked to the genre and an obsession in them with retributive violence colours a number of his non-Western films (although by no means all). As Will Munny rides out at the end of *Unforgiven*, threatening to visit devastation on the town if they do not bury Ned properly, the stars and stripes can be seen hanging limply behind him in the

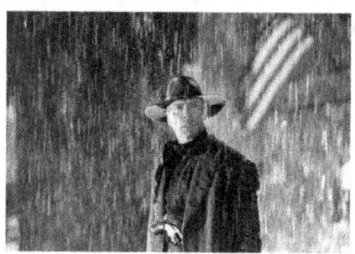

driving rain. This brief linkage of 'good' violence with the symbol for America is explored at feature length in the first of his two films about the capture of the island of Iwo Jima from the Japanese in 1945, marking a yet further stage in his career: TV actor – actor in spaghetti westerns – Hollywood star – Hollywood director – Hollywood director of stars beside himself [Kitses,'Horizons West' (London: BFI Publishing 2004), pp.305-6 has an incisive vignette on Eastwood's career]. In *Flags of Our Fathers* and *Letters from Iwo Jima*, he is now prepared to engage with the facts of twentieth-century American history rather than its legendary nineteenth-century dimension, although, to complicate matters, the Marines' capture of Iwo Jima has become the stuff of military legend.

Eastwood's ambition is marked by his venture into territory that was new to him, the battle movie. One might be surprised that an actor and director so fascinated by masculine violence had not taken on a war film before now, but he preferred to give his imagination rein in fictional settings: to make films about contemporary battle ties you, at least to some extent, to historical facts and realistic scenes of men at war. If this project has come late in his career, does it release feelings that have long gestated inside him? Stephen Spielberg and Terrence Malick had both recently made striking films about World War Two, *Saving Private Ryan* and *The Thin Red Line*, set respectively in Normandy in France and in Guadalcanal in the Pacific. Eastwood might seem of their generation, so that like them he wished late in his career to mark the heroic efforts of his parents' generation in the war. There is however a small but important difference between them: whereas Spielberg and Malick were born in 1947 and 1945 respectively, Eastwood was born in 1930, and so would have been 15 at the time of Iwo Jima, old enough to have read about this epic battle and old enough to recognize the photograph of raising the flag of Old Glory on Mount Suribachi as an iconic moment in America's progress towards victory. This would make *Flags of Our Fathers*, the story of Iwo Jima from the American point of view, a personal one. What the 60-year gestation in making it also does is to prompt Eastwood to do something unprecedented in the history of the battle movie, namely to make a companion piece about the battle as seen from the Japanese side, *Letters from Iwo Jima*.

The capture of the island was marked by extreme violence: 6821 Americans killed and 20,000 wounded (out of an invasion force of circa 70,000), while on the Japanese side, virtually all of the 21,000 defenders were killed or had committed suicide. But there is no retributive element in Eastwood's treatment; rather both sides fight because they have to in the way they have been trained. For the Americans that includes motives of courage and comradeship; for the Japanese that includes a sense of shame in surrender: both are versions of military honour. In general, how the cinema has enlarged our sense of what infantry battle looks like, even feels like, is discussed in the next chapter. Eastwood's films make an excellent introduction to it as they come at the end of a long line of American World War Two movies, and in their own way form a commentary on them.

The first point to make is a controversial one. Putting the photograph of the raising of the flag on Mt Suribachi at the centre of *Flags*, and its subsequent use in a drive for war bonds in 1945 which involved three of the Marines concerned, enables Eastwood to make some pointed comments on his country – how a symbol like a flag can be exploited for shabby ends, how the showbiz nature of the war-bonds drive was both successful and inappropriate, how racism kept surfacing in the treatment of the Indian Marine, Ira Hayes, how a photograph is not what it might seem, and the truth that how the conquering hero feels and how he is perceived can be two different things; all contribute to the melancholy fact that post-war adjustment for returning soldiers can be difficult. By the end you doubt that fighting for the flag is so glorious, when the victory is so costly in terms of lives and trauma.

One of the virtues of the project is the way one film mirrors the other, both starting from innocuous documents, the photograph in the case of *Flags* and the Japanese letters home, written but never sent, in *Letters*. *Flags* ends with a shot of the U. S. Memorial on Mount Suribachi; *Letters* begins with the Japanese memorial. The landings in particular are seen from the two angles. Both break the narrative with flashbacks (*Letters*) and flash forwards (*Flags*). Specific narrative links are few, but the glimpse in *Flags* of Japanese soldiers who had committed suicide by blowing themselves up with grenades is explained in a gruesome sequence in *Letters*. But the tilt of the films is significantly different too. The flash forwards in *Flags* are substantial and bear the weight of the narrative, while the flashbacks in *Letters* are peripheral to the story of the defence of Iwo Jima. Secondly, *Letters* devotes most of its time to the clearing-up operation in the month following the fall of Mount Suribachi, while battle action in *Flags* is confined to that single part of the campaign to capture the island.

Letters from Iwo Jima, while drawing on two Japanese books, has still been conceived by the American victors, which is a constant of Hollywood's preoccupation with battle over the last hundred years. Eastwood creates a sympathetic portrait of General Kuribayashi charged with the defence of Iwo Jima, who had spent time in America as military attaché in the early 1930s [see Wikipedia s.v. 'Letters from Iwo Jima' and 'Tadamichi Kuribayashi']. An American sensibility has also shaped the depiction of Saigo, the reluctant and indeed incompetent Japanese soldier, who is saved from punishment or death three times by Kuribayashi, and who survives at the end, a reward (if reward it be) for the scepticism he had felt for the business of defending the island. While not exactly non-violent, his incompetence with a rifle gives a hook for pacifist audiences to hold on to. Late in his film career, Eastwood wants to praise vulnerability, not just the recoil from violence by brave and capable men, but also the futility of war for an outsider like Saigo. There are no heroes or villains therefore, only complexity.

Spielberg co-produced the two films, and the documentary feel of his *Saving Private Ryan* stands behind the sequence showing the Marines landing on the beach at Iwo Jima and moving inland. A common denominator in many American battle films is a view of the soldiers on the landing craft preparing to hit the beach, and *Flags of our Fathers* is no exception. But the film is shot in black, silver and grey, drained of colour, as if it was gravitating naturally to the landing in the black and white film, *A Walk in the Sun* (1945). Despite the vividly coloured blood, war is fought in black and white, the tonality of the 1940s.

Except that tonality is illusory. The credit sequence at the end of *Flags* is made particularly poignant by running a series of photographs taken during and after the combat itself. After the filmic storm of steel, and the aural assaults of re-created battle, there is something generically different about these still photographs. They are mementos of a real event, but they remind us that the film is also a memory but of a different kind. Since violence has a particular fascination for film-makers, the violence of war has been magnificently portrayed in the cinema, but the temptation to exploit violence, to make it lurid, which is the path the gangster film and horror film are much of the time drawn down, is more naturally resisted in the twentieth-century battle movie: the subject is too weighty for such exploitative treatment.

3   LIGHTS CAMERA ACTION AND THE POOR BLOODY INFANTRY

War has always been a favourite subject of literature: the story of David in the Book of Kings (maybe tenth century BC) in the Bible is made vivid by the recurrent element of armed conflict; the drama of Homer's 'Iliad' (seventh century BC) takes place in war and its warrior protagonists are defined by their fighting prowess; Thucydides' 'Histories' (end of fifth century BC) document war and the causes of war, which he deems inevitable because it is innate in human nature for one state to seek to have power over another [Thucydides 1.76.2. The quotation is from a speech by the Athenians to the assembly in Sparta, but the sentiment is part of Thucydides' mental outlook]; Books 7 to 12 of the 'Aeneid' of Vergil (the Roman 'Iliad', end first century BC) deploy Roman rhetorical poetry to describe battle. If these authors are treasures of European civilisation, it is because that civilization has been forged in the geographical crucible of multiple nation states jostling for position and status in a crowded area divided by mountains, rivers, seas: battle came naturally to its occupants, and after battle reflection in literature and art. More recently, war is in the foreground and the background of many of Shakespeare's history plays and tragedies, and the iconic novel of the nineteenth century is 'War and Peace'.

Writing well about falling in love, or family conflicts, may not be easy, but at least these situations are familiar to readers. The subject of battle on the other hand poses a ticklish question: how do you convey the reality of it to the many readers who have never been in one? How do you make readers feel they were there? Shakespeare, with his acute artistic intelligence, used the question to kickstart his drama about King Henry V with an invitation to the audience to use their imagination. When the Prologue craves apology for the inadequacies of the stage – "a kingdom for a stage", "Can this cock-pit hold the vasty fields of France?", "Into a thousand parts divide one man", "Turning th'accomplishment of many years into an hour-glass" – Shakespeare was encouraging the imagination the audience would bring: "O for a Muse of Fire, that would ascend the brightest Heaven of Invention," "Let us. . . on your imaginary forces work," "Peace out our imperfections with your thoughts", "Make imaginary puissance", "For 'tis your thoughts that now must deck our kings." When the Prologue appears to seek indulgence – "gently to hear, kindly to judge our play" – does he in his heart of hearts boast at the amazement his audience will feel? And when Laurence Olivier films *Henry V*, and the English countryside serves in a passable fashion for the vasty fields of France, and he shows us the wooden O, the theatre in the round, as the field of Agincourt, he gets the best of both worlds, like the man of the theatre and the man of cinema that he was, so that he can both cherish the little stage for these great events, and yet bow to Ben Jonson's jibe about presenting history with the help of "three rusty swords", transforming the stage into a battlefield with arches and horsemen. We do not have to imagine the horses "printing their proud hooves i' the receiving earth", for we can see them do so and on the soundtrack hear the overwhelming thunder of the hoof beats.

Would Shakespeare have written for the cinema? Yes, no doubt, for the money, but reluctantly: surely he would have taken the purist line that to use words to underpin images was to dilute their power? Cinema as an artistic expression of battle seizes its audience in a quite different way from the theatre: it defines battle, in essence does the spectator's imagining.

This chapter picks up the discussion of Clint Eastwood's *Flags of our Fathers* and *Letters from Iwo Jima* at the end of it to argue for the success film-makers have had in extending the boundaries of this particular area of the human imagination, for in one particular way literature and painting, in their long history, have failed to do full justice to the reality of battle: they honoured the heroism it brought forth and the pain it caused, but depicting its physical reality has proved beyond it. Film on the other hand, the art of the common man for the century of the common man, can pitch the spectator into the front line, where battles are won or lost not by the warrior heroes of Homeric warfare but by the "poor bloody infantry". Also, the focus is on conventional battle on land, not on war at sea or war in the air, which require their own treatment, nor on irregular war, such as guerrilla or partisan war such as the resistance films recalling Occupied Europe. These exclusions mean the omission of such notable works as *Paisà* (1946, especially the last episode), *The Battle of Algiers* (1965) and *Army of Shadows* (1969). Then there are the flying scenes of *The Battle of Britain* (1969) and the remarkable *First Light* (2010), one pilot's story of that contest with fine combat footage. John Ford is the film poet of battle, witness his cavalry trilogy and the outstanding *They Were Expendable* (1945) – but the former is nineteenth-century irregular war (as it might be described) and therefore outside my terms of reference, while the latter is largely naval warfare.

War films can usually be put into one of two categories. The first group aims to convey the physical reality of battle, the second to explore the mental reality – what effect the sights and sounds of physical action have on soldiers in the thick of it. The two categories do not exclude each other, for a film aiming to get an audience to feel the effects of battle on mental states will want to convey the appearance of battle to the senses, nor can a film engaged in reproducing battle easily avoid showing human reactions to it. This topic is made the more lively because public feelings about war have been hugely influenced by films, so that rightly or wrongly conceptions of what, for example, twentieth-century battle looked like are shaped by such films as *All Quiet on the Western Front* (1930), *The Sands of Iwo-Jima* (1949), *Apocalypse Now* (1979) and many others. But it is more than the imagination that has been shaped, for public attitudes have been powerfully moulded as well, something both pacifist film-makers and militant governments have firmly grasped in the way they have promoted anti-war and pro-war sentiment through the cinema. Politicians arguing for war have the harder job, for two reasons: narrative focuses on individuals so that we identify with them and when in war they suffer, so we suffer too and conclude that war is a bad thing. Secondly, the cruelties of technological war in the twentieth and twenty-first centuries undermine human heroics, human courage being eclipsed by 'smart' bombs, 'smart' shells and 'smart' bullets.

When the century turned in 1900, the cinema had just been invented. Soon afterwards war erupted on a scale and with an awfulness that was new to mankind. Besides its colossal carnage, the First World War redefined war for Europeans and beyond Europe, as not just the clash of arms in the hands of humans, but the clash of armaments, metallic, impersonal, unthinking, and quite indiscriminate in their effects. When it ended in 1918, the shock of the war's effects, which included literal shell-shock, caused public silence as if the combatants did not dare to recount what had happened, and non-combattants were too divorced from the experience. When writers recovered their voice, books began to pour out. In Britain (for example), 'Goodbye to All That' (1928), 'Undertones of War' (1928), 'Journey's End' (1928), 'Death of a Hero' (1929), 'Memoirs of an Infantry Officer' (1930) entered the public domain from the late 1920s on, and their effect became cumulative as the century wore on.

In France, Henri Barbusse's 'Le Feu: journal d'une escouade / Under Fire: story of a squad', immersed the reader in the experiences of the front line and won the Prix Goncourt– but this was in 1916, during the war itself. After the war had ended memoirs and journals were published in numbers, as well as novels inspired by personal experience of combat. The experience in Germany was different, except that the war did produce one masterpiece, 'In Stahlgewittern / Storm of Steel' by Ernest Jünger. First self-published in 1920 it was frequently and heavily revised subsequently, as if the author was wrestling with how best to preserve the sense of lived experience. Jünger was uniquely qualified to write it, having volunteered in August 1914 and having fought throughout the war, surviving several woundings. It makes a fascinating comparison with David Jones's 'In Parenthesis': Jones too served for much of the war, from 1915 to 1918, but unlike Jünger his memoir, after marinating in his mind and being delayed by nervous breakdown, was only published in 1937. Because of its poetic and mythological content, mixed in with closely observed documentary detail, it is different from all other literature on the war, and while it has not been filmed, it has been made into a striking opera by Iain Bell to mark the hundredth anniversary of the Battle of the Somme in which Jones had fought. It was just one of the considerable number of works commissioned to mark the centenary of World War One, a period which, at least in the UK, provoked an intense national remembrance, with two notable film contributions at the beginning and the end. In 2014, the BBC screened a three-part series, each one-hour long, 'Our World War', focusing on the infantryman's experience on the Western Front. The third part, *War Machine*, recounts, from the unpublished account by Private Charles Rowland written when he was 80, the experience of the tank battle at Amiens in August 1918 which marked the start of the end of the war. Shot in the visceral style that Spielberg pioneered in *Saving Private Ryan* (see below), it pitches the viewer into the action with claustrophobic, jolting shots of the men inside the tank, and it is unafraid to verge on non-realism with Private Rowland's hallucinations. The ignition of the tank's motors uses a digital re-creation in close-up of the spark starting up the engine, a device which helps dramatize the tension of the moment when the engine fails and has to be restarted, otherwise the tank becomes a sitting target for the enemy artillery. Monochrome colour is used to offset the vividness of fire flashes, and the soundtrack has been meticulously designed to alternate a pounding ostinato with quietness, and at the end a melancholic rock song to convey a sense of 'lostness'. There is too a strong script by Joe Barton bringing out the tensions between the men forced to work as a team. As they stumble out of the tank at the end, an officer asks, "Anyone wounded?" The wounds he wants to know about are physical not mental, and those emerged more in the decades following the war than during it.

In 2018 a quite different commemoration of the war came out: Peter Jackson, the New Zealand film director whose grandfather had fought in the war and for whom the event is something of an obsession, oversaw a project to digitize and colourize newsreels held in the archive of the Imperial War Museum in London. The 100 hours of film he looked at were then distilled into a film of 100 minutes, i.e. a ratio of 1:60. Because the soundtrack uses archival interviews with combatants, the film has an unmediated quality – the images feel fresh and novel, and there is no distancing authorial narration, just a balance between verbal memory and visual memory. Fittingly the release of *They Shall not Grow Old* close to the centenary of the Armistice produced a culmination to the four years of remembrance, going back to the first visual recordings of the war, to make the point that "their faces and voices live for evermore".

*

America's entry into the war was late but decisive. Four million military personnel were mobilised and the event had enough of an impact for Hollywood to broach the subject in *The Big Parade* (1925) and *What Price Glory?* (1926), to give two examples. Then in 1930 two notable treatments, one American, one German, the first one celebrated, the latter obscure, were able to make use of the new technology of sound to make a new kind of film about the First World War, and indeed about battle. Erich Maria Remarque's 'Nicht Neues im West' had been published in 1929 and has subsequently sold hundreds of thousands of copies. It was aided in this by its filming in 1930 by Hollywood as *All Quiet on the Western Front*, the reputation of which is not necessarily easy to pin down. It is famous because of its pacifist message, articulating a denunciation of the war as not just terrible to fight, but grossly deceptive in the way soldiers marched off joyfully, and came home either dead or with morale shredded to pieces (and in Germany's case, defeated). This was unlike *The Big Parade* stirring 'snatches of all-American whimsy' [Milne in 'Time Out Film Guide'] into its portrayal, or *What Price Glory?* mixing in comedy. Rather it was an assault on militarism: in a scene near the beginning the flower of German youth, at their school desks, is stirred into battle by the oratory of their teacher who does not shrink from reciting the Roman poet Horace: "Dulce et decorum est pro patria mori" ("it is a sweet thing, and an honourable one, to die for one's country"), the words conveying a special bitterness to an audience whose memories of the war were still fresh. Yet nowadays the tone of its pacifism feels mannered as a result of its hectoring, histrionic tone.

So should it be famous for its realism? In the scenes on the front line, the director Lewis Milestone and his set designers bring to the fore the ruin of war, its squalor, and its mud – which Napoleon had called 'the fifth element' in battle. What is more, the very recent invention of sound cinema means that the effect is not just visual but acoustic as well, bringing to audiences an idea of the horrific sound world in the trenches. The cinema did not just reveal what the exotic, the unfamiliar and the unknown looked like, but what sounds it made as well. *All Quiet* was released in August 1930. Three months earlier, a German film, *Westfront 1918*, had appeared with enough similarity of content to suggest that UFA, the German studio, wanted to make their own version of *All Quiet*, but finding Universal had got to the film rights first, they commissioned Ladislaus Vajda to write a fresh script incorporating a number of elements in Remarque's book. This is only speculation, but note the following common elements: the camaraderie among soldiers in the trenches including harmonica music, fraternizing with the French women including sleeping with them, return to their homeland where there is mental dislocation, disembodied hands (on the

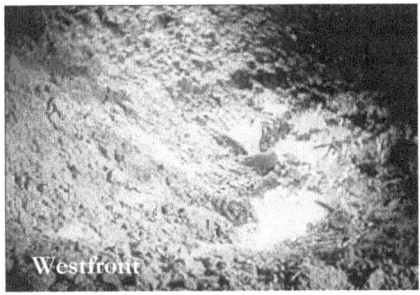

wire in *All Quiet*, sticking out of the mud in *Westfront*), French attack on a German trench followed by a retreat, Franco-German peace-making (in *All Quiet* Paul in the crater giving drink to the Frenchman he has bayoneted as he dies; in *Westfront*, the French soldier announcing to Karl at the very end he is 'camarade, pas ennemi'), and the hospital in the ruined church. In the event *Westfront 1918* was eclipsed at the time, and has been ever since, by *All Quiet*: since it is a German not an American film, its promotion and distribution was significantly weaker, and it lacked the underpinning that the title of Remarque's bestseller gave to the film of *All Quiet*. Yet it ought to be as celebrated, not least because it mirrors the pacifism of *All Quiet* at several points: it centres on a group of German soldiers, narrating their disintegration as a group and how they died; its message is that World War One was an insane waste of human life. At the same time, it achieves a greater realism than *All Quiet*. Its director GW Pabst paid particular attention to capturing the quality of the landscape of battle by means of a visual eloquence about the mud, and in making the camera as mobile as the early sound technology permitted. He deliberately eschewed filming from inside a stationary soundproof booth, and instead allowed the camera to move by opting to use a mobile 'blimp' (a soundproof casing around the body of the camera). This visual quality was matched by using sound creatively, once again within severe constraints since the technology of mixing sound from different sources did not exist. "Consequently, the sound of artillery bombardment had to be eliminated to insert lines of dialogue. . . . This crude method required numerous painstaking trials and errors before an acceptable synchronization could be achieved." [See Attwell and Geister.] The result of Pabst's methods is that *Westfront 1918* feels more realistic, two sequences in particular standing out: the first is of German soldiers going into the trenches at night in silence, which is then broken by a barrage opening up. When two of them are trapped underground in the bombardment, others try to rescue them fruitlessly. This is an eight-minute sequence told solely in image and sound. A second sequence later in the film, some seven minutes long, also wordless, well illustrates the fog of war: a long shot of some two minutes' duration shows a French attack across the mud and the wire of no man's land, leading to Germans being overwhelmed in the trenches. Then suddenly the French withdraw, leaving their dead. The sequence is made more vivid by the presence of tanks bulldozing their way through until they are immobilized.

All Quiet has its own effective realism too: one ghoulish touch shows the French advancing across no man's land and being machine-gunned; when one soldier is blown to bits we get a glimpse of his severed hands hanging on the wire. But this realism is secondary to its real strength, which is the narrative of the career of Paul as a soldier, from student ardour to mental isolation in the trenches and death – that is to say, an account of the mental journey Paul makes, in which he both grows up and suffers the pain of withdrawing into himself. Paul's relationships change: he responds to his teacher at the beginning but when on home leave he returns to the school, he tells an unconvinced class that it is "dirty and painful to die for your country". His friends gradually die off until only he and the old soldier Kat are left. When Kat is killed, Paul withdraws completely into himself. The dialogue in the film feels stilted much of the time, expressing convincing inner thoughts in an unconvincing way. For example Paul's moralizing speech to the French soldier he has bayonetted and with whom he shares a crater as he dies is delivered theatrically at the corpse, when what is needed is a voiceover of Paul's thoughts while the camera focuses on his impassive face. This is a clumsiness stemming from inexperience of how to use the new sound technology, and in reaching an appreciation of the film the viewer needs to make allowances for it as an element of the film's style. As we shall see, Milestone was to learn from this experience in making *A Walk in the Sun* fifteen years later.

*

Books and films do not cause wars, *pace* the Vichy spokesman who said in 1940: "If we have lost the war, it's because of *Quai des brumes*" [Sadoul p.205]. Perhaps he was thinking that that film's desperate atmosphere at the end of the decade was a natural conclusion to the pacifism of *All Quiet on the Western Front* at the beginning of it, Jean in *Quai des brumes* being as mentally isolated as Paul at the end of *All Quiet*. It is possible therefore to argue a connection between *All Quiet* and the feeling of 'never again' that prevailed in the 1930s for example in Britain and France. Ever since, film (and now television) has been at the forefront of the process of connecting the public with the nature of the war that their country has been engaged in. This has been true of all wars fought by the Western powers in the twentieth century in one way or another, the paradigm for which has been the Vietnam War. This process of historical interpretation and understanding takes place at the most substantial level in writing about the war, but this cannot be divorced from the visual imagination which people bring as well. First of all the Vietnam War is famous for the fact that even while it was being waged, news cameramen and still photographers were bringing its horrors into the living room in a newly immediate way, quite eclipsing the one (notorious) pro-war film to have been made during the war, John Wayne's *Green Berets* (1968). When the war ended for the Americans with the fall of Saigon in 1975, within five years both *The Deer Hunter* (1978) and *Apocalypse Now* (1979) had newly defined the war in hallucinatory terms, as if the "veracity" of news images needed supplementing. The late 1980s then saw a spate of Vietnam battle films, including *Hamburger Hill* (1987), *Full Metal Jacket* (1987), *Platoon* (1987) and *84 Charlie Mopic* (1988), seeking to convey the intensity of battle and its brutalizing effect on those fighting it. (Alongside these efforts there has been the complementary group of 'Vietnam veteran' films, which as a subject for the cinema has arguably been more potent as vehicles to explore the mental impact of the war.) Yet it is the documentary method that has produced the two works that move rather than numb, as if the primary relationship between the visual material and the events they portray give them an authenticity which challenges fictional re-creation. These are *Dear America* (1987) and the television documentary *Two Days in October* (US title) / *How Vietnam was Lost* (UK) (2005). Both rely on newsreel and amateur footage as the visual ground over which speech is used as a counterpoint, in *Dear America* as voice-over (the soldiers' letters home) and in *Two Days in October*, the surviving protagonists commenting on the action in which they were involved thirty years later. In both films, the subject is thickened by the mixing of domestic elements. In *Dear America* one layer of the soundtrack is given over to countercultural anthems of popular music, many of them created in reaction to American militarism especially in Indochina. The effect is in the end muddying, as though countercultural expression at home was equivalent to the experiences in the Vietnam jungle, when patently they were of a different order. *Two Days in October* (based on David Marraniss's book 'They Marched into Sunlight') achieves far greater clarity by cross-cutting two simultaneous events from 1967: an incident in Vietnam when American GIs were ambushed and lost sixty-one of their number, and the student protest at the University of Wisconsin-Madison against the presence on campus of recruiters from Dow Chemicals (who were involved in the manufacture of napalm), a protest that turned violent, so that these two Americas come face to face in the way the two unfolding events crisscross each other, ratcheting up the pain and emotion they still cause even now.

Portrayal of the Vietnam War is significant in the history of the cinema for another reason: the films are made in colour, the particular attraction of which was that it made the appearance of war more vivid: an explosion is much more spectacular in colour than black and white. The Hollywood action films that came out of the Second World War (for example, *Guadalcanal Diary*, *Objective Burma!*, *The Sands of Iwo Jima*, *Battleground*, *The Story of GI Joe*) were made largely in black and white. It is really only in the 1960s, with the advent of the blockbuster war film (such as *The Great Escape* (1962), *Battle of the Bulge* (1966), *Army of Shadows* (1969), *The Battle of Britain* (1969), *Tora! Tora! Tora!* (1970) and *A Bridge Too Far* (1977)) that colour begins to be used to add a vividness to the story. (This is not to deny that the studios were schizophrenic about the merits of colour and black-and-white: the milestone film in this development was *The Longest Day* (1962), which Daryl Zanuck chose to make in black and white, and subsequent blockbusters such as *The Train* (1964) and *Paris brûle-t-il?/Is Paris burning?* (1966) were made in black and white.) To appreciate this most fully, we need to go back from the twentieth century to the nineteenth, to the spectacular Soviet version of Tolstoy's 'War and Peace' that was made as an eight-hour film in 1967.

The western front of the First World War, while containing a number of key battles, comes to us as a state of mind and body rather than a sequence of incidents, four years of continuous mud and slaughter, a permanent stalemate. The conventional view of warfare on the other hand is that winning battles is the key to victory – and this is well-suited to the capabilities of the cinema, to show the beginning, middle and end of an encounter, to give an overview of the engagement rather than the eye view of a particular protagonist. When Tolstoy described the Battle of Borodino in 'War and Peace', he portrayed it through the eyes of Bezukhov and Bolkonsky. Because Bezukhov travels over the battlefield as a free agent, present at but not a participant in events, Tolstoy has a means of giving some sense of the whole.

In making the film version, the director Sergei Bondarchuk goes beyond giving merely the fixed viewpoints of Tolstoy's two heroes: Bolkonsky with his regiments behind the lines, waiting to go into battle; and Bezukhov, principally with the battery at the Raevski redoubt. Secondly, Bondarchuk reinterprets Tolstoy's historico-philosophical framework: Tolstoy writes about the opposition between Bezukhov/goodness and Napoleon/badness, and Napoleon's destiny to stumble and fall at the hands of the Russians who embody History. Bondarchuk elevates these ideas further, making of the Russian army an embodiment of moral superiority, of the battle a symphony in praise of war, and of Kutuzov the visionary general who can see beyond the 'defeat' at Borodino to the final ruin of Napoleon and the French army's dreams. As an example of this elevated tone, he copies faithfully the striking scene in Tolstoy during preparations for the battle when the icon of Our Lady of Smolensk is paraded among the army at work. Everything comes to a halt and common soldiers, officers and the general, all fall to their knees in veneration. The soundtrack on the film allows a dimension denied to Tolstoy: a Russian choir singing a hymn of prayer to the Virgin for victory and salvation. A liturgical chant sung by a choir is heard off-screen; we are then shown a closer view of the procession as a prelude to close-ups of soldiers crossing themselves fervently and singing. Kutuzov pays his respects to the icon by falling to his knees, and the sequence concludes with a shot of an intense blue sky, the religious banners silhouetted on the horizon and a cloud drifting across the late afternoon sun. The choir that had begun off-screen, then revealed as on-screen, is now heard again as an off-screen accompaniment.

The section dealing with the Battle of Borodino lasts some thirty-five minutes. The first impression is of something enormous, carried out on a huge canvas, 'canvas' being the necessary word in view of the painterly effects the film achieves, nineteenth-century painting that is: infantry and cavalry in movement,

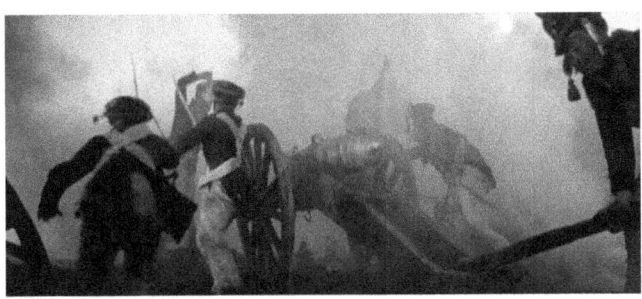

battle in the sunlight, the visual poetry of plumes of smoke from artillery and from rifles. Once the battle is fully underway, fire seems to become the predominant element, reflecting the way that the order of battle has become confused and turbulent. It appears that Bondarchuk filmed a huge amount of material, the editing of which then became a crucial stage in completing the film: we see lots of individual actions – soldiers marching and firing, an artillery salvo, a cavalry charge, i.e. men following their particular orders in disregard of the activity going on around them, symbolized most acutely by Bolkonsky's regiment at the rear of battle, unflinching from their positions as their numbers are decimated by French cannon: the soldiers remain heroically obedient to orders. As the battle progresses, this order breaks down, marked vividly by a group of riderless horses passing across the screen. The dead bodies pile up, and the battery of guns on the Raevski redoubt begins to run out of ammunition. At the opening, the camera is comparatively static as the movement occurs in front of it. As battle progresses, Bondarchuk uses elaborate tracking shots giving it a movement which doubles the movement on screen. At the climax of the sequence, and following the mortal wounding of Bolkonsky and the encounter with his rival for Natasha in the dressing station, the voiceover becomes more lofty yet in tone, and a sequence of freeze frames follows: of the faces of the artillery men at the redoubt, and overhead shots of the battlefield after the battle.

It is fitting that the Soviet cinema, in which the theories of montage had been most assiduously practised, should have produced this essentially visual depiction of battle with a bravura piece of direction, of cinematography and of editing. It aspires in effect to be symphonic, aided in the process by the score of Vyacheslav Ovchinnikov which is used for much of the battle, mingled with the noise of gunfire and explosions, the sound of horses' hooves. The effect is achieved with some discretion: the music is never allowed to overwhelm the image, and the battle sequence eschews the use of a Russian choir (presumably a temptation to its makers which they rightly rejected) to add a sentimental affect to the proceedings.

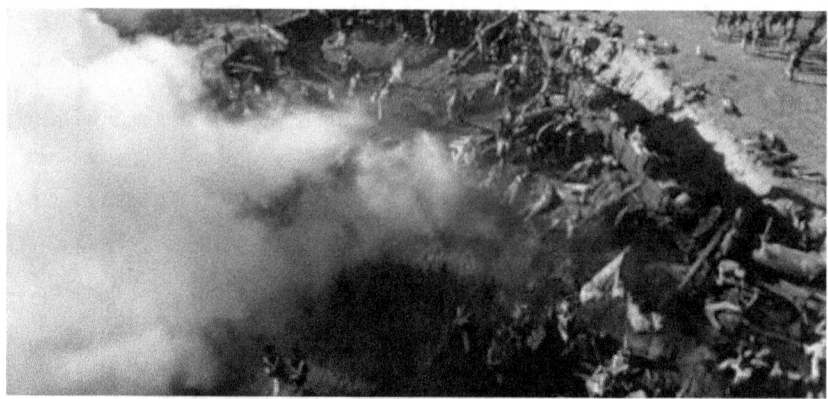

Two criticisms need to be made: for all the colour, as it vividly recreates a nineteenth-century canvas in which the palette, even while muted, is very colouristic in effect, the film shows little

blood, even when soldiers lose their limbs or die. In this respect, the first section of *Saving Private Ryan* (see below) is its antithesis, an antithesis that lends the heroics of that film an 'anti-war' feeling compared with *War and Peace* which glorifies its battle, even though the D-Day landings were as crucial to the defeat of Hitler as Borodino was to the defeat of Napoleon. Secondly, while great symphonic music combines vivid passages of music-making with the creation of a whole structure, so that the listener is drawn through the music in time (exposition of theme, development of musical ideas, the elaboration of suspense as to where the music is going, the resolution of ideas), such a satisfying totality just eludes *War and Peace*. There is some structure, as indicated, but there is a certain disjointedness in the editing of the sequences as well: after the battle disintegrates as it were, we are shown an orderly charge, or very arrestingly, aerial shots of the soldiers in the square formation. Are these from an earlier stage in the battle? From another part of the battlefield? Is their insertion justified by the movement from one shot to another? The answers are not immediately obvious.

Taken as a whole, the sequence is coherent enough and when it ends with an aerial shot high in the clouds, with the Russian landscape visible far below, it gives a proper sense of the immensity of the battle which is true to history, to Tolstoy's novel, and to the Soviet military effort in the Second World War. Just as significantly and in fact much more than any painting could, it enlarges our understanding, our imagination of what a major nineteenth-century battle might look like.

*

In Tolstoy's novel, the primary purpose of describing the battle is to explain its effect on Bezukhov's personality, his interior space. In the film, Bezukhov's view of battle is of a heroic encounter not of the pain and waste, and ultimately it locates the interior reaction on the public plane, sacrificing it as it were, in line with Communist ideology that private feelings can only be at the service of the state. It therefore cannot by definition reflect the interior quality that a quite different kind of war book and war film can evoke. Interestingly, a key novel to illustrate this point is Norman Mailer's 'The Naked and the Dead'. While Mailer consciously set about writing a novel displaying Tolstoyan compassion as he understood it, encompassing both the good and the bad in human beings, severe in order to avoid being sentimental, but aiming for the reader to "feel strengthened by those who endure, and feel awe and pity for those who do not" (as Mailer put it in his 1998 introduction), the book's strength is in the way it portrays the intensity of battle on a Pacific island as something felt privately by the infantryman, beyond the reach of the officers giving the orders.

It is a truism of battle that the big picture is denied to the individual actually fighting it. The point is made by Terrence Malick's *The Thin Red Line*, the promotional tagline for which, 'Every man fights his own war' (a consideration not extended to the Japanese, who remain the almost faceless enemy), could equally well have been used of 'The Naked and the Dead', and is true to the spirit of James Jones' novel on which the film is based. Jones, who had participated in the Guadalcanal campaign, published his novel in 1962 (when it was immediately turned into a film) and the narrative concerns the actions of C Company in landing on a Pacific island and capturing a ridge held by the Japanese; the company then engages in a gunpoint-to-gunpoint encounter with the Japanese and overruns them; the third encounter with the enemy results in the sacrificial death of Private Witt. Although these actions are set in the larger context of American efforts to capture the island of Guadalcanal from the Japanese, this big picture, which in hindsight we know not just to have been successful but to form a turning-point in the Pacific War, is scarcely referred to. This is very much an infantryman's war, and focuses on the story of Witt, seen at the opening of the film as AWOL on a South Sea Island, experiencing his own version of paradise. When the US Army finds him again, they put him back in the ranks. Witt's private war is trying to square the physical experience of battle with his own mental confusion about the loss of goodness, where hatred comes from, "this war at the heart of nature". This spiritual dimension in him, an awareness of another world, is in contrast to his alter ego, Sgt Welsh, who insists that this world is the only one that exists – a dialogue between a theist and an atheist in which the word God is never mentioned. When after Witt's death he is formally buried in the jungle, and the other soldiers drift off, Welsh remains behind to grieve. Every man fights his own war.

"Where does this emotionalism come from?" one might muse in Witt-like manner. There are several answers. Firstly it comes from Malick himself, who does not intend an anti-war film, but aims to get audiences to understand the pressures of battle on individuals, to articulate the tragedy of the common soldier's situation. There is always a public argument about why the infantryman is there in uniform with the task of defeating the enemy in this particular situation, such public argument revolving around defending the homeland, asserting the values of the society in which he exists, emphasizing the community of effort that the war involves. Yet Malick does not engage these questions, but instead focuses on private hopes and fears, as if to assert that the ordinary infantryman cannot know the public reasons why he fights. Secondly, between Guadalcanal and Malick's film has come the reverse of American arms in Vietnam, the war that made the American soldiers' private feelings public. Malick imports into the Second World War a post-Vietnam sensibility. Is this a permissible anachronism? It would be too strict a judgement to say no, and in any case, *The Thin Red Line* deliberately adopts a particular stylistic approach, which could be considered 'timeless', namely to put into dialogue and facial expression feelings and thoughts that were surely suppressed at the time. To take a clear-cut example, in the first encounter with Japanese bullets, a soldier in C Company dies. In the confusion, someone suggests to another that he is the appropriate person to write to the dead man's wife, a proposition from which the other demurs. This feels untrue to reality: under fire among the still-hot dead and wounded and with an order to execute is no time to be discussing letter-writing, but the incident is still true to an inner realism, that a soldier on seeing for the first time one of his buddies killed in battle could well have flashed through his mind the thought that someone was going to have to write to the widow and it was not going to be him.

The central figure of Witt largely gives his thoughts through voiceovers as well as flashbacks to his paradise in the South Seas. Private Bell is shown with constant visual memories of the wife he has left behind. But apart from these two the other soldiers largely express their feelings through dialogue, delivered in various American accents and mumbles, and accompanied by an array of tics and mannerisms, the most particular of which is turning the head away from the person being spoken to. The film therefore very much belongs to the actors as well as to the director, reflecting the conditions in which it was made. The actors underwent a nine-day boot camp (hosted by two Vietnam veterans) followed by a five-month shooting schedule in which (very unusually for a big commercial film) the film was shot in sequence from beginning to end. The ensemble and the relationships between the characters, and the relationship to the director, became important. This is a powerful ingredient in the film, provided any wish for simple looking and simple speaking, one man to another, as in a previous generation of Hollywood war movies, is put on one side. It feels like the difference between classicism and mannerism, both styles requiring creativity to be successful, but with the inherent risk in the latter of flaccidity of execution tipping it into the pit of hyperbole. This is certainly the case with the opening set in Witt's paradise, some nine minutes long, when a judicious selection of single images would have cut it by half and yet made the point about Witt's otherworldliness more cogently.

The Thin Red Line came out almost simultaneously with Steven Spielberg's *Saving Private Ryan* about the US landings in northern France in 1944 and the subsequent push inland. Both were hard-fought victories, and Spielberg and

Malick were of the same frame of mind in the sense of representing the generation born after the war coming to terms with the heroism of the Second World War. They have another social purpose as well, probably quite accidental, to go behind the defeat of the Vietnam war to a war in which American military virtues were triumphant. Their joint appearance makes an unconscious political point about the Second World War, that only the USA managed successfully to achieve victory in two major theatres, the Pacific and the European. In a way, they represent a post-Cold War zenith in conveying American global power.

But as cinematic depictions they make a very important contrast in illustrating the two poles I have explored in this essay: do you focus on the external appearance of battle or on the private experience of it? *Saving Private Ryan* is in three parts, the first of which is a re-creation of the US landings in the Dog Green Sector on Omaha Beach on 6 June 1944. In this section there is only the sketchiest delineation of character in individual infantrymen, sacrificing that for a concentrated attempt to pitch the viewer into battle, to give a direct experience of its extremities. To achieve this, the camera is variously used: it is static, reflecting pauses in the action when a clear view of individuals is possible; it is hand-held, imitating the narrow focus of soldiers running without regard to what is happening around them, and it is 'blurred static', portraying the fractional but doubly arresting glimpses of action, Spielberg (left) here drawing on

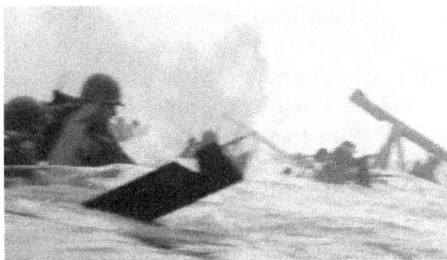 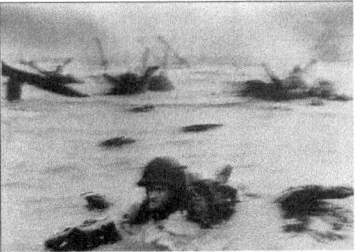

Robert Capa's photographs (right) taken at the Omaha Beach landings, which gain urgency from being out of focus. The editing is rapid, so that the sequence comprises short strips of film, exploiting the paradox that the less time you can see them, the more vividly they play in the mind. Just as Bondarchuk's *War and Peace* drew visual inspiration from nineteenth-century painting, so the visual quality of *Saving Private Ryan* draws on war photography to create a convincing visual patina, a point underlined by the way the illusion of seeing is disrupted by sand, water and even drops of blood hitting the camera lens. But the sequence could also be described as 'painterly' in quite a different way from *War and Peace*: the rapid montage creates a visceral effect such as you get in some twentieth-century portraiture, where the paint 'comes onto the senses' in a way that photography is unable to achieve. The chief example of this style is Francis Bacon, but one thinks of De Kooning, Auerbach and others. [The point is explored further in chapter 8.] As already noted, battle is an aural as well as a visual experience: after the period of waiting for battle, when sounds drop away, the bullets and shells create their own startling aural vocabulary which words such as whizz, zing, boom, crump etc. only inadequately describe. The final point to make concerns the narrative structure, as the first part of the film is exceptional in showing with great clarity the particular military objective, to land on the beach and knock out the German gun emplacements at the head of the cliff, and in illustrating visually how it was achieved.

Unfortunately, the subsequent two parts of *Saving Private Ryan* lapse into more conventional heroics, so that overall *The Thin Red Line* manages to achieve a greater resonance as a depiction of war, in the way it conveys, as does *Saving Private Ryan*, the sheer physicality of coming under fire and of fighting back, but balances that with the portrayal of the states of mind of those involved, their reflections on experience, their anxieties, and in Witt's case his mental detachment coexisting with his physical involvement.

The genre of the battle film in Hollywood, into which *The Thin Red Line* falls, even if it seeks to transcend it by its length and its philosophical content, was developed in the aftermath of the Second World War, and is further stimulated both by the Korean and Vietnam Wars. This period is marked too by the impact on the military of the ideas of SLA Marshall, who joined the American Historical Teams in interviewing individuals and groups fresh from combat in the Second World War. These are discussed in John Keegan's book, 'The Face of Battle' [Keegan pp. 71-3], including Marshall's ideas about the 'ratio of fire' and his conclusion that only a minority of soldiers on the battlefield actually fire their weapons at the enemy. These ideas subsequently proved very controversial, but were influential at the time, and my point in referring to Marshall's work is that it exerted influence not just in army thinking but in battle films of the era. The interviews form the basis of the American campaign histories, from which Marshall drew for his first book, 'Men Against Fire', published in 1947. This reached conclusions about how soldiers might deal with their fear on the battlefield, and how it was necessary for the American army to foster a sense of bonding among groups of GIs, with the practical purpose of getting them to support each other physically and emotionally, to help overcome feelings of cowardice. Put crudely, the emphasis is switched from it being noble to die for one's country to honour being found in defending one's friends, which may well involve being a casualty, whether wounded or dead. This 'band of brothers' strain (going back to where we started with Shakespeare's 'Henry V') is common among many of the battle films since the end of the Second World War, indeed to the point where it is almost a defining feature of the genre: even a film focused on the externals of battle should make some attempt to characterize individual soldiers so that we as audience can empathize with what they suffer or appreciate the motivation behind their heroism. The strength of this idea made the explicit basis of the HBO TV series, *Band of Brothers*, which was screened in ten episodes in the autumn of 2001. The involvement of Spielberg and Tom Hanks (director and star of *Saving Private Ryan*) gives a clue to its approach: how might the filming methods of the first part of *Saving Private Ryan* - the beach landings – be applied to the subsequent land campaign? The series follows the exploits of E (Easy) Company in the 2nd Battalion of the 101st Airborne Divi-

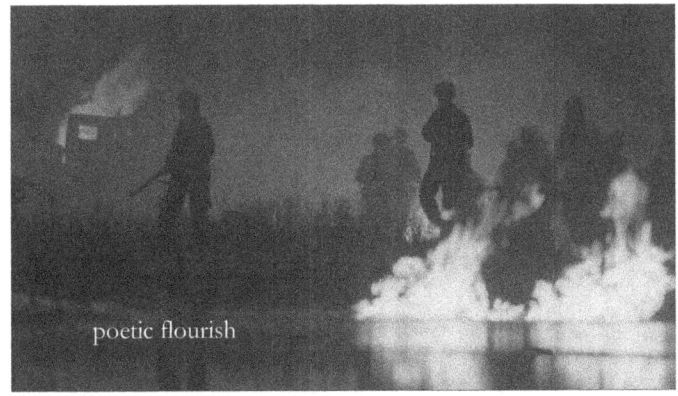

poetic flourish

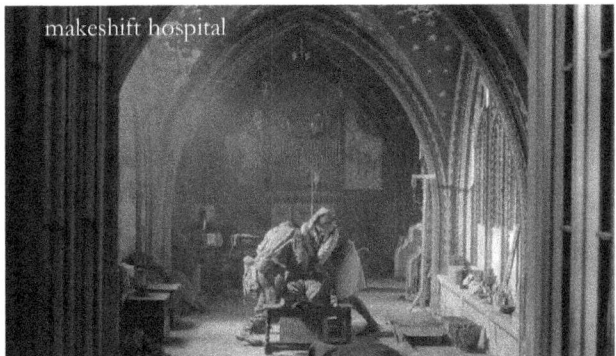

makeshift hospital

Band of Brothers

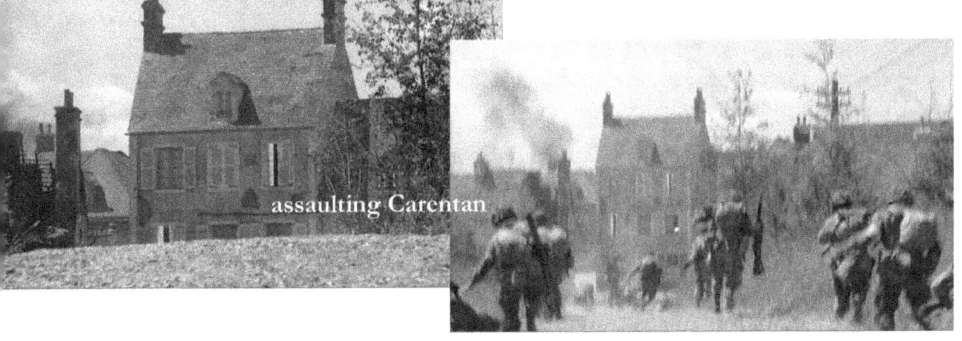

assaulting Carentan

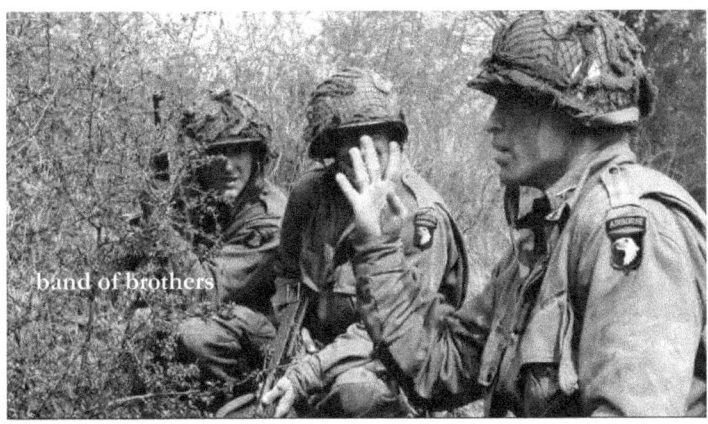

band of brothers

sion from D-Day itself through Operation Market Garden, the Battle of the Bulge and beyond up to the occupation of Berchtesgaden, Hitler's mountain lair, in May 1945. In turning history into legend, the series made a superlative fist of filming infantry battle, and gave a convincing exposition of the idea that soldiers fight for each other quite as much as for a cause.

Band of Brothers' length of ten hours gave the film scope to focus on psychology. In depending on each other, the soldiers had to form a bond, and the main test of whether the bond would hold was in performance on the battlefield. Hence new recruits drafted into replace casualties (episode four, 'Replacements') faced an initiation test of initial hostility before being accepted. Besides depending on each other they had to depend on their commanders: in episode seven, 'The Breaking Point', at a low point in the American campaign to reach Berlin as the army strove to push on after the German failure to win the Battle of the Bulge, whose epicentre Bastogne was a crucible in which Easy Company took part, Lt Dykes' lack of command of his platoon leads to unnecessary casualties and near failure, the situation being rescued by the reckless heroism of Lt Speirs. The narrative is thinly explained, and which soldier is which, and what his motivations are, is not consistently clear. (A particular dimension to Lt Speirs' heroism is that our first introduction to him in episode two shows him disencumbering his unit of German prisoners-of-war by shooting them in cold blood.) In the event it does not matter as the framework of the action is readily assembled and understood, even as the spectator is trying to gain a physical understanding of where the enemy is and what the Americans have to do to drive them back. Episode two ('Day of Days') is much more finished in this respect. Lt Winters is detailed to take out a German battery at Brécourt shelling the US troops landing on Utah Beach. Through deft use of visuals, both the challenges explained and the carrying out of the tasks involved makes for particularly vivid action scenes – for example, showing how machine-gun fire shreds the leaves in a tree – while the tactics remain comprehensible.

One strength of the series derives from its attention to detail in the sets and costumes. It also takes the spectator into the extreme risks the soldiers had to run, especially in episode three ('Carentan'), and into the crises caused by major wounds on the body (episode six, 'Bastogne'). In the manner of *Saving Private Ryan*, the camera is often hand-held and shaky, backed up by rapid cutting, action glimpsed rather than shown, less an explanation for the head, more a blow to the innards (in Latin *viscera*, hence 'visceral').

The soldiers depended on each other and, one of the slogans claimed, "The world depended on them." *Band of Brothers* came to television at the peak, as it were, of American power, between the end of the Cold War and the invasion of Iraq in 2003 when the USA (and Britain) stumbled so badly. The series needs to be watched in that light since subsequent war movies set in Iraq or Afghanistan links soldierly heroism with much darker experiences. For example, *Lone Survivor* (2013) depicts an unsuccessful Navy SEAL mission in Afghanistan. *The Hurt Locker* (2008) is about the stresses experienced by bomb-disposal experts in Baghdad, and *Zero Dark Thirty* (2012) gives a gripping and disturbing account of the premeditated and carefully planned quest to find Osama Bin Laden and annihilate him. Its concluding image of Maya, the CIA analyst heavily involved in the hunt for Bin Laden, boarding a transport plane back to the USA as its sole passenger, is one of cavernous solitude, at the other extreme from "they depended on each other, and the world depended on them".

*

Since the end of World War Two, as this chapter shows, not just military strategy has changed since then, especially so since the end of the Cold War, but the tactics are different. *Band of Brothers* may be viewed as marking a high tide which from that point began to ebb. That flood tide was in full flow when one of SLA Marshall's books, 'Pork Chop Hill: the American fighting man in action, Korea, Spring 1953', published in 1956, was made into a solid example of the genre, *Pork Chop Hill* (1959). Its specific focus is on the military action involved in retaking a strategically useless hill and how the officer in charge drives his men to carry out this task. The idea is reprised in *Hamburger Hill* (1987), about the capture of a hill in Vietnam in 1969 in fearsome conditions: the film ends with a shot of surviving combatants sitting desolately on the desolate hilltop. The mood at the end is one of despair. The strategic purpose of capturing the hill is never explained, as if it was irrelevant to the men's motivation; nor does it even resort to the platitudes such as that tacked onto the end of *Pork Chop Hill* – "Millions live in freedom today because of what they did."

Pork Chop Hill was directed by Lewis Milestone, who as we have seen made his name with *All Quiet on the Western Front* (which incidentally brings to the fore the way the German soldiers in the trenches supported each other in the fighting, distant from the high command and even more distant from the misconceptions about trench warfare on the home front), and is an excellent example of Milestone's virtues as a film-maker – and his vices, principally that of speechifying at the audience to press a message home that battles are for useless ends. Having created two parallel stories, one of the battle to take the hill, the other of the protracted negotiations between the USA and China at Panmanjom, it neglects the latter in favour of the former when there was a striking opportunity to inject suspense into both stories, and to make crystal clear the way the strategically valueless hill became a pawn in the negotiations to the cost of many lives. This causes the film to lose direction in its last third. However, the middle section, from the start of the attack to the capture of the top of the hill, has an exemplary quality: it is comprehensible tactically in explaining the way the three platoons are deployed, and in using a model of the hill at Battalion HQ to explain what the attack is meant to achieve; it touches at various points on Marshall's preoccupation with how soldiers are motivated to fight, even motivated to use their weapons; it gives a convincing picture of the battle-scarred hill and its trench system (which must have given Milestone a feeling of *déjà vu* in the way it recalls the First World War landscape of *All Quiet*). Because of this clarity, a real suspense is generated as to whether the attack will succeed or fail.

Almost exactly in the mid-point between this film and *All Quiet*, Milestone made another battle film, *A Walk in the Sun* (1945), which is his master-

A Walk in the Sun

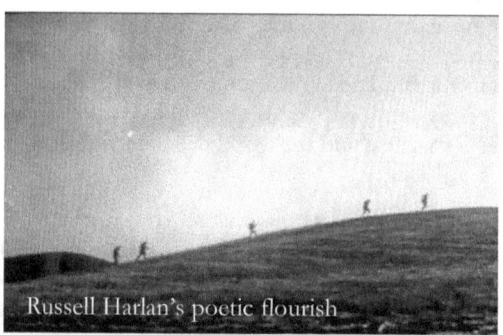
Russell Harlan's poetic flourish

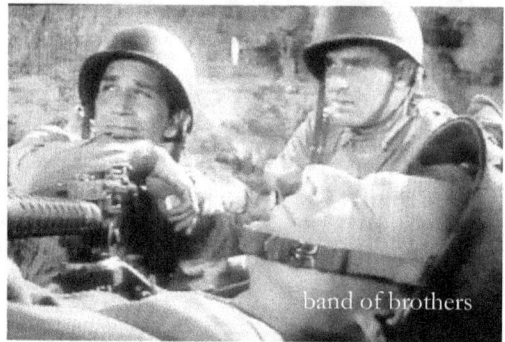
band of brothers

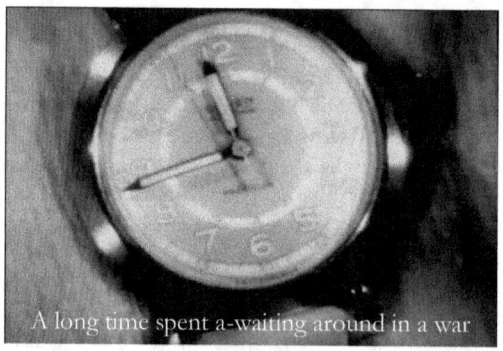
A long time spent a-waiting around in a war

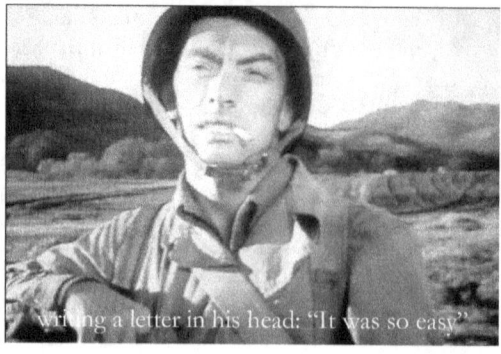
writing a letter in his head: "It was so easy"

piece, and which may be taken as the introduction of the 'band of brothers' strain into the American war film. While *All Quiet* was a notable early sound film, *A Walk in the Sun* is vastly more sophisticated in its use of this element of film-making, deploying sound and internalized speaking in a way that conveys the thoughts of the characters in new ways. The story concerns a platoon of common GIs in the Texas Division at Salerno, south of Naples, in September 1943. Given the task of landing at the front on the beach and taking a German-held farmhouse six miles inland, it only achieves its objective at the cost of several lives. At the end, Windy, the introspective GI, composes a letter to his sister: "It was so easy, so terribly easy." It both celebrates the force of American arms while confronting the casualties of war, the dead, the bleeding and even the mad: Sergeant Porter, pitched into command by the deaths of an unnamed young lieutenant and Sergeant Halverson, breaks down and relinquishes his command to Tyne. The film is at the other extreme to the openly heroic, a dark war film made in the flush of American victory in the Second World War.

This disjunction between the official (heroic) version and the harsh reality of the achievement is achieved by interiorizing the thoughts of the GIs as they move from landing barge to objective, dawn to noon, the prime example being Windy composing laconic letters in his head. The film gathered several talents, bringing out the best in each: the story was by Harry Brown, who seems to have specialised in stories about beach-landings, witness *The Sands of Iwo-Jima* (1949) and *D-Day 6 June* (1956), and who had worked on *The True Glory* (1945), a large collaboration on the Allied invasion of Europe; the screenplay was by Robert Rossen, who came from the New York Theatre, and whose best written work, as in this film, understands the need for men to create a hard-boiled carapace which cannot prevent human sentiment breaking through; the director, Lewis Milestone, achieved early fame with *All Quiet*, but with this more muted work could be said to have achieved something more lasting, a study of men coping not with the extreme horrors of trench warfare but inner demons in a more conventional military setting. Milestone produced the film as well, which may be an indication of his personal commitment to what he had to say about war. Mention should also be made of the cameraman Russell Harlan who can probably be credited for giving the film some striking visual flourishes, and of the title song, sung by Kenneth Spencer, that helps to fix the film in the memory by echoing the understated nature of the action: a landing, a 6-mile hike, the knocking out of a German foxhole and the blowing of a bridge were just a stroll, terribly easy.

Wars, the film argues, are fought as much in the mind as in open battle. While the assault on the farmhouse at the end lapses into incoherence in terms of the action, the script and Milestone's handling of his actors focuses on the relationships between the GIs, their obduracy and their strength of character. Nothing is witnessed of the landing (apart from a brief long shot of the landing craft coming ashore, possibly newsreel footage) except what is visible to the platoon. Later there is an encounter with an armoured car, and finally the GIs' assault on the farmhouse. If the film is weaker in the action sequences, the film is particularly good at the inaction which comes in between and characterizes so much of war: waiting for the landing barge to hit the beach, waiting behind the beach-head to move on, waiting in a ditch, waiting behind a stone wall to go over the top and storm the farmhouse. The lugubrious song comments on the mood: "It's a long long time a man spends a-waiting, a-waiting around in a war." And in this downtime, the men converse sporadically, wise-cracking, periodically needling each other, thinking of home. And in this fog, they get only a glimpse of the big picture: only the whine and snarl of shells in the darkness indicate to the men in the landing barge that they are nearing the beach; the German planes dropping bombs on supply ships are not seen, only the black plume of smoke going into the sky points to what is happening; a reconnaissance motorcyclist offers to check the road up front and report back, but they never see him again (as Tyne remarks: " It's a funny thing, how many people you meet in an army that cross your path for a few seconds and you never see 'em again") ; only the machine-gun rattle coming from the farmhouse reveals that Germans are holed up there. McWilliams, the medical orderly, expresses it well: "That's the whole trouble with war, you never get to see nothing, you fight 'em by ear." Tyne responds, "You gotta guess what's going on." Shells are heard before they are seen to explode; planes are sounds until they suddenly appear on top of you. As spectators, we are afforded no wider view, merely the means to identify with the characters, all well individualized in Rossen's script. At the end, in showing Tyne, crawling on his stomach, leading his men against the farmhouse, Milestone uses not a long take, but a montage of shots of his face, subtly blended by the device of a wipe, and voicing his monologue on the soundtrack. At the end, Tyne, fearful to the pit of the stomach, sees the landscape spinning, a wholly interior spell, broken by an explosion and the eruption of action.

As spectators, our involvement is bought by the film rather than presented on a plate. The Salerno landings were heroic, the platoon's capture of the farmhouse is worthy of a Congressional Medal of Honour, but by the end we have been sucked – by the script, by the quality of the ensemble acting, by the use of interior voices and sound – into the ambiguity of war: are they murderers? Or "selling democracy to the natives"? "Nobody dies" the GIs tell themselves, yet several are killed; they have been given a clear objective, but waiting in the beach-head, they also feel they've been forgotten; Tyne is thrust into command because Porter cracks, having fought "one battle too many"; if landing in Italy is like this, what will the invasion of Normandy be like? Censorship did not allow Rossen to have the GIs use the f-word on screen, so Rivera keeps saying "loving" instead. We have eyes and ears to see and hear, but Milestone and Rossen make us put them to work.

*

Thucydides wanted his history of the Peloponnesian War to be considered "useful" by those wanting to understand what happened (and, he added, will be repeated in the future) [Thucydides 1.22.4]. Even though many film-makers are moved to express the horror and pity of war, passing over into expressing a judgement on those who conduct war, there is a gloomy sense that the most successful films reveal the fact of battle in the front line, rather than the why of it, or how it came about. There is an even more melancholy conclusion that doing this well is commercially speaking a sound proposition: there is a mass audience for battle scenes. Making the situation murkier still is the entertainment value in killing, as portrayed in films like *The Lord of the Rings* (2001-3) and *300* (2006), with the risk that the documentary reality which *Saving Private Ryan* strives for requires the audience to disentangle it from fantasy films, a process that becomes foggier as history moves forward. Portraying D-Day remains vivid history, even to those born just after it. This element of history is still present in the Battle of Borodino in the Soviet *War and Peace*, but our response includes the feeling that battles are no longer fought in that way and so the events begin to drift away from fact. *Gladiator* (2000) descends into fantasy in the digital manipulation of the scenes in the arena in the latter half of the film, yet it opens with something much more interesting. While using digital blood and guts to depict the battle between the Roman army and German tribes somewhere in a dark Teutonic Forest about 2000 years ago, the film does draw on ancient evidence, notably the vivid scenes on Trajan's Column in Rome of the Emperor Trajan defeating the Dacians, to document Roman technological superiority against its enemies (while also wishing to echo American technological superiority at the turn of the millennium). The film therefore bridges two eras, that of the battle documentary and the digital inauthenticity of *Lord of the Rings*.

Yet a realist tradition will not easily be lost, and may well outlast the fantastic re-imagining of battle: see the BBC's *War Machine* (above) and the fact that it was Peter Jackson, the creator of *The Lord of the Rings*, who masterminded the documentary insights into how World War One was experienced by those who fought it in *They Shall Not Grow Old*. And in 2017, just as the negotiations for the UK to exit the EU were getting seriously under weigh, Christopher Nolan released *Dunkirk* which had nothing to do with Brexit because he had apparently nursed the project for decades and pre-production began in January 2016 before the referendum had taken place; yet the coincidence is a neat one. Nolan intercuts three stories set on land, sea and air, and then as the film progresses he speeds up that intercutting in his aim of creating a visual symphony. The dialogue is largely inaudible and when the words spoken by the diction-trained Shakespearean Kenneth Branagh are audible, an abrupt change of mood occurs in the film, and a drop in the temperature. On the other hand, the reading out of Churchill's famous post-*Dunkirk* speech from a newspaper report is a masterstroke, as the words are read in an anti-Churchillian manner and suit the 'desperate-heroic' tone of the film.

Two notable features make the film stand out. It was made particularly for the IMAX screen and only that sort of viewing can do it justice; secondly Nolan deals with three time-frames: a week for the infantryman, a day for Mr Dawson and his boat, an hour for the flight of three Spitfire fighter planes, and they all come together at a key point around three-quarters of the way through.

As they progress, the three stories have not been signalled by Nolan that they will come together, so when they do and the links between them are made, the film reaches a climax. The infantryman has got off the shore in an old boat riddled with bullet holes so that as it sinks he and the others have to abandon ship. Secondly a Heinkel bombs a minesweeper and hits it so that the crew and all the rescued infantrymen aboad have to abandon it; the Heinkel is then pursued by the Spitfire. The sight of all the men in the water then brings in the third strand of Mr Dawson steering his small boat to go to their rescue. The scene is an apocalypse of a kind: a sinking minesweeper, soldiers struggling in the water some of whom are engulfed by flames from burning fuel, and Dawson having to retreat from the flames and the oil-clogged sea.

This breathless narrative is achieved not just in short sections of film – moments of action and brief shots of the main actors in this drama – but in the rapid intercutting of the narrative, piling moment upon suspenseful moment: who will be drowned and who saved? Chance has brought these stories together, and the end looks like the outcome of chances, but individual acts of will count as well: infantryman finding a way to get off a sinking ship; Mr Dawson using his boat to maximum extent to save men; the Heinkel bombing the minesweeper, and the Spitfire shooting it out of the sky.

The innovative brilliance of Nolan's style and the enduring appeal of the subject has meant that *Dunkirk* has grossed some five times its budget, to confirm the commercial impulse in making war movies. But, as we have seen, there is a clear technological one as well, the challenge of using the resources of the cinema to depict battle: long shots, close-ups, sound (bullets, half-heard shouts, explosions etc), battlescape design, mobile cameras, rapid editing, special effects, digital imaging and so on. The cinemas themselves have changed: when *Saving Private Ryan* is screened to an audience in comfortable armchairs experiencing the images on a very large screen with sound filling all portions of the darkened chamber, this offers a new experience from watching a routine black-and-white Hollywood war movie in an empty flea-pit or on a second-hand television in a bedsit.

So money and technology have a big part to play, but there is surely a more enduring and more compelling motive in the drive to expression of truth about the human condition. *A Walk in the Sun* has an arresting detachment in being sceptical about heroism and about the larger war being fought, and a close attachment to the humans who have to fight. *All Quiet* is more famous as a film with a pacifist message, but the fifteen years separating the two films mark a maturing of views. *All Quiet*'s messages are unmistakable, whereas *A Walk in the Sun* catches us unexpectedly, so that on subsequent viewings *All Quiet* begins to grate in its obviousness, whereas the subtlety of *A Walk in the Sun* becomes more striking. It has also been more influential because it achieved several 'firsts' for a battle film : the first to show a story about a platoon; the first to start with the infantry in the landing craft before hitting the beach; the first to use a group of young actors fairly early in their careers (e.g. Andrews, Conte, Ireland); not the first to alternate action and stasis, but the first to make convincing the anxiety that waiting can cause, where 'each man fights his own war' – in the mind. Finally it also in my view exemplifies the virtues of a restrained style of film-making that is now all the more striking when put alongside the hyperbolic styles of the present day.

Yet there is surely scope for greater profundity. In this respect, *The Thin Red Line* is more interesting than might first appear. Consider its final section. The transition to it is marked with a prologue, of Sgt Welsh and Private Witt on a verandah talking about "this world and another world", flesh and spirit. Then it is evening, with the men on the ground smoking, wordless except for Witt's inner thoughts on the soundtrack. It is then day and the men are going up a stream to engage the enemy. When two men are chosen to be sent forward to reconnoitre, Witt volunteers to accompany them. Upriver, the three encounter a platoon of Japanese coming down. When one of the three is wounded, Witt volunteers to stay with him and divert the Japanese, while Fife goes back to send word to the others. Witt leaves the wounded private to float himself back downstream, while he draws the Japanese away deeper into the jungle, where he is surrounded and killed. The film then jumps to Witt's burial, done without any liturgy (no sign of an army chaplain) and bare of any ritual accept the planting of his rifle in the ground, barrel down, with name-tag and helmet hung on it. His fellow soldiers drift off leaving Welsh squatting by the grave, muttering something inaudible and then being swept by emotion. The next shot jumps to Welsh listening to a newly arrived captain lecturing them on how he's going to run the group: we experience a dissonance between Welsh's experience and disenchantment and the captain's voice of authority and commitment. The troops embark on a landing craft and in the evening sun are silent on deck while Witt's voice-over meditates on the nature of his bond with the others, on light and dark being in the same Mind that made the world, shining in the setting sun. A shot of the wake of the boat gives way to natives in canoes in a mangrove swamp, to a ground-level shot of a seedling tree breaking from the shell of its seed, the roar of the oceans behind it. All through, the adagio music overlays and overplays the emotion.

The trajectory of this last sequence is redemptive, and redemptive in the Christian manner. From the evening sequence with Witt and the others lying smoking in the grass (Last Supper), to daytime and Witt volunteering to go into danger (Calvary), to Witt's sacrifice (Crucifixion) in order to rescue the platoon, to his burial (Deposition) and Welsh's grief (Pietà). Finally, the voice-over from beyond the grave, reflecting on the central mystery of Creation, simultaneously light and dark, is a Resurrection, made specific in the final image of the seedling on the beach. This narrative is understated while the emotion is carried in the music, and applies, as already stated, the 'trauma', the wounding that the Vietnam War gave to America, to the clearer certainties of the Second World War. The shell is brittle, the toughness is skin deep. Inside each soldier fighting his own war is a huge well of feeling, of belonging, and in Witt's case, of understanding.

The masterpiece of contemporary land battle, an equal to Tolsoy's 'War and Peace', is yet to be written or filmed. The cinema is certainly poised to do it, offering as it does the resources of words in dialogue and in reflection allied o the extraordinary visual and aural possibilities inherent in making pictures for a large screen, and sophisticated techniques of re-creating battle (although one obstacle to be skirted will always be the propaganda element, making the film either denunciatory of war or laudatory of false heroics). If Shakespeare and Tolstoy are to be our guides, then a battle story woven into a much larger narrative would allow an extra dramatic force to be given to scenes of fighting, an extra way into understanding for spectators who have never fired a gun. As the first line of Homer's epic poem tells us, the subject of the Iliad, set in wartime and punctuated by scenes of battle throughout, is not the public fighting but the Wrath of Achilles, its cause and its costly assuaging. Our putative masterpiece will certainly need to engage with the mental landscape as well as the physical one, encompassing the heroic and cowardly, tenderness and hatred, suffering and redemption from suffering. Focus on the protagonists on both sides will allow the audience to engage with a general human vulnerability, culpability if you prefer, but also on the value of individual fulfilment and meaning, that soldiering and fighting are a necessary part of an existence out of which expressions of humanness, extreme as they may be, can emerge.

*

The filming of battle has by and large not been questioned as a fit subject for the cinema. There are theoretical doubts about the battle film as a form of 'entertainment' alongside the gangster film or romantic melodramas and so on, and there are pacifist doubts about whether battle movies glorify war and killing. But these doubts are overturned in the audience's mind by the way these films engage with people's imaginations and with the 'ethics' of war: the pacific minded will have welcomed *All Quiet on the Western Front* as powerfully making the case against modern war.

The subject of war may be too serious to be mocked. Where films have done so (e.g. *Oh What a Lovely War*, 1969), this is seen as a legitimate tactic for those who wish the human race would never engage in it. But there is another area of shocking human experience where representation in art has proved deeply contentious, that of the Holocaust. It may be one thing to describe it in memoirs and in histories, but another to do so on the screen, where questions of authenticity and therefore of bad faith are thrust to the fore. Holocaust cinema therefore counterpoints battle cinema and poses the question: why try to film the people and events involved?

4   IMAGINING THE HOLOCAUST

Among the aspects of human life to which the imaginative genius of the Greeks applied itself was the torment of eternal punishment. Notably, in Homer's 'Odyssey', when Odysseus visits Hades (to learn from Tiresias of his destiny), he glimpses first Tityos, then Tantalus, then Sisyphus. Tityos is spread on the ground where he is powerless to stop two vultures plucking at his liver; Tantalus stands in a pool, but each time he stoops to drink, the water drains away before his eyes, and each time he reaches for the sweet fruits over his head – pears, pomegranates, apples, figs and olives – the wind tosses them out of his reach; Sisyphus keeps rolling a boulder uphill, but as he reaches the crest so that he can push it over, its weight causes it to roll backwards down to the plain below.

In his 'Inferno', its inspiration triggered by his reading of Homer, Dante likewise strains his imagination to devise perpetual torment, such as the icy rain forever falling on the souls in the third circle, the flatterers lying in excrement in the eighth circle, those in the fifth 'malebolgia' who traffic in public offices submerged in a river of boiling pitch and kept from escaping by a horde of demons, the hypocrites in the sixth malebolgia pacing the ground in copes of lead – "Oh in eterno faticoso manto!" – and in the ninth and bottom circle, the traitors frozen in the River Cocytus.

The human impulse to see crime and sin punished, if not on this earth by human agency then in the afterlife by divine sanction, leads us to imagine what might happen – and in the imagination so much more can be spoken: the unrealistically excruciating can become available to us, far beyond the humdrum laws of physical pain. Furthermore, a bleaker, more cerebral idea can be added: repetition.

When Primo Levi returns to Turin from his own season in hell, nine months in Auschwitz, the word that still rings in his ear is 'Wstavac, get up,' the command to start the day of labour, racked by fatigue, hunger and disease. It is one of the features of the Nazi programme to annihilate the Jews that before annihilation, the victims must suffer in a re-creation on earth of Dante's circles of hell. Only this reinvention is physical and material: the transports of Jews must be organized, camps and crematoria built, guards found, methods of gassing invented, and finally the ashes disposed of.

And after the camps are liberated, the programme halted, and the survivors dispersed, the event lives in their memories, and also beyond their memories, because the human race needs to come to terms with what has happened, to seek some future wisdom from the now-past catastrophe, and for this thinkers, writers and artists are needed. What is more, because it is a twentieth-century catastrophe, and because in the twentieth century film takes over the word as the means of mass communication, it is imperative that the new medium of film is used to express it. It is arguable that of all the ways of imagining the Holocaust for future generations, among them history, literature, painting, it is the cinema that has tackled the subject most persistently, sometimes crassly, often movingly. One can even now talk of a genre of Holocaust film, not just deriving from Hollywood (among other films, *Judgment at Nuremberg, The Pawnbroker, Sophie's Choice, Schindler's List*) but also from Eastern Europe (among others, *The Long Journey, The Last Stage, Passenger, The Pianist, Fateless, Son of Saul*) and from Italy (*Kapo, The Garden of the Finzi Continis, The Night Porter, Life is Beautiful*). Television too has been crucial: the American mini-series, *The Holocaust*, and British made-for-television non-fiction accounts (episode 20 of *The World at War, Kitty – Return to Auschwitz, Auschwitz - The Nazis and the 'Final Solution'*). In a class by itself stands Claude Lanzmann's *Shoah*, initially shown in the cinema, but reaching a wider audience still through television, the making of which is a key part in the whole process of testifying to the Holocaust both for our time and for generations to come.

There is of course a very substantial literature on the Holocaust; indeed one of the twentieth century's key works, Primo Levi's memoir of his time in Auschwitz, 'If this is a man', was published within two years of his return to Turin from the camp. There have followed other memoirs and novels, major scholarly histories, poems, and not least the publication of diaries kept by Jews *in extremis* prior to their murder, and allowing their voices especially to be heard beyond the grave. All these words have been very important for the film-makers, for often the most striking stories, whether factual or invented, have been made into striking films, and their histories have informed the best television documentaries. The literature therefore underpins the cinema and television works, but the latter supersede the written word in giving the subject a presence and a reach that is new to history. This has been desirable, but it has not been without its controversy and its risks: are the visual accounts true? What is the truth in a subject like this? What would the dead victims make of these works, were they to see them? The unease erupted in 1978 when Elie Wiesel attacked the NBC Holocaust series in the New York Times in words that recall the Jewish imagining of Yahweh in the Old Testament as transcendent and unique – and not to be represented in graven images: the Jews after all are a 'people of the book', for whom God has a name but no image. Does this therefore transfer into a general distrust of images when dealing with fundamental things? The question is an important one for anyone seeking to defend the magic of images made in a movie camera: do they put us in a dilemma, between desiring images for their richness, their newness, their extraordinary variety, and suppressing them because they bring the subject into such focus we cannot see beyond them? Hence, the prohibition on images of God, for the Almighty, the Eternal, the Infinite, and so on, cannot be represented in one image, or even a million images. Wiesel himself speaks as a survivor, with deepest feeling. And his plea in 1978 needs to be tempered with what he wrote in 1989 in the preface to Annette Insdorf's 'Indelible Shadows' when he recognized that the film image might express, at least in part, what he felt in 1978 was inexpressible. In reaching this position, he was perhaps struck by the way the NBC series unlocked people's consciousness, for it was watched by some 120 million viewers in the USA, and had a similar consciousness-raising impact in

Germany in 1979. In an echo of the importance of this popular, commercial image-making, survivors in Britain who go to schools to talk about the Holocaust and what it means have remarked that *Schindler's List* "put us on the map" [Haggith and Newman p. 249].

The truth is that cinema can be seen as the dominant element in the story of how the Holocaust has been received, if not the most subtle then the most forceful and widespread. This was a story that began immediately the war ends, even if this initial period was characterized by a loud silence for far from simple reasons. One was the understandable desire to put the war in the past, especially its horrific aspects; a period of digestion was somehow felt necessary, to think 'never again' as being sufficient. (A similar looking away followed the end of the First World War in 1918.) The third reason was the initiation of the Cold War, which for the West meant refraining from pointing a condemnatory figure at West Germany. This was the factor in the demise of a project to assemble a film from newsreel footage of the concentration camps when they were revealed to the Allies and the Soviets in 1945. This was the brainchild of Sidney Bernstein, who had worked for Britain's Ministry of Information during the war, and who enlisted his friend Alfred Hitchcock to oversee the way the film should be structured. Yet it came to nothing. Hitchcock worked on it intensively in June and July 1945, only for him and Bernstein to find that the British government wanted the project shelved so as not to antagonise the Germans who were needed as allies – and not to encourage nascent Zionism and exacerbate Britain's delicate position in Palestine after the war. [See Wikipedia s.v. 'Night Will Fall' and Barr and Kerzoncuf pp. 182-7.] However two films were made in the countries where camps were located: *The Last Stage* in Poland (1948, directed by Wanda Jakubowska for Film Polski, with some scenes filmed in Auschwitz itself) and *The Long Journey* in Czechoslovakia (1949, directed by Alfred Radok for the Barrander Film Studio). However, their impact was very local, a fate which also befell the three extraordinary published accounts which appeared soon after the war: Primo Levi's 'If this is a man' was published in 1947, sold poorly and was not republished until 1958. Wladyslaw Szpilman's account of survival through the life of the Warsaw ghetto and then beyond its extinction was published in 1946, then withdrawn from circulation, only being republished fifty years later. Béla Szolt's 'Nine Suitcases', his story of forced labour in the Ukraine and then escape from the transports of 1944 from Hungary to Auschwitz, was serialized in his journal *Haladás* in 1946 and 1947, but never materialized in book form in Hungarian until 1980. It was published in English in 2004.

This period seems therefore to have the character of a false beginning, but there is a parallel story that emphatically sees the process of memorialization in hand. At the end of the war Simon Wiesenthal began working for the US Army gathering documentation for trials of Nazi war crimes, and helped found the Jewish Documentation Centre in Linz, from which his hunting of escaped Nazis began. In 1953, the Israeli government established the Yad Vashem Memorial Park for the Remembrance of the Martyrs and Heroes of the Holocaust. And it is memory that is the key concept, along with time, behind the film Alain

Resnais makes in 1955, *Nuit et brouillard/Night and Fog*, an intelligent, poetic and philosophical short film that first brings to the visual imagination the potency of Auschwitz as a place of mass annihilation. Inevitably the film generated its own controversy [see van der Knaap] but its currency in the late 1950s and the 1960s had a significant effect in raising awareness of the Holocaust and how it might be represented in art.

The next phase is marked by the Eichmann trial of 1961, which is the event that transformed popular understanding of the Holocaust in important ways. Prior to it, a television version of *Judgment at Nuremberg* had been screened in the USA in 1959, and the interest it aroused led to Stanley Kramer producing and directing a film version for United Artists, in which the use of newsreels within the film as trial evidence harmonized closely with what was happening in the Eichmann trial. The film was released in December 1961, four months after it had ended. Because Eichmann had masterminded the deportation to Auschwitz of 437,000 Hungarian Jews in 1944 and then vanished at the end of the war, Wiesenthal and Israeli intelligence had tracked him down in Argentina, and Eichmann was brought to trial in Israel in 1961, when the testimony of some ninety camp survivors was used to explain the detail of what had happened. The Israeli government allowed news programmes all over the world to broadcast the trial live, which meant that the detail of the Holocaust, and its costs to individuals, was becoming available to the public in new ways.

The war against the Jews, not just the years of Nazi rule, was now in the public domain as it were: the opaque glass screen surrounding these events had now been broken. As a result, in 1964 Sydney Lumet is able to make *The Pawnbroker*, an intense psychodrama about a survivor of the camps who runs a pawn

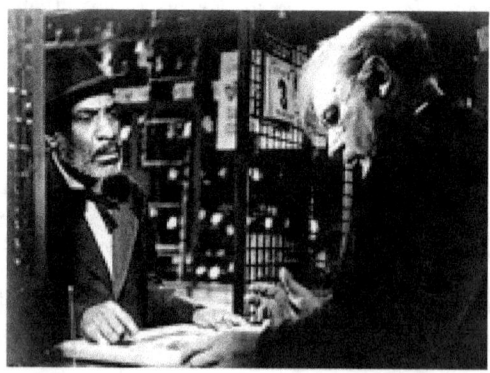

shop in a poor area of New York. As he sees the violence around him, the pawnbroker gets flash memories of his time in the concentration camp (the influence of Resnais' *Last Year in Marienbad* and *Muriel* can be discerned here). These flashbacks, first as flash glimpses, then more sustained, are effective as a way of uncovering the memory in the brain, as if at first they force themselves to the surface of consciousness only to be shut out as quickly as possible, and then recurring and taking over the person they are living inside. This is an analogue for the way many survivors wished at first to black the past out, only for it to refuse to disappear until the survivor realized that he or she might come to terms with it by talking about it.

The historians began to publish their big histories as well: Gerald Reitlinger's 'The Final Solution', first published in 1953, was published in an enlarged edition in 1961, followed by Raul Hilberg's 'The Destruction of the European Jews' in 1967, and Lucy Dawidowicz's 'The War Against the Jews 1933-45' in 1975. With these written works and the availability of newsreel film in the archives, at least on the Western side of the Iron Curtain, the episode on genocide in the *World at War*, produced by Jeremy Isaacs and Michael Darlow, was screened on commercial television in the UK in 1974.

The next milestone is *The Holocaust: the story of the family Weiss*, a miniseries screened on NBC-TV in America in 1977, which brought to the surface the debate as to how you bear witness being as important as the facts to which you bear witness. As mentioned, Wiesel expressed his concerns strongly, but his reservations can only be described as swept aside by the fact that one in two Americans watched the series and when it was shown shortly afterwards in Germany, its effect in educating a new generation was enormous – "It had more impact than the original." (Anonymous comment quoted by Michael Berenbaum in a highly informative television feature 'Imaginary Witness: Hollywood and the Holocaust' from 2004).

However, Wiesel's point that only those who had survived the camps could speak about them had its echo: *sotto voce*, as it were, the voices of the survivors continued to speak and be heard. Diaries and testimonies were being stored at Yad Vashem; the Eichmann trial had brought the pain of remembering into the open. In the late 1970s, Peter Morley, a freelance producer/director, made for Yorkshire TV *Kitty – Return to Auschwitz*. Kitty Hart-Moxon, aged 12 in 1939, was on the run in Poland for four years before landing up in Auschwitz with her mother in 1943. Morley met her in 1978 and persuaded her to participate in a 90-minute TV documentary on the subject of her going back to the camp with her son. Of the first transmissions, Morley has said: "The word-pictures Kitty painted in people's minds were far more graphic than old newsreel film. Extraordinary." [Haggith and Newman p.159.] The remark echoes the way Resnais had made *Night and Fog*: description at one remove proves more powerful than unfettered revelation.

Morley's technique had been to let the camera follow Kitty around the camp as she talked to her son David. The observer is an audience to what is being said, and this technique it appears allowed her to speak as much as she did. A similar challenge faced Claude Lanzmann in making *Shoah*, but his strategy is different. His motivation is a pure expression of Wiesel's approach: only those who were there can speak of the camps, but he extends the testimony from survivors to those who drove the trains to the camps, those who farmed and lived nearby, even some of the Germans who had a role in running the camps. Its epic quality signals a high point in the process of remembering. Lanzmann seems to have wanted to have delivered the definitive statement on film of the Holocaust, and was openly dismayed by the appearance of Spielberg's *Schindler's List* in 1993. *Shoah* had embodied in pure form philosophical notions about the 'limits of representation', to use the title of Saul Friedlander's book about the Final Solution, so that *Schindler's List's* attempt to depict the totality of the event as the context of his story about Schindler and his Jewish workers was criticized by some as a "transgression". However, it stood out as Hollywood's most notable statement on the subject so far, and reached audiences in a way that other films had been unable to do. It initiated a new phase, both in encouraging other film-makers to tackle the subject (for example Roberto Benigni's *Life is Beautiful* (1997) and Tim Blake Nelson's *The Grey Zone* (2001)) and in causing agonized debate about the ethics of making films on the Holocaust: the proceedings of a symposium at Philadelphia in 1994 was published in 1997 [see Loshitzky] which among other things deals with the polarization between *Schindler's List* and *Shoah*, between showing and witnessing, the wider question of filming history, and of the reception of the film not only in the USA but Germany, Israel and France as well. As a background to this was a rising realization that survivors of the Holocaust would not live forever, and since there was a risk of there being no remembrance because there were no survivors, and with the fiftieth anniversary of the ending of World War II coming up in 1995, plans were laid and brought into effect to create Holocaust museums. The Memorial Museum in Washington D. C. opened in 1993 after many years of planning and fund-raising, and the Jewish Memorial in Berlin, first proposed in 1988, opened in 2005, a monument that also contains a Visitors' Centre. In London the Imperial War Museum's Holocaust Exhibition opened in 2000. In the meantime Yad Vashem in Israel continued to document the lives of victims, and had completed three million in 2005. The USC Shoah Foundation for Visual History and Education, based in Los Angeles, and established in 1994 by Spielberg following the reception of *Schindler's List*, has now recorded more than 55,000 interviews with survivors and witnesses.

Shoah and *Schindler's List* stand either side of the ending of the Cold War, which opened up new archival material from behind the Iron Curtain, and gave a momentum to new publications, notably of Szpilman's 'Death of a City', which Polanski filmed in 2003 as *The Pianist*, another consequence possibly of *Schindler's List* in its expression that there are other stories to tell beyond *Schindler's List*, and in the fact that Polanski, himself a survivor, had the credentials to create something more fastidious, even with autobiographical touches in order to add to its authenticity.

There is now some excellent writing on Holocaust cinema, notably Annette Insdorf's 'Indelible Shadows: Film and the Holocaust', the collection of essays in 'Spielberg's Holocaust', and the essays collected in 'The Holocaust and the Moving Image'. Analysis of films *Night and Fog, Shoah, Schindler's List* and *The Pianist* shows that, although they have been extensively written about, yet there are still points to make about how they work on our imagination.

*

The French documentary, *Nuit et brouillard/ Night and Fog*, made in 1955, had an emphatic cultural impact in Europe, especially on those too young to have participated in the war and on those born just after it. It was made by Alain Resnais, whose *Last Year in Marienbad, Hiroshima Mon Amour* and *Muriel*, his first three feature films, caused sufficient of a stir among cinéastes (in distinction to the mass audiences of popular cinema) that they sought out the documentaries Resnais had made before embarking on these features and already notable in France, chief of which was *Night and Fog*. This film, like the three features, is an exercise in memory. It is not a straightforward account of the Holocaust, although it is structured in three chronological parts (the building of the camps, the functioning of the crematoria and the liberation), but an appeal to the memory through the showing of the death camp buildings at Auschwitz, the 'shower' rooms and the ovens, as they were 10 years after the end of the war, and by the remains, a pile of women's hair, of spectacles, of shaving brushes. Jean Cayrol's voice-over for the film culminates in a question, "Who is responsible?" implicating not just the executioners but a whole society, a whole culture in which such things could take place. A particular poignancy derives from filming the site in summer sunlight. The opening shot shows a pleasant rural landscape, in which the camera pulls back to reveal the barbed wire of the fences. It is from these remains that we have to conceive in our imaginations the conditions of living and dying in the camps. Resnais was a film editor by profession and juxtaposes the contemporary shots with documentary footage and photographs. It is only in the last section which includes newsreel of the near-dead inmates taken at the liberation of the camps that the horror comes visualised rather than imagined, as if at the end we needed to see in order to gain more of an understanding.

Night and Fog's seriousness in recognising the elusiveness of its subject is a prelude to Claude Lanzmann's desire to set clear parameters as to how the Holocaust should be represented, and like Resnais he uses the actual sites as a starting point, to create something epic and face-to-face with the nature of the deaths and of the survivals. *Shoah* is nine hours long, the size and weight of it striving to match the enormity of the history it tries to recount, but the true impact of Lanzmann's work is yet to be assessed, for he shot an estimated 350 hours of film. Beside *Shoah*, four other films have been released subsequently. *A Visitor from the Living* (1997) about a Red Cross representative, Maurice Rossel, who in 1944 wrote a favorable report about the Theresienstadt concentration camp; *Sobibor, October 14, 1943, 4 p.m.* (2001) about Yehuda Lerner, who participated in an uprising against the camp guards and managed to escape; *The Karski Report* (2010) about Polish resistance fighter Jan Karski's visit to Franklin Roosevelt in 1943; *The Last of the Unjust* (2013), an interview with Benjamin Murmelstein, a member of the Judenrat, or Council of Elders, in Theresienstadt. No one has done more than Lanzmann to engage with the reality of what happened in the annihilation camps and yet it is only a small fraction of his material collected in *Shoah* that has any sort of currency.

Lanzmann addresses the question of <u>how</u> you bear witness in as pure a way as possible, in doing so picking up where Resnais had left the subject. Eschewing all use of newsreel, he approached it only through the present day. We are shown the camp at Chelmno (now just an open space in a pine forest), Treblinka (made into a stark monument with its forest of rough-hewn stone slabs on which are inscribed the names of the places from which the victims had come) and Auschwitz-Birkenau, much of which still stands]. We travel the railways on which the trains carrying deportees arrived. We see the Jewish houses and synagogues in Poland which now have other occupants, other uses. Above all, under Lanzmann's probing, torturing questions, witness is born from survivors, from railway workers, from villagers living adjacent to the camps, even from German S. S. soldiers involved in the running of the camps. It runs for nine hours and its story resists paraphrase: it has become the Everest that has to be scaled in order to embark on understanding. The most important testimony comes from camp survivors, whose factual account of life in the death camps is spoken not to a family, nor to a court, nor to a historian, but to the world. It is true that Lanzmann fully understands the poignancy of the visual memory such as the erased camp at Chelmno and the former Jewish houses now occupied by Poles, the railway lines snaking through endless fields and woods to the broken crematoria of Auschwitz, but it is the <u>words</u> of the survivors such as Simon Srebnik, Richard Glazar, Filip Muller and a number of others, rather than Lanzmann's images, that stir the deepest emotions, and convert the intellectual imagining of the event into one of feeling, that might begin to create a proper authenticity, to address the question of <u>how</u> as much as <u>what</u>. Yet, to add a paradoxical twist, the most powerful moment is the account by Abram Bomba, a barber in Czestochowa before the war, a barber in Israel after it, and a barber in Treblinka shaving the heads of deportees prior to their annihilation. Under Lanzmann's sympathetic but insistent questioning, Bomba tells us much of the horror of Treblinka (where 850,000 Jews died), but when he reaches the point where a friend and fellow-barber recognizes his wife and sister among the deportees, Bomba stops and when Lanzmann gently cajoles him with "Go on, you must go on," Bomba seems to be getting ready to do so, but remains speechless. For three minutes, we hear the sound of barbers at work, we watch Bomba at work, but no words are spoken. There is a rhetorical device called 'aposiopesis' in which speech stops and the listener must supply the rest. *The Pawnbroker* ends with it when the Jewish pawnbroker gives a silent scream, the shock expressed not in the sound but in the picture. In editing *Shoah*, Lanzmann had the artistic choice of whether to cut this section of Bomba's testimony, but he chooses instead to make use of this rhetorical device, recognizing that its unplanned, unscripted, unacted nature imparts a much greater force than Lumet and Steiger were able to achieve in *The Pawnbroker*.

Following *Shoah*, the film-makers had to consider whether any story recreating the circumstances of the Holocaust – be it a fiction or a true event from history – should be undertaken at all. The question has been set aside, judging by the number of narrative films that have been made since *Shoah*, and indeed it had to be: to veto all such efforts would be to act like the philosopher-kings in Plato's *Republic* who wished to suppress artistic representation in the state on the grounds that it was only a copy of reality, and therefore inferior, and it led to bad morals. Even if these two arguments had force, the effect of such a veto would be to deny the necessary comfort that art can provide. Although 'comfort' feels an inappropriate word to use about Holocaust fiction, the search for expressing the truth of this event, even as it falls short of perfection, is more comforting than being prevented from saying anything at all. *Shoah* moved this question centre stage and after it the film-makers had to take more seriously than ever the how of portraying events from the Holocaust. It was at this point that Steven Spielberg made his remarkable intervention with *Schindler's List* (1993), slipped into his schedule after the huge financial success of *Jurassic Park*. *Schindler's List's* gross worldwide of $321 million (against an estimated budget of $25 million) is a crude indicator of its impact.

The real-life story of Oskar Schindler was a complex one, well reflecting the morally fluid nature of his character. Born a Catholic in Moravia, he grows up in the 1930s trying his hand at business and failing. By 1939, he is thirty-one. The war brings him his chance to succeed: he buys assets for virtually nothing and employs his labour for virtually nothing, because his workers are Jews in no position to contest the terms of their employment. As the war progresses and Schindler witnesses the plight of the Jews in Kraków ghetto, he sets up the Deutsche Emalia Fabrik using Jewish labour to produce enamel goods for the German front. When the Nazis liquidate the ghetto in March 1943, depriving him of his work force, Schindler goes to the Plaszów concentration camp, to which they have been transferred, and negotiates the setting up of a factory for 900 Jewish workers in Zablocie, making (defective) bullets for German guns. It is there, in the latter half of 1944, that he compiles his list of essential Jewish workers, in a plan to rescue them from extermination. In October 1944 he relocates the factory to Zwittau-Brünnlitz in Czechoslovakia, by which time his wife Emilie is playing a key role in keeping the operation going. In this way, 1100 Jews are saved. Yet the contradictions of his life do not end there: at the end of the war, aware of the accusations that would be levelled at anyone collaborating with the Nazis, he leaves Brünnlitz to evade Soviet justice, and travels to the American-occupied zone in Germany, surviving there in part on the gifts from the Jews he had saved. From there he emigrates to Argentina with Emilie in order to start a new life, but it does not work out: his businesses fail and his marriage breaks down. He returns to Germany in 1958 where he survives on some pensions from Schindler Jews in Israel, and small pensions from both the German government and the Israeli government. He dies in 1974 and is buried in a Catholic cemetery in Israel.

This richly dramatic life became history when a Canadian journalist, Herbert Steinhouse, stumbled on the story in Germany after the war, and met Schindler in Munich in 1948, holding four interviews with him and six with Schindler's accountant, Itzhak Stern. After sending it to his agent in New York, he found that no one was interested in printing it, another example of the amnesia concerning the Holocaust that settled on the immediate post-war world. It was only when the Australian author, Thomas Kenneally, turned the story into a historical fiction with his book 'Schindler's Ark' published in 1982 that this piece of history, now distilled as story with reinvented characters and dialogue, took on a wider currency, especially with its capture of the Booker prize in that year. This was how it came into the hands of Steven Spielberg, who purchased the film rights soon after publication and then waited for the right moment to make the film, in order to give himself time to mature as a film-maker and thus allow the production to have full impact. Nor is there any doubt about that impact: possibly no single document about the Holocaust – whether it be memoirs, fiction, newsreel or film, even Lanzmann's *Shoah* – has brought home to people around the world the enormity of the event, enlarging horizons and provoking journeys towards understanding.

This commercial success, based on Spielberg's attunement in his own sensibility to popular desires and expressions, has attracted particular opprobrium, that he has 'Hollywoodized' the subject -- as if in so doing he had indulged in a particular display of bad taste, which in view of the subject is in a way harmful. But this is unjust: Spielberg is a story-teller by vocation and has been drawn to telling the essential story of Schindler's life because it is a compelling drama of good and evil, of horror and salvation. The 'Hollywoodian' contribution is to reduce the ambiguities involved, to print the legend replete with hero and happy ending – or as near to it as the story would allow. But the film does retain its ambiguities: 1100 Jews may have been saved but the film does not flinch from the annihilation going on around them; the heart of the story is the relation between Schindler and Hauptsturmführer Amon Goeth, S. S. commander of Plaszów, the truth of which has surely been quite lost, and replaced by Spielberg and his screenwriter, Steven Zaillian, with something possibly much more complex and interesting.

Despite his Hollywoodian faults – not felt to be such, I am sure, by the masses of people who saw the film – Spielberg is a gifted film-maker. Four points can be made on this score: firstly, he made the bold decision to film in black and white, a decision brilliantly executed by the cinematographer, Janusk Kaminski. The choice was successful, partly because audiences associate black-and-white film with the 1940s, but it is more. Chiaroscuro is appropriate to the darkness of the story, and the ambiguity of Schindler: when he rescues his female labourers from Auschwitz, Schindler sits opposite Rudolf Höss, the camp commandant, and bargains with diamonds. Why should these women be preserved? "Allow me to express the reason," says Schindler, against the dark background his face painted in light from a single overhead source, who then spreads a set of

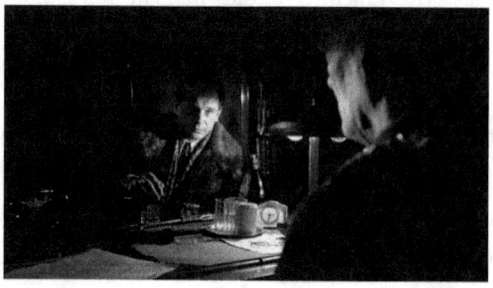

diamonds on Höss's desk , even more seductive in black and white than in colour, Spielberg and Kaminski investing the cliché of *film noir* with new meaning.

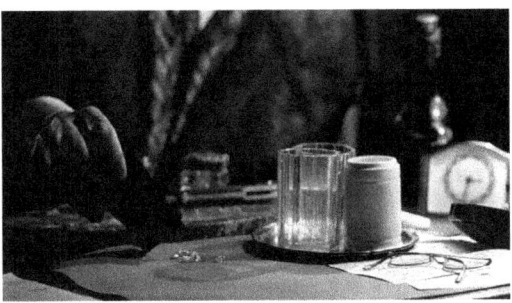

Secondly, this choice allows for several pictorial *coups de cinéma*: the remarkable re-creation by set designer Allan Starski of Plaszów, in which the drabness of the factories and of the concentration camp is conveyed in newsreel greyness so that the filming uncannily recreates the banal monotone of the surviving photographic documents. By the use of colour at the end to show the surviving Schindler Jews honouring his tomb, when the fiction suddenly becomes documentary, Spielberg signals that the story is in the past, that the world has changed, that survival even of such events as these is possible.

Thirdly, the 'red coat' of the liquidation of the Kraków ghetto is an imaginative leap of a high order. Or was it Spielberg's imagination? In 'East-West Street', the author Philippe Sands tells of his meetings with Niklas Frank, son of Hans Frank, the governor-general of Nazi-occupied Poland. Sands was shown by Niklas some home movies of his father at work including scenes in the Kraków ghetto. "In one short scene, the camera lingers on a girl in a red dress. Looking straight into the camera, she smiles. . ." [p.231]. Was it just coincidence, Sands muses, that Spielberg used this idea in *Schindler's List*? If it was a red dress, the home movie must have been in colour: so if Spielberg had seen the clip or just been told about it, his intelligence was to pick out the redness of the coat in a black-and-white film. The scene rivets the spectator: as the mayhem goes on around her, a little girl lost wanders through it all, and we follow her from afar, our eyes caught by the fact that her coat has been tinted red. Her final fate is then revealed later in the film when the bodies of the massacre are exhumed at Chujowa Gorka (in order to be cremated, as the Nazis take a further step to eliminate these people from physical existence), and we see her dead body, still in her red coat. To the accusation that Spielberg's film of the Holocaust focuses on two Gentiles, Schindler and Goeth, thus missing the point, this piece of fiction is surely a rejoinder. He knows he is up against the 'limits of representation' but that the imagination can convey something of what happened, for one corpse focusses the reality of death for "a world entire". That it is a child's death adds poignancy to the horror.

Fourthly, while it seems that the Schindler-Goeth relationship is what most intrigued Spielberg the story-teller (as well as Zaillian), it is the Holocaust story as a whole that captures his soul as a Jew. Hence he opts for an epic dimension for the film – giving it a duration of 195 minutes – as if the subject demands no other choice. Yet epics always pose a challenge to the preservation of temporal unity, especially for a subject which has been so well documented by historians. While the film works spatially because Spielberg concentrates on the ghetto/camp world of Kraków, Plaszów, Auschwitz and Brünnlitz, all in comparative close proximity, and refrains from the distraction of showing events on the Russian front or the western invasion of Europe, yet time is dislocated. The events in the film run from 1939 to 1945, but spectators need to keep their own awareness of the passage of time, that we are seeing the highlights of the story, and not the grind of hunger and suffering in between. For example, after the creation of the Kraków ghetto in March 1941, we are shown scenes of how the factory operated, how Schindler bribed Germans, how he treated his wife Emilie (preserving the cake of marriage while eating it by enjoying a stream of mistresses). There follows a sequence showing the rescue of Itzhak Stern from deportation to South Russia which is given no date but must have happened about a year later (well after the German invasion of the Soviet Union in June 1941). And then in the next scene, we are shown the arrival of Goeth at Plaszów in winter 1942. This criticism may seem pedantic, but if you film a historical subject, you face the problem of the truth of history getting out of harmony with the truth of the story. I believe there was a solution, that despite the difficulties in doing so, the film could have explored some of the month-in month-out suffering of those in the ghetto. There would even be scope for irony: was the rescue of Stern from deportation for the agony of life in the ghetto really a blessing?

Rightly or wrongly, Spielberg is striving in his epic to deliver the conclusive, definitive viewpoint. To aid him in this, he wants to create archetypes: Goeth embodies all Nazi evil; Helen Hirsch, Goeth's Jewish mistress, is Biblical Judith before Holofernes, Jewish feminine beauty as the victim of Gentile lust; the evacuation of Kraków ghetto stands for all such evacuations; Stern is the repository of Jewish patience and intelligence in the face of tyranny; Schindler is the man of action whose righteousness redeems the world -- the film's slogan, "Who saves one life saves the world entire" is a triumphalizing of what Schindler has achieved, just as he beats his breast that he has not saved more.

Archetypes risk becoming stereotypes, reducing complexity rather than increasing universality. In a film like this, too, a part must stand for the whole, yet the encompassing of the Holocaust as a whole required a further effort of imagination to preserve complexity. While the spectator needs to understand the context of Schindler's and Goeth's actions, the opportunity for deepening them is missed. For example, Schindler was brought up as a Catholic, and buried as one, and while he appears to reject this upbringing entirely, both his attempt to honour his marriage to Emilie and his guilty breast-beating at the end reflect an ingrained Catholicism, which gives greater piquancy to his actions.

A bigger hole yet is the portrayal of Stern, played with as much subtlety as he can muster in an underwritten part by Ben Kingsley. Stern was in a powerful position in Schindler's factories, and must have been faced with multiple dilemmas of whom to save and whom to decide he could not save. The Judenrät

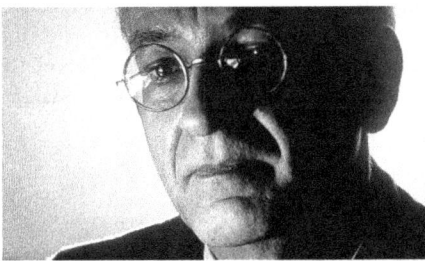

set up by the Nazis in the ghettos, to do their dirtiest work of arranging who lived and who died, found themselves excoriated for collaborating: their efforts were largely brought to nothing both in the fact that those whom they preserved were later annihilated – and they too themselves. One of Primo Levi's most compelling reminiscences, told in 'The Story of a Coin', is of Chaim Rumkowski in the Lodz ghetto and his relationship with the "shady German industrialist", Hans Biebow, a connection that does not save him from the gas at Auschwitz. Rumkowski lives in Levi's 'grey zone' of survival, indeed revels in it, for his presidency or eldership of the ghetto was "an amazing tangled megalomaniacal dream of barbaric vitality and real diplomatic and organizational ability". The echo is uncanny, for in Kraków and Plaszów, Schindler supplied the barbaric vitality and Stern the organizational ability. *Schindler's List* cries out for a portrait of Stern that is as revealing as Rumkowski's, even though at the end he was saved from death.

Because Spielberg wants a totality to his story, and because of the many camps in the Nazi Reich (for imprisonment, for slave labour, and for annihilation) Auschwitz is perceived as the most notorious, he cannot refrain from showing it. Although Spielberg was not allowed to shoot inside the camp he shot sequences outside its gates. The rescue of Schindler's female workers from Auschwitz comes as a penultimate climax to the story, and makes for compelling cinema – but also for a signal failure of aesthetic choice, and possibly an offence against the truth of what actually happened. The scene between Schindler and Höss referred to earlier deftly reveals the sordid circumstances of Schindler's operations and of his perilous role. But the decision to show the women naked in the showers bathed in water when the spectator is brought to the edge of the horror of expecting death by gas, even if it is through the illusory lens of the camera, is a violation of respect. If ever at any point in the film circumstances required a witness to the scene, rather than the scene itself, it is here.

The episode is made more problematical still by the possibility that it did not actually happen. Kenneally acknowledged that the whole affair is clouded with uncertainty, and Herbert Steinhouse, when talking to Schindler and Stern just after the war, understood that the women had been sent to Gross Rosen, a concentration camp in East Germany, rather than Auschwitz.

If it is legend rather than fact, Spielberg is true to his Hollywood milieu in seeking to print the legend. As a climax it provides a fitting prelude to the operatic showpiece he stages at the end when Schindler addresses both his workers and the German guards as well. This is factual, because a transcript taken by his secretary appears to exist of what he actually said. There is a special irony here because the grandiose sentimentality of the episode rings as false as anything in the film, and yet it certainly appears to have taken place.

Despite these criticisms, the film will continue to compel audiences for a long time to come. One final aspect should be mentioned that turns the film into something more philosophical and universal. It is in effect a critique of capitalist enterprise, and it is revealing that Spielberg said that in portraying Schindler he was thinking of the head of Warner Brothers when he first went to Hollywood. Schindler's business is bad because it sustains the German war machine; good because in doing so it chose to make defective munitions; it is bad because war profiteering is repellent; good because it creates the surplus necessary to bribe Germans and thus gain work and life for his Jewish work force. Ultimately it is good because it saves a portion of the world. Schindler's enterprise is focused on money, because he needs an experienced accountant, Itzhak Stern, to make it survive, but Schindler changes during the film to the point where money is only of value insomuch as it saves life. The bottom line ceases to be profit but life. At the very end, Stern tells Schindler that his business is bust, but Schindler has achieved a moral purity, a literal redemption of 'buying back' his Jews from death, even as we know that the suitcases of marks Goeth receives from Schindler will not deflect the retribution of arrest and hanging for crimes against humanity.

Since the Holocaust is a key event for all Europeans, not just its Jewish members, the global impact of *Schindler's List* is important. But if it is conceived of as unique, and only to be interpreted by Jews who survived, then from this viewpoint the credentials of *The Pianist* are impeccable, for the story of Wladyslaw Szpilman's survival through six years in a Warsaw crammed with Jews then finally cleansed of them was recounted by Szpilman himself in a book, and filmed by Roman Polanski in 2002, Polanski himself as a young Jew having experienced at first hand life in the Kraków ghetto.

Again, how the details of Szpilman's life came to be known sheds remarkable light on the way the Second World War and the Holocaust in particular came to public consciousness. Before the war, Szpilman was an accomplished pianist in Poland, and indeed had experienced German musical culture at first hand during his time at the Berlin Conservatoire in the early 1930s. Aged twenty-seven when the war broke out, he and his family stayed close to each other through the successive torments of the imposition of racial legislation against the Jews, confinement in the ghetto, and its painful shrinking in size, until finally he is separated from them in the Umschlagplatz, the place from which the rounded-up Jews were sent for extermination in Auschwitz. In the second half of the war he escapes from the ghetto and survives outside it until Warsaw is finally liberated by the Russians. He resumes his career as a pianist and composer, playing on Polish radio and composing many popular songs. As already noted, his account of his survival was published in Warsaw in 1945 but does not seem to have made much of a ripple, certainly not outside Poland, and in any case the new Communist government quickly suppressed it. Szpilman's son tells of how his father did not talk about what had happened, and it was only after the fall of Communism that the book saw the light of day again. Its fame then began to spread. When exactly it came to Polanski's attention is unclear, but in filming it, he made one of the subtlest of narrative films about the Holocaust, and as with *Schindler's List* created a huge wave of interest in what had happened at the heart of the Nazi extermination process. So far it has grossed $120 million worldwide.

Why subtle? In part because of its detached tone, which is well transferred from the book to the film. While Szpilman's account does not match the profundity of Primo Levi's 'If this is a man', which poses so insistently the question of why one was saved while another was drowned, probing the behaviour of men in extreme conditions, and agonizing that he survived, the questions are implicit in Szpilman's account. He writes simply with occasional flashes of sardonic humour and warmth about individuals, fellow Jews and the Poles who help him. The book also has an extraordinary absence of anger. Every great story needs a climax too. As it turned out, Szpilman did not need to engineer one. He, seemingly the last Jew in the city after the murder of half a million, meets the one Nazi among a host of murderers with sufficient compassion to help him with food and a coat, and the news that the Russians would shortly be coming.

Many readers will have embarked on the book knowing that Szpilman survived. As with Bresson's account of Devigny's escape from the Gestapo prison at Montluc in *A Man Escaped* (1956), the fact of his salvation is not in doubt, only the means [see also chapter 1]. Furthermore there is a shadow story behind the personal one. When first published, Szpilman's book was called 'The Death of a City', since it is an inside account of how Warsaw was stripped of its Jews, how the Jewish Uprising led to the physical erasure of the ghetto, and how ancient, historic, beautiful Warsaw was then devastated by the Nazis during and after the crushing of the Polish Uprising in 1944. Towards the end he reflects on the six Christmases and New Years he had lived through during the war. "And now I was lonelier, I suppose, than anyone else in the world." On the final page of the book, two weeks after his rescue by the Russians, clean and rested, a free man, he walked towards the Praga district of Warsaw, now all that was left of the city. "I was walking down a broad main road, once busy and full of traffic, its whole length now deserted. There was not a single intact building as far as the eye could see."

In lesser hands, the film might not have done justice to the book, but in Polanski who had been looking for a suitable subject from wartime Poland, the time of his childhood, the book finds its inspired interpreter. He puts it into the hands of the playwright Ronald Harwood to sharpen the dramatic detail. For example, after his escape from the ghetto, Szpilman stays in a flat where he only learns of the Jewish Uprising in 1943 through the sight of smoke rising from the direction of the ghetto and what he reads in the Polish underground papers. In the film, on the other hand, his flat has a narrow but direct view of the ghetto, and through this eye-piece he and the audience receive glimpses of what is happening, enough to allow us to imagine the rest. The film creates a

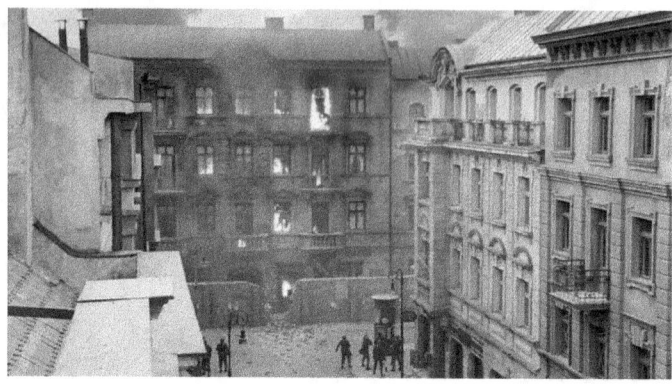

relationship with the Polish woman he meets in 1939 when the Polish Radio building is evacuated during the blitzkrieg, which is not in the book. When the retreating Germans occupy the house in the attic of which Szpilman is hiding, in the film, but not in the book, he hears the sound of Beethoven's 'Moonlight Sonata' coming from below in an obvious, perhaps too obvious evocation of German musical culture, which he will counterpoint by performing Chopin when the German officer Wilm Hosenfeld confronts him.

The finished film also eschews certain visual details in the book which might have been profitably added: Mrs Szpilman in the ghetto scrutinizing her children for lice when they come in from outside, Szpilman kissing the first Pole he meets after being liberated. On the other hand at the Umschlagplatz, the film (but not the book) shows Henryk Szpilman, Wladyslaw's literature-loving brother, reading Shakespeare's 'Merchant of Venice' and quoting Shylock, "If you prick us, do we not bleed?"

Both book and film have this unusual two-act structure: act one up to the separation of Wladek from his family as they are herded into trucks for 'resettlement' in the death camps; act two is Szpilman's new life, first working outside the ghetto and then living and surviving outside it. The first part ends in despair with a scintilla of hope because he has survived by the intervention of a member of the Jewish police who chooses to save him, and the second in hope of a devastated kind: he is alive and able to resume his career as a pianist, but his family and his Jewish background have been rubbed out.

Neither book nor film dwells on the philosophical questions the story raises, but they are there for all to read and see: why were the Jews singled out for this treatment? What could they have done to save themselves? What hand had Szpilman had in his survival? As Clive James has pointed out in his essay 'Chamber Music of Horrors', we need to eliminate the idea that Szpilman's will to survive was sustained by 'music', whether understood as an abstract ideal to which he was committed, or as something much more specific, his desire to carry on playing and composing. If those were motives for him to carry on, they are articulated neither in the book nor the film itself. And yet there was scope to make something of this idea, which the film shies away from. For example, the piece Szpilman plays for Hosenfeld is Chopin's Ballade No. 1 in G Minor, in an abridged version for the film. In the book, what Szpilman plays is the Nocturne in C Sharp Minor, which is what he is playing in the radio station on 23 September 1939 when he is interrupted by the German bombardment of Warsaw, and the piece Szpilman chose to play when Polish Radio reopened after the war. Why the change? Perhaps the Ballade is Polanski's favourite piece of Chopin. Yet for a production team who seem to have convinced themselves that it was Szpilman's desire for music that helped him to stay alive, the playing of the Nocturne would have offered a neat link between what Szpilman played in the studio in 1939, what he plays for Hosenfeld, and what he plays on the radio when it reopens in 1945. (The film further dislocates the truth by ending with Szpilman and orchestra playing Chopin's 'Grande Polonaise Brillante'. Is the choice of a Polonaise Polanski's assertion of his Polishness?) Although the idea of Szpilman drawing the instinct for survival from a love of music seemed to have been a significant element in the film's publicity at its launch, it seems a diversionary and unhelpful piece of marketing.

So why does he survive? On more than one occasion it is his intuition that saves him. Or perhaps it is the decision taken in freedom of the man who engineers a contact for Szpilman with a safe flat outside the ghetto, or of the Poles who chose to shelter him (for which the penalty on being discovered was death). Or was it his reputation as a pianist that gave him a special role that people wanted to preserve, for his divine playing of Chopin was as much an expression of Polish patriotism as anything? Or was it all really blind chance at virtually every turn? Compare the book's (but not the film's) account of Goldfeder, with whom Szpilman played concerts in the ghetto. He too managed to escape the ghetto and to survive in hiding for two years, except that "a week before the Soviet army invaded, he was shot by Germans in a little town not far from the ruins of Warsaw". Goldfeder's fate is a curt reminder of how ill chance might have ended Szpilman's life too.

There are two particular differences in Polanski and Harwood's handling of the film as opposed to *Schindler's List*. While details of the story may have changed, they are very close to Szpilman's version of his narrative, namely that all the events are filtered through his involvement with them. Whether a spectator comes to the film knowing something of the historical background or being ignorant of it, the film points them to the larger context, either illuminating what is known already, or posing urgently the necessity of learning more. Spielberg's film on the other hand takes a cosmic view, seeking to recount the whole Holocaust through one story, while the film of *The Pianist*, like the book, displays a certain modesty in this regard.

Schindler's List has been praised, rightly, for its bold use of black-and-white cinematography at a time when colour film had become the universal medium for commercial cinema. Many spectators commended this choice, as if almost to dare any subsequent film-maker to re-create, to 'imagine' a Holocaust story in anything but black and white. If so, Polanski proves them wrong. While there is a deliberate intention by Polanski and his costume designer, Anna Sheppard, to create a monochromatic atmosphere in the ghetto scenes, using not just browns and greys but colours with the brightness washed out of them, yet through the film colour helps to give life to the story, whether it be the yellow armbands forced on the Jews to wear, the flames of the burning ghetto, or the moonlit winter streets of a devastated Warsaw with their other-worldly blue-toned quality. Like *Schindler's List* the sets and costumes pay effective attention to how the ghetto and Warsaw looked. Another contributory factor is the performance of Adrian Brody as Szpilman. His face remarkably preserves if not the 'letter' of what Szpilman looked like, then certainly its spirit. A photograph taken for his identity card in 1942 (at the age of 31) shows a man with refined features, a high forehead, a finely sculpted mouth serious at the corners but ready to break into a smile. Brody's face is similarly striking and suggestive of a certain distance between him and the spectator, while real sensitivity of expression is achieved through the piano. This allows Brody to give a muted performance, which is more eloquent than a loud, showy one.

Finally, it is worth criticizing *The Pianist* for failing, like *Schindler's List*, to convey the passage of time. A whole year passes in the ghetto, marked by nothing more than a title with a new date; months are spent in hiding in different flats with little or no attempt made to convey the fact. Yet if the temporal dimension is not fully fleshed out, the physical aspect is superbly realized. Although old Warsaw was erased almost completely by the war, Polanski's production designer Allan Starski, something of a specialist in Holocaust films for he had been designer on *Schindler's List* (on which Anna Sheppard had done the costumes) and before that on Jack Gold's *Escape from Sobibor*, made use of the Praga District of Warsaw, on the east side of the Vistula, which still has streets and buildings from the period. In addition, modern buildings were dressed as old ones. Secondly, the Babelsberg studio near Berlin was used to create other streets. Thirdly, to show the devastated Warsaw of the final sequences, a former barracks of the Soviet Army near Berlin was used. Since it was scheduled to be destroyed, a deal was made with the company that owns the site whereby the buildings were 'wrecked' to look like a war-torn city. Making a feature film requires creative collaboration at many points, and while it is clear Polanski had definite ideas about how the film should look, the director has to rely too on the work of designers to realise those ideas, to 'imagine' them on the director's behalf. Polanski, Starski and Sheppard made extensive use of photographs and newsreel footage, to which Polanski brought his childhood memories as well. Just as Carné, Prévert and the set designer Alexandre Trauner made their version of Le Boulevard du Temple (also known as 'Le Boulevard du Crime') in *Les Enfants du paradis*, recreating in a Nice studio a particular corner in 19-century Paris, their masterpiece of 'poetic realism', so Starski can take a significant credit, along with Polanski and Sheppard, for his contribution to the film's overall atmosphere. When Szpilman escapes from the former hospital building being torched by Germans with flame-throwers, he clambers over the wall at the rear. As he does so, the camera, mounted on a rising crane, lifts itself to reveal him stumbling away down the deserted street, lined with houses half-derelict from burning and shelling. The scene is eloquent of the death of a city and Szpilman being "lonelier, I supposed, than anyone else in the world," sans family, sans city, sans people.

*

Immediately following the war, it was a devastated Berlin rather than Warsaw that must have burnt itself on the imagination of the Allied forces who were involved in administering post-war Germany. The city's destruction is intimately linked to Hitler's last days in his bunker. Again, the historical details have been in the public record ever since the publication of Trevor-Roper's meticulous account in 'The Last Days of Hitler', first published in 1947, but it took the making of *Downfall* by Olivier Hirschbiegel in Germany in 2004 to create for a large audience a memory of that time. The layout of the bunker is well-documented and comparatively easy to fabricate in accurate terms. But the film interweaves the claustrophobic scenes in the bunker itself with a different kind of claustrophobia, the physical and moral chaos on the streets of Berlin as the Russians close in on the Chancellery, and Hitler, refusing to surrender, insists on the collective suicide of the German nation as the only end to the war. The film's designer (Bernd Lapel) recreates the necessary patina of buildings shelled and burnt, and the landscapes of rubble in the streets. This artifice, creating the illusion of ruin, is a physical counterpart to the collapse of the Third Reich. Compare Roberto Rossellini's *Germany Year Zero*, made in 1946, and filmed in the open air of Berlin's streets and the ruined Chancellery: no set designer was needed for these scenes. The flat 'documentary' lighting of this cityscape has a different effect from the re-created, studio-lit images of *Downfall*: here Rossellini is not obliged to persuade us to believe that Berlin look like this, for its appearance is incontrovertible. [A devastated Berlin was also the effective setting of *Berlin Express* (1948, d. Jacques Tourneur) and of *The Man Between* (1953, d. Carol Reed).] But like *Downfall*, *Germany Year Zero* has a purpose to communicate, a moral judgment to make, pressing with some urgency, for the question of German guilt for what was done by the Nazis in their name is typically asked by Rossellini as crucial, as requiring an examination that does not flinch. His humanism makes him focus on the struggle for survival by a twelve-year-old boy seeking to support his family, including a father who is ill and an elder brother who, having served in the Wehrmacht, is now in hiding.

The film is the third in Rossellini's (unintended) war trilogy and represents a philosophical impasse for him. After the cruelties but also the heroic martyrdoms in *Rome Open City*, the vividness of the sketches of Italy in *Paisà*, the bleakness of the episode of the partisans' life in the Po delta tempered by the episode in the Franciscan monastery, *Germany Year Zero* pitches Edmund into an ethical hell which is beyond his years to understand. Encouraged by the adults around him who keep referring to the burden placed on them by having to feed their sick father, Edmund administers poison in order to bring about his death.

In its subtle way, this echoes what the Nazis confronted the German people with: the mentally and physically ill, homosexuals, gypsies are all useless parasites who need to be exterminated if society is to be healthy, and above all the 'Jewish infection' must be eradicated once and for all. The citizenry responded impassively in moral ignorance, and like Edmund, some actively translated this theory into action.

Edmund's action so troubles him that the story in progressing to its bleak conclusion – for in the final sequences, we see Edmund wandering through the shell of a tall building and then suddenly killing himself by leaping off it – does achieve a troubled redemption, that the only response to murder by the perpetrator is his suicide. Only in this way can time, history and civilization begin again from the Year Zero.

Rossellini is an Italian addressing the question of German guilt. How would German writers and film-makers come to terms with the enormity of the years 1933-45? The most monumental film to try and do so has been Edgar Reitz's *Heimat* (1984 to 2006), comprising some forty-eight hours of film, and divided into three distinct sections. (In 2011 he added a prequel set in the nineteenth century, *Die andere Heimat/Home from Home.*) The second section, *Die Zweite Heimat* (hereafter referred to as *DZH*), released in 1993, covers the lives of a group of music students and their friends in Munich between 1960 and 1970, a period of musical experimentation, radicalism in student politics, and above all the coming to maturity of a generation born after 1940, innocent of the Nazis today but feeling its presence in the lives of their families and in their history.

DZH has a rich gallery of characters, with Hermann and Clarissa central to all 13 episodes, while a number take centre-stage in particular episodes, with even more coming in and going out of the story. While *Heimat 1* and *Heimat 3* are family sagas, certainly of very great accomplishment but with several antecedents in literature, *DZH* is much more original: the portrait of a generation linked not by family but by friendship and acquaintance. *DZH* has a strongly autobiographical feel to it, even if the particular events and stories which Reitz narrates are fictitious. One of its most striking qualities is the way the full history of the characters only emerges by the most careful watching of the film. It is like a palimpsest. Indeed re- and re-viewing are essential to appreciating its weight, perhaps most of all in the way it deals with the Nazi past. It is worth looking at biographies of five characters in particular.

The first forms a particular link with the past, since she is twenty years older than the others. Elizabeth Cerphal is in her forties during the 1960s but is both the 'eternal daughter' of her father who keeps the family history from her so that she exclaims, "Everything loathsome and bloody has passed me by", and the eternal student who responds without hesitation to the new generation of artistic students coming to Munich to the extent that she opens up her villa, the Fuchsbau, in the smart Munich suburb of Schwabing for them to use as a place for meetings and for parties. The deep, dark something in her family which Juan (see below) surmises is that one of the partners in Verlag Cerphal founded by her grandfather and father in 1910 was a Jew, Herr Goldbaum. The Fuchsbau is the original property of Goldbaum: when, in 1935, the firm helps him to leave Germany for Haifa, it is Elizabeth's father who takes over the villa with a written promise to restore it to Goldbaum in due course. Elizabeth calls Goldbaum 'uncle' because her great friend is his daughter, Edith, a friend now lost because Edith was 'betrayed' by her husband, Herr Gattinger (see below), and imprisoned in Munich. From there she went to Ravensbrück from which Gattinger and the Cerphal family got her moved to the work camp at Moringen. When the camp is closed in 1944, she dies in some unknown way, in some unknown destination.

She survives in her daughter, Esther Goldbaum, who makes a vivid appearance in parts 10 and 11, when she has an intense affair with Reinhard, a young film-maker, and when she and Herr Gattinger, her father, look for traces of her mother in Dachau – only for her to learn from him that Edith was never in fact in Dachau. Reinhard is Reinhard Dörr, born in 1943, whose father was a fighter pilot who had helped bomb Guernica. He has had a rootless youth, moving five or six times when young. He is as burdened as any of the student group by Germany's Nazi past, and his film script on Esther's life is his way of trying to understand it. He becomes the main story himself when he disappears on the Ammersee near Munich, missing presumed drowned, presumed by his own will.

Reinhard especially distrusts Gattinger, who has become Elizabeth Cerphal's chaperone, a man apparently without character, which has enabled him to slither through the murky depths of Nazi racial ideology even while fathering a daughter by Edith Goldbaum. Even Elizabeth Cerphal calls him "a bad cheque, like the Third Reich". His defence to his daughter is that he has admitted what he has done.

Finally, there is Juan, a mystery himself, capable of discerning mysteries in others. Juan is Juan Ramon Fernandes Subercasseaux, born in Chile, to (I think we are to imagine) a Catholic mother, whose surname he adopts, while his father is a 'Protestant from Virginia' and his grandfather a Russian Jew. Juan is gifted – multi-lingual, gymnastic, highly musical. He is refused entry to the Hochschule because his music is too 'folkloric': he plays Bach on the marimba. He befriends both Hermann and Clarissa, and as a result of his charm befriends Frau Cerphal and Herr Gattinger and through this familiarity learns that the Fuchsbau originally belonged to Uncle Goldbaum, and makes the fact explicit to Elizabeth: "Your father got the house from Goldbaum in order to return it after the war. He took his fortune and gave nothing back. A great injustice." Juan is the outsider, fascinated by Germany but detached from it. When (in episode nine), Elizabeth is taken to a police station (as a result of a misunderstanding about her presence one evening in her father's publishing house after it has closed for the day), on her release she remarks to Juan, "I owe everything to my father, including this house. Can you imagine that they took me for a criminal?" To this Juan replies without pause, "Yes."

There is then in *DZH* a direct engagement with the Holocaust in the person of Esther Goldbaum's mother, Edith, and with the results of Nazi racial ideology in the expropriation of the Fuchsbau from the Goldbaum family. This act links the German middle-class to the deep ambiguity of the Holocaust, for while it was carried out under a reign of terror, so opponents were frightened into not acting or acting only in secret such as arranging for Goldbaum to go to Israel, rescuing Edith from Ravensbrück (only to lose her), and secretly arranging for Esther to be looked after in Switzerland, yet when the war ended, and Elizabeth's father holds a written promise to return the Fuchsbau to the Goldbaum family, he does not do so (despite being in written communication with another Goldbaum daughter in Israel), and on his deathbed gets Elizabeth to tear up the written contract promising to return the villa, and urges her not to countenance any outside claims to ownership.

DZH, in all its thirteen episodes, provides a deep insight into the philosophical, cultural and moral nature of the new generation maturing after the war. The film has two principal begetters, one in Edgar Reitz who wrote and directed its twenty-six hours, and the other the composer Nikos Mamangakis, who has broken new ground in using music constantly through its whole length to illuminate the cultural background in a country where classical music has always reflected German 'seriousness', both having the music arise internally as it were from all the rehearsed and improvised performances we hear in the film, and as an external element to add an atmosphere to the film. He also makes musical links between episodes, binding the events together in the same way as the characters do.

This is not to detract from the fact that Reitz is the major author of DZH. While assisted by Mamangakis and Robert Busch, responsible for casting the film (achieved with extraordinary aplomb) and credited as co-director, it is the brilliance of Reitz's epic narrative conception, of his scripting, and of his visual imagination that make DZH one of the masterworks of twentieth-century European culture. Reitz does several things to give the narrative cinematic depth: he is always showing us visual things that enlarge the narrative, whether it is the non-verbal communication that enlarges what the characters say to each other, or the portrait of Munich that provides the setting for so much of the film, or the addition of a visual sensuousness at so many points. For example, when Reinhardt meets Esther in Venice and they have an intense affair, it is embroidered by Reitz's pleasure in the sight of the backstreet canals that punctuate the episode, especially a tracking shot along the canal into the sunlight, and as Reinhard and Esther probe each other's characters on the bed, the sight of the half moon at night waxing over the canal. Venice is a much filmed city, but it has never been made so romantic and yet so disturbing. [For other Venice films, see for example *Death in Venice* (1971, d. Visconti), *Don't Look Now* (1973, d. Roeg), *Comfort of Strangers* (1990, d. Schrader), *Monday Morning* (2002, d. Iosseliani).]

A bare account of the characters' biographies makes DZH sound like a novel, and indeed Reitz has the novelist's gift for characterization, but his film manages to interweave and to layer these stories as only the cinema can do so well. The whole twenty-six hours is a miracle of cross-cutting that does not just take the viewer from A to Z, but from G to N, from R to W, and indeed from P to B and so on, because the film works backwards as well: earlier episodes are more fully appreciated by the knowledge gained in later ones. This lends depth at both the visual and verbal levels, and it is especially powerful in changing our perceptions of events. Episode nine is particularly devoted to Elizabeth Cerphal's story. When she goes to Verlag Cerphal and is officially welcomed by the firm's staff one says to her, "Your family's history would be an incredible record of our times." As spectators we quickly realise the unconscious irony of this remark for the fate of the Goldbaum family would make it a disturbing one. Then later in the episode, we are taken aback that Elizabeth's generosity in letting the new artistic generation use her house is abused by its enforceable 'occupation' by a group of radical students, this being 1968. Their leader says to her, "You're probably very nice, but you are perforce propertied class," while not realizing (as we realize) that she owns the property by her father's own act of occupation, different from that of the students but more lasting.

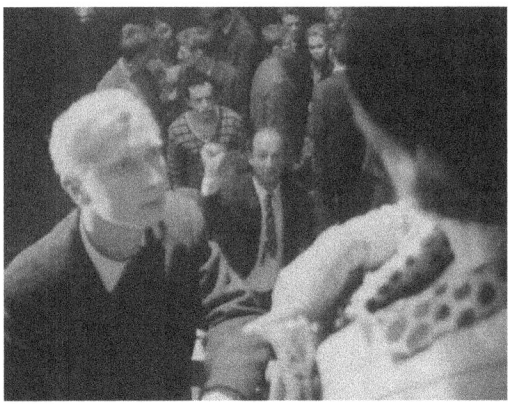

Reitz manages to turn this building, the Fuchsbau, into a major character, which like the human ones, changes its role through the story. In letting the students use it, Elizabeth shares its handsomeness with others but as Hermann guesses early on, "The generation with houses like this were Nazis," so its qualities are therefore polluted. Elizabeth's dreams of creating a cultural community centred on the villa are both realized and then shattered when she feels she has had enough and is moved to drive them out, commenting that the

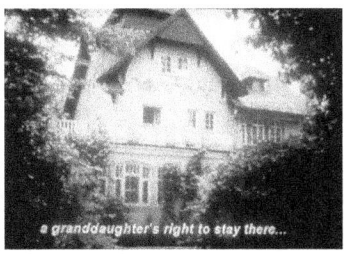

a granddaughter's right to stay there...

Fuchsbau years are over. She allows Gattinger to arrange a deal for the site to be sold for redevelopment as a block of flats, which at a stroke greatly enlarges the ex-Goldbaum fortune, and leaves the students to lament its destruction in a requiem composed by Hermann and performed in the grounds, now a building site: the loss of the house becomes a metaphor for the breaking up the group, as they change, grow up, move on.

Because the characters are artistic (film-makers, actors, composers, musicians), they are motivated to express themselves in stories, to realize their imaginations. This adds a background dimension which the audience has to imagine for itself, namely that in telling all these stories, Reitz is telling his own as well as someone of that generation seeking to come to an understanding of Germany. Like Reinhard 'becoming a story' after he disappears, Reitz does as well in completing the film. This is something which in itself provides hope. When Reinhard and Esther try to confront their history, Reinhard writes his script and falls into despair, while Esther, searching for her lost mother, visits Dachau and, finding no trace either of her or of "all the people mercilessly tortured to death here", realizes that it is a site merely for tourists photographing without understanding. As a result she exclaims that she is giving up photography. Reitz is prepared to recognise the argument that an artistic account of the Holocaust is an impossibility, that knowledge can only bring silence, while being ready to continue getting inside it himself, to seek an understanding that does not shirk the truth while humanizing the people taking part in its history, in the belief that the effort must be made to enlarge the spectator's imagination of this fact of twentieth-century history through creating a monument of extraordinary complexity, deploying in multiple layers character, images, sounds and music. The scale of this artistic enterprise is proper to the questions it explores.

*

The purest reaction to the Holocaust, the reaction of the purists, is philosophical: What happened? Why did it happen? How was it allowed to happen? But the human brain works in many different ways, and it is the medium of the story, rather than of the philosophical or metaphysical essay, that for many people manages to convey knowledge, even partial, and a portion of understanding. For this reason, we need memoirs, and not just memoirs but fiction as well: the former give us a glimpse of the real, but fiction, for all the risks it offers of being unreal, can show us truth even if it is not real. The extraordinary stories of survival can help to redeem the event for us, give us something to cling onto in the wreckage and take us through the turbulence. Those of the Jews protected by Schindler and of Szpilman the pianist are two of them, but there could be others.

Primo Levi died before he could see those two films, and indeed his own account of survival in 'If this is a man' offers some crumbs of comfort too, but it is doubtful whether he would have accepted that there could be any sort of true redemption to be found in stories about the Holocaust. The tone of his writing is at all times modest and strives always to observe with detachment, but there is evident too a constant distress right up to 'The Drowned and the

Saved', the last book he published before his death in 1987. It is probably the case that a film worthy of his book is an impossibility, although an effective television version of Anthony Sher's one-man adaptation for the stage has been made (*Primo*). Its simplicity and lucidity are sufficient in themselves, and could be marred by a conventional transposition to the screen. It would run the risk, as do all narrative films that seek to portray Auschwitz, of creating a synthetic grimness compared with the actual, of a false understanding of behaviour and motive. The film by Lajos Koltai, *Fateless,* illustrates these pitfalls: the film recreates Auschwitz (briefly) and Buchenwald in an honourable manner, but the point of its source material, Kertesz's memoir – what did it mean for me to be a Jew and so chosen for deportation, and to be a Jew and survive, and return to Hungary as a surviving Jew? – is philosophical, which gets mostly lost in the re-created agony of the camps.

It was another Hungarian film that more strikingly enlarged the genre of the Holocaust film, László Nemes' *Son of Saul* (2015). He confronts head-on 'the Lanzmann problem' (that direct representation of the Holocaust is impossible, perhaps even a blasphemy of a kind) by going not just into the death camp but into the crematorium where the newly arrived Jews are murdered. The focus is on the *sonderkommando* Saul, one of the Jews selected to carry out the industrial process of murder. The challenge of filming this runs straight against the question: how do you convert the banality of making a film into something that will capture the horror of the process? Nemes does it by something new, namely focusing on one man Saul, whose action and expression is set against a background out of focus. We know the violence that is taking place because of the words heard and the sounds made and the screams heard, but also, because we can see movement behind Saul: we know clothes are being removed, and naked bodies being urged into the shower rooms. The violence is reported rather than shown. This approach has other echoes besides that of the second of the Ten Commandments. Greek tragedy evolved the convention that violence (such as Clytemnaestra's murder of Agamemnon in Aeschylus, Oedipus blinding himself in Sophocles) should be reported not shown. From this convention it derives massive force: the horror is horrifying but made less superficial by being mediated. *Son of Saul* works the same way.

Jack Gold, initially reluctant to make a film about the uprising in Sobibor death camp which brought it to an end, in the end did so in *Escape from Sobibor* (1987), because it was a story that needed to be better known. Unfilmed still is the story of Rudolf Vrba's and Alfred Wetzler's escape from Auschwitz, their contact with the Jewish Council in Slovakia, and the creation of the Auschwitz

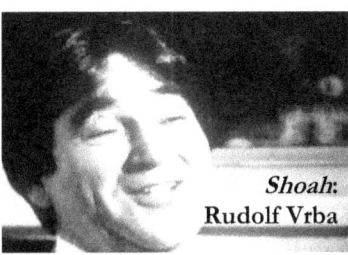

Shoah:
Rudolf Vrba

protocols which were instrumental in creating pressure on Miklós Horthy to stop deporting the Hungarian Jews. There is also Béla Szolt's account in 'Nine Suitcases' of his escape from those same deportations, which has that quality of blind chance to be found in *The Pianist*, with the opportunity too of conveying Szolt's macabre humour. One could conceive of the two narratives – of Vrba and Szolt – being told in parallel, and posing at the end the urgent question: was enough done to save the Hungarian Jews from deportation?

Is there a story woven into the massacres of the Jews at Babi Yar in the Ukraine? Dramatization in film form runs a tremendous risk: in showing bodies being stripped naked, then beaten and herded to the edge over a ravine and shot, reminds us of the fact of the event, but at the same time casts doubt, as we are brought face-to-face with the illusion of film-making, with the act of re-enactment: is the whole thing just an illusion? The massacres of Jews in the Ukraine needs to be approached circumspectly, to be told off-screen, revealed in other ways then direct telling. In *Schindler's List*, as I have mentioned, Spielberg was on the mark in <u>not</u> showing the death of the little girl in the red coat.

Because films and television have the widest reach of all artistic media, it is important that they are used to create an understanding of the Holocaust. The graphicness of the cinema can convince audiences, it can make the intellectual, the abstract and the rarefied concrete and immediate. Its very crudity, the way it can do the imagining for a person, alleviating him or her from the trouble of active thought, is for once an advantage in helping them confront the seriousness of what happened. Primo Levi wrote that to help others understand we have to simplify: "A certain dose of rhetoric is perhaps indispensable for the memory to persist." [Levi, 'The Drowned and the Saved' p.8.] But Levi was always troubled in a particular way, whether anyone but survivors could deal with the subject, and not even survivors because only "the worst survived, the selfish, the violent, the insensitive, the collaborators of the 'grey zone', the spies. . . The best all died." [Levi, ibid. p.62.] Reference to the 'grey zone' gives a twist to Levi's reticence. It was the phrase he used to describe the ambiguity of relationships inside the lager, an ambiguity you had to adopt to have a chance of survival. Without making it explicit, he proposes a hierarchy: those who died, those who survived, those who had not been in the camps or the ghettos.

In Plato's 'Republic' he criticises painting and art in general of being at two removes from ideal reality, proposing a hierarchy of Perfect Form (the ideal table), the table existing before us (a copy of the ideal) and the painting of the table (a copy of a copy of the ideal). One can get a sense here of Levi's strictures on the inauthenticity of representation of life in the camps in which an analogous hierarchy could be created: description of the grey zone by those who observed it but were detached from it, and hence died; a compromised description by those who were part of it and yet died; and representation in literature and film of this compromised description, itself compromised when its creators were themselves survivors, and compromised even further when they were <u>not</u> survivors.

But the construction is surely perverse. Fiction allows identification between audiences and participants, with cinema offering a special route into the physical, more 'real' reality, so that imagination is made concrete. This is a further argument that Holocaust stories should be filmed. And even the ambiguities of the grey zone can be brought home through fiction, presenting its audience with the viewpoints of victim, executioner or bystander. In particular the moral dilemmas can be explored in a way that turns the observer into a participant. If human beings can truly learn from history, then the identification may help us to understand how we should act.

Leon Wieseltier has written a striking commentary to do with a story of a pious Jew from the Warsaw ghetto who in his last act before the final annihilation of the ghetto after the Uprising concluded that God had hid his face, and delivered to Him an admonition that this had happened rather than conclude from it that He did not exist. This brief fiction by Zvi Kolitz – initially received as having actually happened rather than being a fiction – is entitled 'Yosl Rakover talks to God'. Emmanuel Lévinas had published a short commentary on it in 1963, and it was of this commentary, as much as Kolitz's story, that Wieseltier had offered a critique. In it, he touches on the question of the 'uniqueness' of the Holocaust to argue that it is specious. He sees in it a continuity with the "fate of the Jews in other European times and other European places". It also, as he puts it, "has the consequence of ripping the disaster so far out of history that it becomes incommensurable, in the way that the sacred is incommensurable." One is reminded of Elie Wiesel's distress as expressed in 1978 at the NBC television mini-series. Wieseltier argues that imprecision is not necessarily false, and may be useful as a means of stimulating moral thought and moral action. Jews are human beings, and their history is not precluded from being universal by being unique. "Let us avail ourselves," he writes, "of all the faculties of the mind and the heart. Let us hear all the theories and all the stories. . . . ." [Wieseltier p.92].

Kolitz's story touches on what is the most troubling question raised by the Holocaust: if He exists, why did He allow it to happen? This metaphysical dimension is not something that film has been able to capture at all, and may never do so, since it may only take a verbal argument, not a visual depiction, to elaborate and explore what is at stake. And yet a cinematic way of doing it may yet come to fruition. Consider Bach's musical Passions: most originally his music does not just dramatize the story, but interleaves it with musical passages reflecting on what has happened. Something similar might be possible on film.

In general, four barriers to filming the Holocaust can be listed, and ways found to overcome them. First is that while film can reproduce the surface grimness of the ghetto or of the camp, the 'interior' grimness for the victims can only be glimpsed: the physical cruelty of torture by starvation, the moral cruelty of saving oneself at the expense of another, the mental cruelty of knowing your family has been killed, of witnessing the suffering of children, and so on. Yet great writing and film-making must give us a route, even an imperfect one, into understanding.

Second, it is desirable that only survivors should create these accounts, and this means that only Jews should write and direct the films. Yet survivors are dying off and we shall still need stories to help us remember. It is one of the dimensions of W. G. Sebald's novel 'Austerlitz', published in 2001, about displacement and memory, key themes to a Jewish understanding of the Holocaust, that it is written by a (non-Jewish) German. This novel is a Chinese box, discussing architecture and history, and describing a variety of places (the countryside of mid-Wales, the east end of London, Paris, Marienbad, and so on), but at its climax is the story of the concentration camp at Teresin /Theresienstadt, and the disappearance of Jacques Austerlitz's parents, his mother to Teresienstadt and thence on a transport east, his father to Paris where all trace of him is lost. Jacques himself only survives on the *kindertransport* to England in 1939. This poetic, melancholic, almost comfortless book by a German seems perfectly in tune with the deep and lasting pain that the Holocaust inflicted on the Jews and, by extension, on non-Jews seeking to understand the events.

Thirdly, the Jewish prohibition on images in the second commandment should not be used to sacralize the Holocaust, as Wieseltier has pointed out in the passage already quoted. The imagination is "an indispensable instrument for the consideration of tragedy" and we need to recognise that it can go wrong. To give an example: Primo Levi, in his courteous way, is harsh about Liliana Cavani's *The Night Porter* (1973) about a hotel porter and a hotel guest in 1957 recreating their relationship from the camps, where he was an SS officer and she was an inmate as a child. Caviani felt that we are all victims or murderers, on which Levi comments that to confuse the German murderers with their victims is a "moral disease or an aesthetic affectation or a sinister sign of complicity" [Levi 'The Drowned and the Saved' p.62]. One could call it therefore a failed Holocaust film, but it is a failure that still contributes to understanding, even if only in the rebutting of it.

A fourth reason to make films starts with a question: what if the films and television works I have been discussing were the only documentation left of the event? It is true that any historical version of the events constructed from such works would be riddled with imperfection, and we would still need proper histories. But while Shakespeare's history plays are an inadequate guide to what actually happened in late mediaeval England, they offer a brilliant insight into the political turbulence of the times and their consequences for individuals. Films of the Holocaust still allow us to construct a version of the historical events that would contain omissions but also many truths. We need further creations therefore to fill in the gaps in our understanding and to assist in preserving a memory of this event. Such a reflection brings us back to Sebald's 'Austerlitz'. This book of words is intensely visual, not just for its prose so full of images, but for the photographs he uses in the text which both ground the reader's understanding of what is being described, and also set in train their own sense of what is poignant and inexplicable about the lost past. What is more Sebald writes about the darkest sort of Holocaust film, the one that denies the event, one that makes the darkness darker. At the climax of the book Austerlitz encounters the fragment of the film made by the Nazis of the camp at Teresienstadt. Following a visit by the International Red Cross in 1944 when the Nazis blinded the Red Cross representatives to the fact that it was not just a cruel place in which to survive but a staging-post for deportation to annihilation, they followed this up by making a 'documentary' of the camp under the heading *Hitler Presents a Town to the Jews*. The film disturbs us for the circumstances of its making, and we need its emphatic contradiction in literature and film. But Sebald is still able to make something consoling from it. Jacques Austerlitz watches the film desperately searching the faces of the inmates in the hope of seeing that of his mother Agata. Because of "the impossibility of seeing anything more closely in these pictures" [Sebald p.345], Austerlitz has the idea of having a slow-motion version of the fragment made, lasting an hour, in order to "reveal previously hidden objects and people, creating, by default as it were, a different sort of film altogether, which I have since watched over and over again". This is a radically new way of watching film.

We should not therefore regret what films have been completed, recognising that there is more to be written and more to be filmed, that the potency of some of the films discussed here has by no means been exhausted. Understanding of the past is a journey from a little knowledge and a little learning to a stage where we realise that we have learnt much but still know very little, yet the less we know, the wiser we become.

PART TWO

5   IT'S IN THE ACTING

The first part of this book has explored how the new invention of the cinema has opened up new dimensions to the imagination, whether pleasurable or terrifying, even seeking to tackle the subject of the Holocaust and doing so at the risk of upsetting those purists who take the view that the subject is not a fit one for artistic representation and that all efforts to depict it are doomed to failure. That failure however is permissible on the grounds that it is the cinema more than any other medium that has conveyed the terribleness of the event; failure is justified if it leads to 'better failure'. In developing this account, I have drawn on examples from the spread of film history and film culture in order to undertake forays into human imaginative worlds, especially its darker side of eroticism, horror and violence. This is a journey into the creative imagination of film-makers themselves into which the imagination of the spectator finds itself being drawn too. We have therefore been exploring the what of the imagination, whereas in the second half of this book the underlying theme is the how: how we watch films, how they stimulate us, how style is a key component in conveying substance. At the end I shall try to weave the two strands together, the what and the how, to explore what the possibilities might be for a more subtle and complex way of telling stories in the cinema.

This is the right moment therefore to say something about film acting, since for many people the quality of the acting comes before any other criterion in judging a film. It has therefore to come first.

*

Reference has already been made in chapter 2 to Scruton's distinction, with reference to the painting of nudes, between 'fancy' (which is bad, ultimately pornographic) and 'imagination' (which is good, ultimately respectful of the nude portrayed), and between the realm of painting (the imagination) and the realm of fancy (photography and film). Scruton is also the author of a much more explicit attack on photography and film in his 1983 essay, 'Photography and Representation', where he argues that photography is quite distinct from painting as a means of representing all appearances, never mind nudes, and much inferior. All it can do is create a record of how something looked, so that any curiosity we have about the photograph is in what it depicts. Painting on the other hand has an 'intentional relation' to its subject, separating what is represented and what exists, so that it can give scope to the imagination and to the deployment of style in a way that photography can never achieve. Not only are questions of the truth and falsity of a painting vital, but also our interest in a picture is not just in the thing represented but in the way it is represented as well with the result that the literal truth of a painting is only the beginning of our interest, whereas in photography it is the end of it. This can hardly be right since taking a photograph is the result of a number of creative decisions (what to photograph, from what exact point to photograph it, whether to use black and white or colour and in what way, what to frame, what lens to use, what aperture to use etc. etc.), but this does not prevent Scruton from then taking an even less carefully argued swipe at the cinema, that as an art it is wholly dependent on the theatre, and a 'good' film is only good by virtue of its dramatic qualities, since, like photography, its only interest is in what is represented of its theatrical origins, not in the way these are represented. As an example, he cites Ingmar Bergman's *Wild Strawberries*, blithely ignoring the contribution of for example cameraman, editor, sound recordist and art director, not to mention the contribution made by Bergman's cinematic consciousness – as if *Wild Strawberries* would be an arresting film even if directed by a non-entity whose sole gift was in the direction of actors. The truth about Bergman is that he is a man of the cinema as much as he is a man of the theatre, with the ability to conceive his films in his own head without relying on literary or dramatic sources, establishing enduring working relationships with his cameramen, notably Gunnar Fischer and Sven Nykvist, in order to achieve the effects of light and dark that give a characteristic patina to his films, and giving his films a fluidity in the editing that creates a steeliness to the narrative beyond their verbal qualities. But in admiring Bergman as a director, Scruton (like many others) ignores these aspects and is really in awe of the casting and direction of his actors, and for the talents they themselves bring to the films, a point validated superficially by the fact that Bergman was a notable theatre director as well as a film-maker, spending half the year devoted to one art, and the other half to the other. [See his 'The Magic Lantern' (1987) and 'Images: my life in film' (1995).] This, Scruton seems to be saying, is the best that the cinema is able to achieve – good, but not as good as what can be achieved on stage.

Now consider the following sentiments written by a celebrated film-maker which on the surface appear to lend support to Scruton's position: "the high relief of theatre"; "acting [in the theatre] adds to real presence, intensifies it"; "but also when it is homogeneous can yield truth (theatre)". And indeed the following quotation harmonizes directly with Scruton's argument: "the photographed theatre or CINEMA [capitals in original] requires a metteur-en-scène or director to make some actors perform a play and to photograph these actors performing a play; afterwards he lines up the images. Bastard theatre lacking what makes theatre: material presence of living actors, direct action of the audience on the actors."

The author of these sentiments is Robert Bresson, who never in fact worked in the theatre, and in his thirteen feature films created a unique style which he called CINEMATOGRAPHIC (in capitals because he liked to underline the Manichean nature of this opposition to CINEMA), and created in his 'Notes on the Cinematographer' one of the three most original aesthetic statements in the twentieth century that emanated from practising film-makers, the other two being Eisenstein's 'Film Form and Film Sense' and Brakhage's 'Metaphors on Vision'. Common to all three books is an idiosyncracy of style that is positively off-putting: we feel a long way from the lucid philosophising on art in Plato and Aristotle, or in modern philosophers like Wollheim or Scruton.

Bresson's particular stylistic source is that rebarbative philosopher, Blaise Pascal, of whom Bresson said in the interview conducted in 1965 by Jean Luc Godard and Michel Delahaye: "Pascal est tellement grand pour moi, mais il est grand pour tout le monde." ['Cahiers du cinéma' May 1966]. As if to emphasize the importance of Pascal "for everybody", the 'Notes' are arranged like Pascal's 'Pensées', but also because Bresson practised in his films an ordering of images and sounds which gained crucially from their position and relation to other images and sounds: "From the clash and sequence of images and sounds, the harmony of relationships must be born." [329] [Note: the numbered references to the 'Notes on the Cinematographer' throughout this chapter are to my own sequential numbering from 1 to 453 of the individual notes in Bresson's English text from 1986.] This works magnificently in the films, but has an irritating effect in his book because it obscures, or seems to obscure, the force of what he is trying to express. An initial reading introduces you to the important distinction he makes between Cinema and Cinematography and between 'actors' and 'models', but to feel the full force of what is in effect a polemic, you need to pick out his statements on these particular topics and stitch them together. The result is as follows.

What the camera captures in *models* is their "being" [6], what is there "behind their forehead, cheeks" [8], and film-makers (to use a neutral term that Bresson eschews) must in their direction of models "suppress intention" in them [43]. This is because ninety per cent of our movements obey "habit and automatism, not will and thought" [69] and the film-maker's task is to mechanize them externally, allowing them to be internally free [161]. Expressiveness must come from the model involuntarily [245], and Bresson rejoices in the paradox that it is the flattest and dullest parts of the model that have the most life [225]. The charm of models is that they "do not know what they are" [308] and, since Bresson was terrified that once the model had seen his or her performance all their future 'modelling' for the screen would be ruined by self-consciousness, models were nearly always used in only one film.

Now *actors*. What the camera captures in actors is "seeming" [6]; they are "illusionists" [204]. While Bresson is particularly contemptuous of the star system in which "men and women exist as phantoms" [125], his repeated reproach of actors is that they are unable to be wholly the roles they play [149], and that their acting seems to exist apart from the actor [113] with the result that their expressiveness means they get "further away" on the screen [193]; the acting masks the actor making him or her unrecognizable [231]. A screen actor in a storm simulating fear of shipwreck "inhibits belief in actor, ship, storm" [59]. Actors are like piano virtuosi who make us hear the music as they feel it, "not as it is written" [334].

One's initial reaction to this tirade is that Bresson is too puritanical in his judgement on acting, and too autocratic in his direction. In praising the charm of models "who do not know what they are" as opposed to the "assurance" of actors [308], Bresson seems to be brooking no opposition to his ideas on set. It is his role to set the limits within which models "exercise their power" [316] as he seeks to penetrate their "unknown and virgin nature" [208]. Even his language has overtones of sexual violence. He is therefore the quintessential auteur, since he conceives and orders his own material which he then turns into a film with as little as possible of the collaboration that marks so much of commercial film-making.

The reality is very different, certainly more complex. Bresson was not alone among film directors in making demands on his actors: the reputation of Mizoguchi in this regard is very severe [see Richie]; Hitchcock seems almost to have relished putting Tippi Hedren through the humiliation of attack by birds in *The Birds* [as Hedren revealed in an interview]; John Ford has John Wayne, Pedro Amendariz and Harry Carey Jr battle through a sandstorm in *Three Godfathers*.

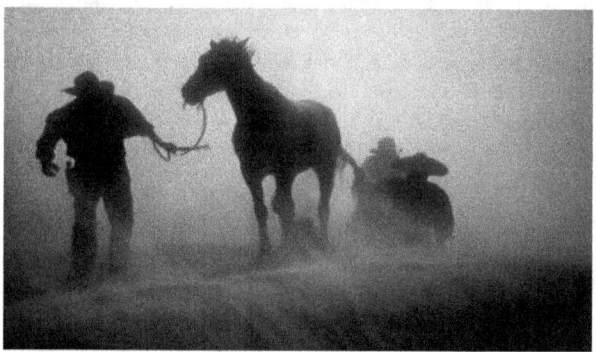

And Bressonians can argue that the results justify the rigours involved in achieving automatism of movement through endless practice: for the simple shot of Michel mounting the stairs to his attic room in *Pickpocket*, Bresson made Martin Lassalle do this some forty times before he was satisfied. The purpose was to achieve this automatism, but it is necessary to understand that Bresson only finds what he is looking for when he sees the results on screen and when he places the shot in relation to other shots, in the creation of a rhythmic structure. He especially liked the "scrupulous indifference" of the camera [84], which is a quality of the tape recorder as well. The result in *Pickpocket* is unexpectedly haunting. But for remarkable 'involuntary performance' one can think also of Claude Laydu as the country priest in *Diary of a Country Priest*, Leterrier as the prisoner willing his escape in *A Man Escaped*, Nadine Nortier in *Mouchette* as the put-upon girl who "loses her body but preserves her soul" and Christian Patey in *L'Argent*.

What Bresson was seeking to achieve in his models was more in the nature of a liberation than a suppression of their person. In giving things to them, he as a director receives from them, creating a "secret and sacred trust" [311] between director and model. He is seeking by means of the camera to find their "pure essence" [152], something unique and inimitable in each of them [173], the "non-rational, non-logical I" [259]. He may mechanize them externally, but internally they are free, because he and they between them reveal the constant and the eternal beneath the accidental [161]. He speaks of the model as having

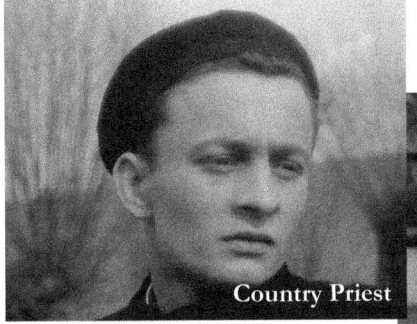

Country Priest

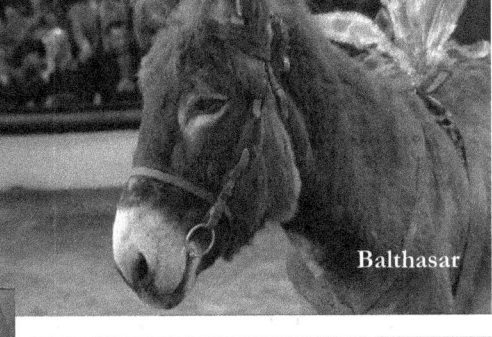

Balthasar

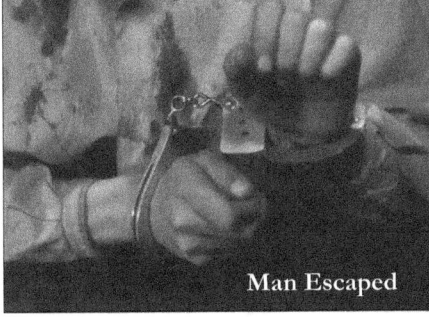

Man Escaped

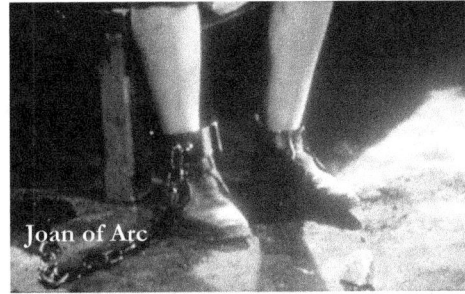

Joan of Arc

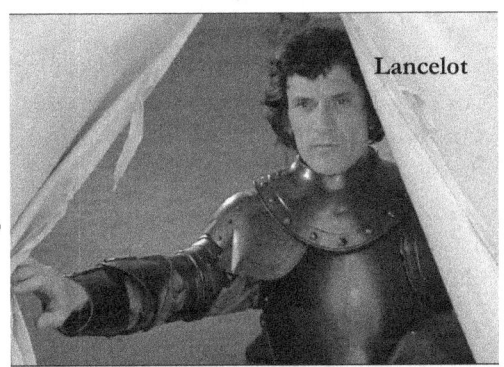

Lancelot

Images showing Bresson's aesthetic of 'involuntary expressive', which extends to hands and feet - and the donkey's eye

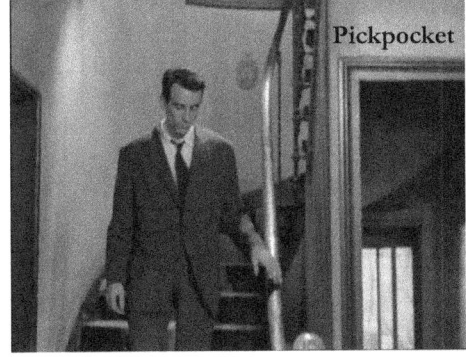

Pickpocket

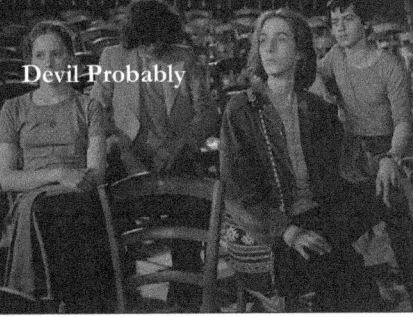

Devil Probably

an inimitable soul and body [166] as if the "illusionism" of screen acting was meretricious precisely because it veiled the soul.

And yet. Even if both his cinematic practice and his handling of models produces such arresting results, his theoretical writing, for all its stimulation, remains provocative – as provocative as Scruton's dismissal of the cinema as only virtuous in its dramatic origins. The provocation in Bresson's case derives from the fact that his 'Notes' point to one conclusion, namely: he knows how to make a film, and the rest of the world does not. This is hardly a tenable position, and it is something of a shock to find beneath that educated, courteous, enquiring and tender exterior such a controversialist. One test would be whether his distinction between 'models' and 'actors' has been taken up by others, so that one could speak of a School of Bresson. Evidence for this is slight, but not negligible. He remains an enormously influential film-maker, especially in inspiring younger film-makers to appreciate the necessary rigours of film-making if they are to realize its possibilities but hardly anyone has adopted his practice with models. [See 'Sight and Sound', November 2007, pp.27-8, where five film-makers talk about his influence. Only Aki Kaurismäki says that he has imitated his style openly.] A rare and fine exception is the use of the singer James Taylor and of Dennis Wilson of the Beach Boys in Monte Hellman's *Two Lane Blacktop* (left), whose downbeat style - 'voluntary inexpres-

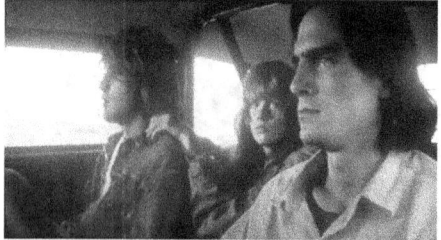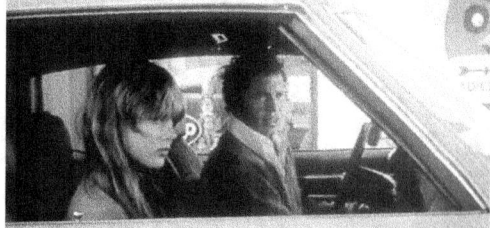

sive' - contrasted with the expressive acting of Warren Oates (right) adds to the tension in the film. One reason for this is that for some film-makers, although by no means all, there is an attraction, having worked successfully with someone, in working with them again, not to mention the pressures of the star system: the audience pays to see faces and mannerisms it likes. Another reason, which raises much larger questions, is that the style was conceived in order to create a 'spiritual cinema', and with the decline of a religious sense in Western society, the idea of embodying grace and salvation in humans may feel outdated. Of contemporary directors, only the Dardenne Brothers and Bruno Dumont occupy this area, at least in part. Alan Cavalier's *Thérèse* should be mentioned, although the complete obscurity of this film seems to prove the point. On the other hand, it is a welcome sign that a film like *Ballast* (directed by Lance Hammer in 2008) consciously draws on Bresson's practice with models, as if his ideas could be resurrected unexpectedly at any time.

There is a superficial understanding of Bresson's theory that may be appreciated by consideration of the film of Robert Bolt's 'A Man for All Seasons'. Because this had been a successful stage play in 1960 (with Paul Scofield in the title role) it was a natural, although unfortunate step, to decide to film it – unfortunate because to make a decent film, the theatrical construction was going to have to be severely tampered with, and a visual bravura introduced. Scofield was retained in the role of Sir Thomas More and the Hollywood director, Fred Zinnemann, was brought in to direct the film, right at the end of his career, and despite his credentials and indeed those of Robert Bolt, who scripted the three David Lean epics – *Lawrence of Arabia, Dr Zhivago* and *Ryan's Daughter* – the film version gets lost in a fog of heritage sets, the bland lighting of interiors, and a suspense-free dramatisation of the big scenes, none of which prevented the film winning Zinnemann an Oscar for Best Direction. The execution scene at the end – a climactic moment, surely – is tacked on as an afterthought, and when in the preceding court scene, Thomas More finally bursts out in denunciation of the iniquity being visited on him, the camera remains in long shot, gawking like a simpleton at the supposed majesty of the scene. Naturally, the production's one virtue is in assembling the cream of British theatrical talent to take the various roles, and there can be no quarrel with the performances, but whereas on the stage they would be hypnotising, on the screen the electricity drains out of them as though all the direction achieved was to earth them so as to reduce the dramatic voltage.

If ever a film met Bresson's description of cinema as 'bastard theatre lacking what makes theatre', *A Man for All Seasons* is surely it. But Bresson's critique is aimed deeper still than that, not just at the mediocre but at films in the classical canon. As it so happens, there is a very instructive contrast between acting and modelling to be drawn between Dreyer's *Passion of Joan of Arc* of 1928 and Bresson's *The Trial of Joan of Arc* of 1963. The story of the life of Joan of Arc has been an immensely popular one for the cinema but these two focus on the trial solely, both drawing on the transcript which survives in the Bibliothèque Nationale in Paris. Dreyer's Joan was famous from the beginning – the point has been made that arguably the greatest film of the silent era was made just as the 'talkies' were about to change the face of commercial cinema. That fame was enhanced by censorship: the Archbishop of Paris insisted on a censored version on the film's release in 1928, and the film was banned in occupied Europe from 1940 to 1944. As post-war critics began to articulate a history of the cinema, by then fifty years old, its reputation continued to grow so that by the time Bresson chose to make his film, one has the sense that it was done as a deliberate correction of Dreyer, a censure almost. When he criticizes a director or an actor in the 'Notes on the Cinematographer', he refers to them anonymously as X. But there is one explicit reference to Falconetti, who played Joan in Dreyer's film: "For want of truth, the public gets hooked on the false. Falconetti's way of casting her eyes to heaven, in Dreyer's film, used to draw tears." [407] I interpret this to mean that the public has a taste for the meretricious, that the film's overt religiosity draws false tears. Elsewhere he says that religious subjects gain "dignity and elevation" from images and sounds, not vice versa [57]. While this cannot be a direct reference to Dreyer's Joan, since it is a silent film, Bresson might be saying that it is Falconetti's emotionalism that gives the film "dignity and elevation" rather than the composition of its images.

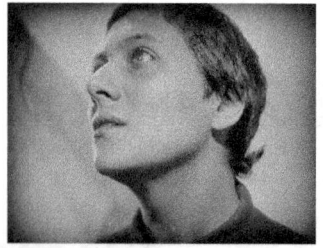

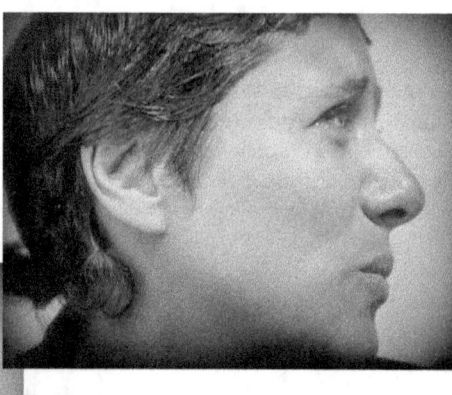

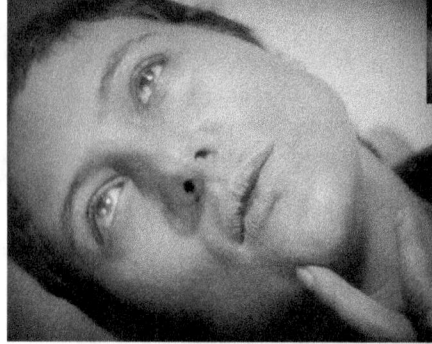

Dreyer's aesthetic of the 'voluntary expressive' in The Passion of Joan of Arc

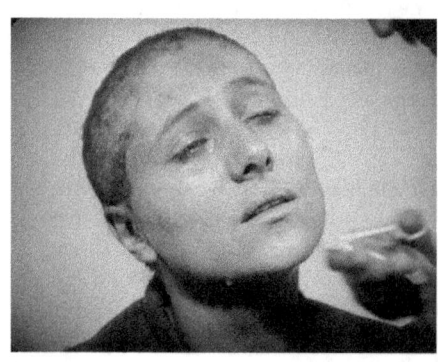

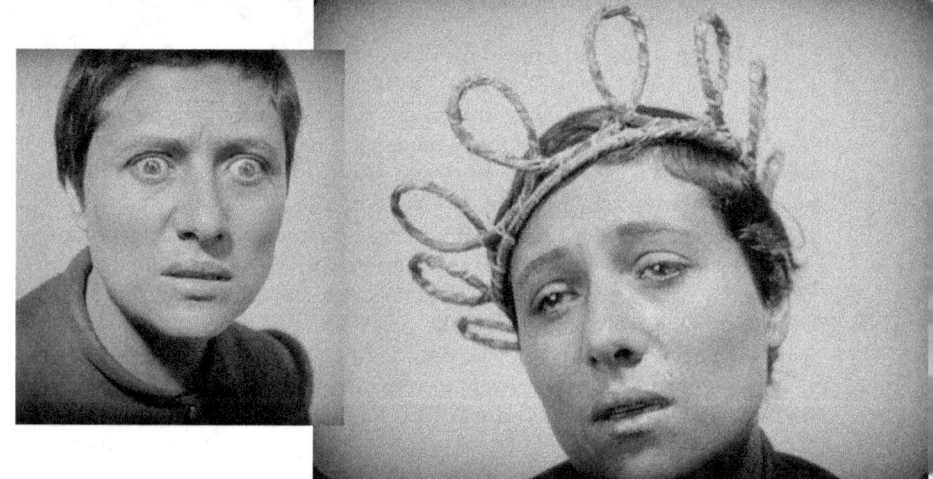

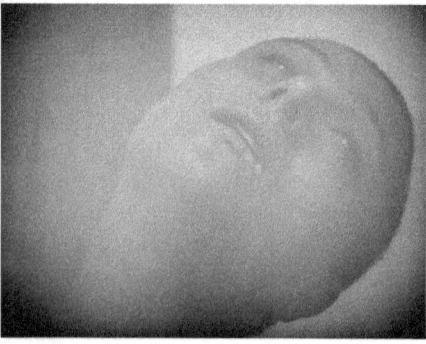

By the time he made his own version, Bresson was well into his middle period and had formulated his aesthetic with perfect clarity. Florence Carrez as Joan, twenty-one at the time the film was made, is an exemplary model. We see her feet chained together shuffling along the pavement, and throughout the film they play an important role in exemplifying metonymically the totality of her treatment at the hands of her accusers. Her face is cast down, and the responses to her accusers are given mechanically, the head lifted to say the words then cast down again. One can feel directly Carrez's drilling by Bresson in delivering the lines like an automaton, more so than in any of Bresson's other films because this one is so full of words. Keith Reader makes the point that the use of direct transcripts from the trial means that the models quote their lines rather than express them "more powerful[ly] than anywhere else in his work". [Reader, p. 63.]

The Trial of Joan of Arc is the only film of his that Bresson refers to explicitly in the 'Notes', saying that he tried in it to avoid "theatre" and "masquerade", to arrive at a non-historical truth by using historical words. It is an element of the seriousness of his aesthetics and of his actual practice that authenticity can only be won by rigour and obduracy. An important contribution to this goal is to ensure that the settings and the costumes do not detract from the principal drama of Joan confronting her accusers, so that the "picturesque" does not hinder the film from "taking off" [247]. The backgrounds therefore are barely visible. He is helped by the priestly costumes, because they are recognizable today having changed little compared to other costumes over the centuries. Only the soldiers' garb risks drawing attention to itself. This leaves the remaining decision of how to dress Joan, but here something problematic is turned to advantage. Because Joan dressed as a man, refusing to wear women's clothes, her unassuming costume, a plain leather jerkin, can become an active element in the drama. Only her hairstyle seems to anchor the film to the time of its making.

Bresson's *Joan* shares an important core with Dreyer's in that for both the historical record of the trial is a springboard to a greater historical truth about Joan's saintliness – her endurance, her resistance to male domination, her fortitude at the stake, the release of her soul at the end, her body destroyed but her truth living on through the centuries. Dreyer's film may be silent (he wanted to use sound but was told that it would be too expensive) but the inter-titles pay considerable attention to using the actual questions and answers from the trial. Bresson has the advantage here in that his film gains in coherence from the synchronisation of image and dialogue. Allowances therefore need to be made for the interruptions that inter-titles create in Dreyer's *Joan*, and I have a suppressed desire for a version that eliminates them altogether, as I believe the film, already intense, would only become more so without losing in comprehensibility. At present they supply an unwanted distancing effect.

Dreyer's set decoration and costumes are more expressive than Bresson's, but he created his own *coup de cinéma* by using an architectural style in the sets that is copied from mediaeval French miniatures. He painted the walls pink, which when filmed in black and white give a balanced tone with the figures revealed against them. This is mediaeval authenticity of a kind, and there is a harmony between the white walls of the interiors and the white skies of the exteriors that give the film a significant unity.

So, we are left with the acting. Dreyer's version is famous for its faces containing the full range of human emotions: anger, guile, despair, joy, hope, bewilderment, fear etc. Many of the images are in close-up, revealing the warts and wrinkles of Joan's accusers, Joan's inner conflict written on her face – even a fly can be seen settling on her forehead at one point – Joan's tears welling from her huge eyes, all at another extreme from the veiled regard of Bresson's Joan. Dreyer had found Falconetti in the theatre and it is her theatrical training that she brings to bear in her interpretation, filtered through the rigours of Dreyer's direction for the cinema screen.

Contra Bresson, in responding to Joan's tears, the spectator is not being hooked on the false, but thrown back on their own empathy with the drama of Joan's predicament. A much more recent film capitalizes on the same approach, again using the skills of theatrical acting and direction to bring off a moment of intensity. Mike Leigh's *Vera Drake* (2004) tells the story of a working class wife and mother who carries out back-street terminations of unwanted pregnancies. While she believes she does it to help girls in difficulty, the terminations are an offence under the law. The *peripeteia* is marvellously handled with a crosscut sequence between Vera participating in a family party to celebrate her daughter's engagement and the police pursuing a trail of investigation that leads to her door. When the knock comes, the family is raising their glasses for a toast. In the ensuing interrogation of Vera, the tragedy of her situation is brought home by her inability to give coherent answers to the officers of the law, a suppression that manifests itself in tears. The spectator is not being hooked on the false, but rather being given a glimpse of the excruciating truth of her predicament, and while the same effect can be achieved through precision of images and a sparsity of means which would suppress facial expressions, Leigh opts to use abundance to equally powerful effect.

"Actors are trained to express complexity," said Ingmar Bergman [in 'Bergman on Bergman' p.59] and maintained that amateur actors on their own could not do it. In pursuit of that complexity in his vision of the human predicament, Bergman formed his own company with whom he worked almost obsessively: Eva Dahlbeck, Gunnar Björnstrand, Ingrid Thulin, Jarl Kulle, Max von Sydow, Bibi Andersson, Liv Ullman, and others. Or take an example from Hollywood: while John Ford worked with many of the most celebrated Hollywood actors and actresses, and had John Wayne in a leading role in thirteen of his films, he was notable for his 'stock company' in bit parts whose characters are drawn with some precision, a process in which the use of regular faces and styles helped: one can mention John Qualen, Jane Darwell, Mae Marsh, Jack Pennick, Hank Worden, Olive Carey, Harry Carey Jr and many others, including his brother Francis Ford. Mention of the Careys – Olive's husband Harry Carey Sr made over two dozen films with Ford in the silent era – and of Francis Ford gives a clue to the extended family relationships he liked to create on the set, with himself as father, grandfather, godfather, and patriarch – authoritarian, even tyrannical, but also loyal and compassionate. To watch Ford's films is to be aware of faces and voices recurring again and again.

The appearance and reappearance of faces is a feature too of Robert Altman's film career. Specializing in films with large casts, such as *Nashville, A Wedding, The Player, Short Cuts, Gosford Park*, again requiring a sharp definition of character through all the roles if audiences are to follow the thread of the film, Altman used a large reservoir of acting talent in America, and Europe too for his films made this side of the Atlantic, to carve out a very different kind of film from the conventional star-dominated product in Hollywood. The films give a

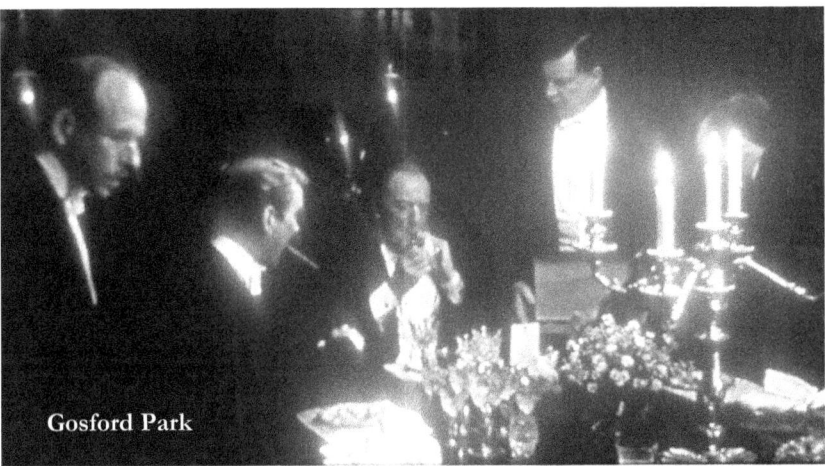

Gosford Park

sense of collaboration between director and actor in the creation of the acting mask that is at the far extreme from Bresson's cinematographic style. And yet the finished result could only be achieved on film, cutting between different individual narratives, whether in the same location (*A Wedding, Gosford Park*) or in several different ones (*Short Cuts*), with the audience seduced into watching them interweave and coalesce in an unsettling denouement.

Altman's method with actors was to use rehearsals to improvise dialogue, getting them to put a 'three-dimensional life' into a two-dimensional script, avoiding being too specific himself. "I'm really looking for something from these actors that can excite me . . . that's valid and truthful" [Thompson p. 132]. Democratic collaboration of a similar kind has been a feature of Mike Leigh's career, who like Altman has evolved a procedure which allows the actors to improvise and help write the character, again at the opposite pole to Bresson's practice of using automatic speech and movement to release the individual personality. Leigh's method has been to work initially with each actor in private, then explore ideas with them in improvised form, leading to a 'dress rehearsal' where critical scenes are performed with an injection of the unexpected.

For example, in the tea party scene in *Vera Drake* already referred to, Imelda Staunton playing Vera was not told that the knock on the door was the detective inspector come to interrogate and arrest her, and the detective inspector had not been told that he would be breaking in on a family celebration [as Staunton explains in the interview with her included on the dvd of *Vera Drake*]. Ideas gained from these rehearsals led to the final filming with a more definite storyline and dialogue.

In the right circumstances, such a procedure can produce a result unique to the cinema, a dramatic freshness when the performance is captured on film first time, that the repeated, perfected performances of a theatrical production would spoil. Bresson however would argue that the film would still suffer from the appearance of so many masks, no matter how skilfully created. He refers to "the public's irresistible need to see, get near, touch the stars in the flesh, a need frustrated by the photographed theatre" [381]. While it is true that there can be an electricity in the theatre between actor and audience which is not reproducible on film (unless it be by Bresson's 'cinematographic' technique of using models to generate a different current), Bresson is failing to appreciate the public's need to dream, on which the star system throughout the world feeds, and in dreaming electrical contact between an expressive face on a screen and the spectator in the audience is commonplace, involving feelings of identity, repulsion, wish-fulfilment. Even the grittiness of *Vera Drake* capitalizes on an empathetic warmth between Vera, as she is played by Staunton, and the audience drawn into her world and her predicament.

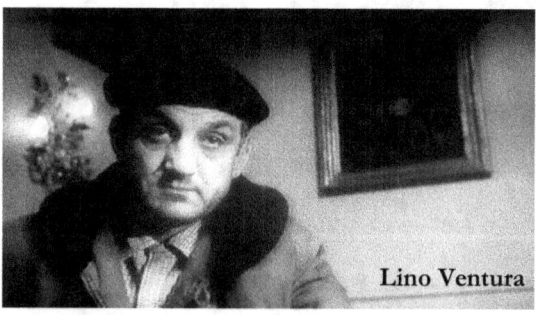

Lino Ventura

In seeking to pinpoint the uniqueness of the art of film, then we have to make room for the larger presence of a Greta Garbo, a Monica Vitti or a Keira Knightley, a John Wayne or a Leonardo DiCaprio, a Setsuko Hara, a Sanjay Dutt, a Maggie Cheung. The parade of cinematic beauty has become a staple attraction, and for many the quintessence of the cinema's *raison d'être*. Movement, gesture and tone of voice enhance the star's inner character and underpin his or her star quality. On the other hand, 'screen acting' that exaggerates that inner truth can falsify it. For Bresson, expression had to be involuntary, and there is an essential truth here, that obviously willed expressiveness can alienate, hence a style of acting developed for the screen that can be called the 'voluntarily inexpressive' to be found in an actor like Randolph Scott in the Ranown Westerns directed by Budd Boetticher who understood especially how to contrast Scott's impassivity with the much more animated, and more empathetic, style of the 'baddies' playing opposite him, such as Lee Marvin and Claude Akins. Other 'voluntary inexpressives' are Lino Ventura in his two films with Jean-Pierre Melville (*Le Deuxième Souffle* and *Army of Shadows*), Clint Eastwood in *A Fistful of Dollars* and Tommy Lee Jones in *No Country for Old Men*. An apt description of this style is 'stone-faced' and perhaps the paradigm for them all is Buster Keaton, whose sobriquet was 'old stone face'.

From 'Notes on the Cinematographer' it can be deduced that Bresson's aesthetics find some of their roots in the neo-realist school of film-making that emerged in Italy at the end of the war. The non-professional factory worker in *Bicycle Thieves* (1948) is famous in cinematic history for a constant expression that conveys the anxiety of existence, as he seeks to trace the bicycle that embodies his aim of achieving honest employment: we all know his face, even if we have

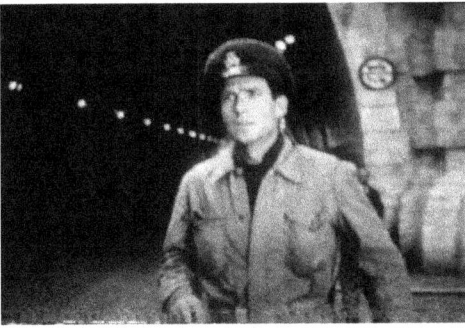

no clue of his name – Lamberto Maggiorani. It is the only film he is famous for, and there is a freshness in his performance that subsequent film appearances risk compromising. It must surely have been an inspiration to Bresson to cast an unknown Claude Laydu in *Diary of a Country Priest*. As famous, and even more remarkable, is the story of Enrico Irazoqui's epiphany in Pasolini's *Gospel according to St Matthew*, best explained in Pasolini's own words, when asked how he chose the figure for Christ: "There was a sudden inspiration involving psychological factors in me, my way of seeing people. I spent more than a year looking everywhere for someone to do Christ, and I'd almost decided to use a German actor. And then one day I came back to the house and found this young Spaniard, Enrique Irazoqui, sitting here waiting to see me and as soon as I saw him, even before he had a chance to start talking, I said, "Excuse me, but would you act in one of my films?" -- even before I knew who he was or anything. He was a serious person, and so he said no. But then I gradually won him around." ['Pasolini on Pasolini', ed. Oswald Stack (London: Thames & Hudson in association with the British Film Institute 1969), p.78.] The face is right, and between them, Irazoqui and Pasolini achieve the necessary visual identification essential to the artistic success of the film. Again, it is important that Irazoqui did not compromise this by making other films. Or consider the case of Sarah Pickering. Christine Edzard's film of *Little Dorrit* assembled some of the finest British stage actors of the 1980s, but for the role of Amy Dorrit, the largest part

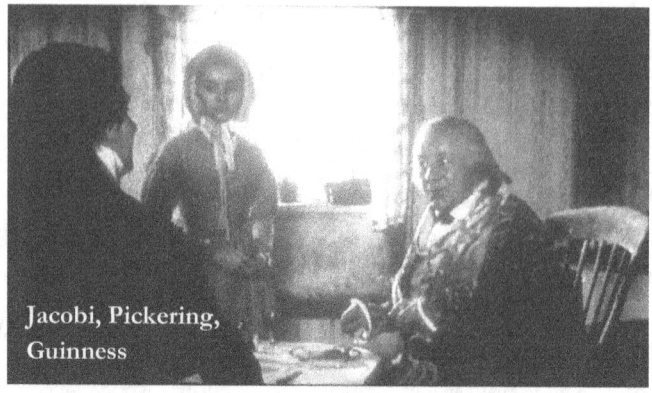

Jacobi, Pickering, Guinness

along with Derek Jacobi as Arthur Clennam, the role was given to a young Sarah Pickering, who had made no films previously. This might be deemed a failure on Edzard's part or that of her casting director, or on Pickering's part, or on the part of the film. In truth, all these judgements would be wrong: Pickering's self-effacement is perfect, a tribute both to her and to Edzard's direction, and this self-effacement is perfect for Dickens's story, in which Amy is the meek, unpretentious touchstone for many of the other characters. We can only celebrate the freshness of the performance, a freshness unsullied by any familiarity with subsequent film roles – for it seems she had none.

So, the use of unknown actors by other directors harmonizes with the virtues Bresson sees in using models, quite apart from the risk in using 'stars' – the public are fickle, and can be quickly bored by familiar faces. But even with Bresson, casting for roles is important: in finding people to play the lead parts in *Pickpocket* – Martin Lasalle for Michel, Marika Green for Jeanne and Pierre Leymarie for Jacques – he was careful in his choosing [as revealed in Babette Mangolte's *Modèles*, interviews with the three actors, which is included on the dvd of *Pickpocket* (London: Artificial Eye 295)], not least in ensuring there was a physical beauty to them, something that is true of all the models in his films. Casting was therefore a key part of the process for him, as it has always been whether in the theatre or in film-making in general. Nowadays credit lists include casting directors, people who specialize in understanding the capabilities of actors and their suitability for roles.

In America, the use of unknowns in this way was – and is – unlikely to appeal: to be unknown and take a major role in a film is a contradiction, for celebrity status deriving from media attention is a corollary of appearing in a movie. (Among the many aspects of film-making that Altman's *The Player* takes a swipe at is the scriptwriter's proposal that for his project there be 'no stars', a batty idea in Hollywood, and one which is jettisoned when the film actually gets made so that Bruce Willis can make an absurd appearance as the hero at the end.) However, it produces a tyranny of a kind: only those who can conform to mainstream ideas of what being a celebrity means are allowed to become stars, a fact which triggered an intriguing version of counter-culturalism after the war.

Kenneth Anger's first film, *Fireworks* (1947), is an anguished self-portrait which projects Anger himself as a star, as the centre of attention. The idea was broadened out a few years later in his *Inauguration of the Pleasure Dome* (1954), a celebration of stardom featuring a list of 'unknowns' seeking to register their presence on screen by taking theatricality and a lush campness to an extreme. It was filmed at the residence of Samson De Brier in Hollywood, and De Brier plays 'Lord Shiva, Osiris, Cagliostro, Nero, the Great Beast 666' – the improbable disguised as an emergency telephone number. Others take roles of a like kind, including the Scarlet Woman, Lilith, Ganymede, Pan, Cesare the Somnambulist. It seems highly unlikely that Bresson would ever have encountered the film, but if he had it is a fair guess that he would not have cared for it.

At the end of the 1950s, Anger published 'Hollywood Babylon', a delirious exposé of the indelicate doings of Hollywood stars, sexual, pornographic, drug-fuelled. In painting this far from pretty sight, Anger was mounting his own attack on the hypocrisies of stardom. On the East Coast of America, another obscure film-maker, Ken Jacobs, was doing the same, obsessively chronicling the bizarreries of a melancholic would-be star, Jack Smith. Here, a celebration of tatty cheapness is mixed into a curious narrative of compassion for those on the underside of celebrity culture. Anger and Jacobs are ground-breaking in their way, signposting a path to Andy Warhol, whose silkscreened paintings of icons of popular culture such as Elvis Presley and Marilyn Monroe led him on to much more interesting territory, using the camera to record the denizens of a bohemian New York world. Warhol exploited the fact that glamour is always superficial to mix star quality with vulnerability by the tactics of fixing the camera on a face and letting the film run, as in his *Screen Tests* made in 1964. This cinematographic stare then both celebrates the self-confident return gaze of the person being filmed, and also as time runs on penetrates the face – assurance is followed by boredom, by nervousness, by a momentary return of assurance and so on, with a result in the long run of our stare and their return gaze ending in mutual boredom. All in all, Warhol's paintings, films (which are further discussed in chapter 8), and the conduct of his life have been influential in the current celebration of celebrity, reinforced by his desire to 'democratize' the idea – anyone can be "famous for fifteen minutes". It has been in perfect tune with an era obsessed with appearances.

This conscious projection of personality in images has been hostile to Bresson's cinematographic aesthetic. Does the latter have a future then? The answer must be affirmative, since apart from any other considerations, it is especially suited to a narrative conducted with efficiency and pace where each sequence, where each shot even, advances the story without diversion or distraction. Bresson referred to 'what happens in the joins' [55] and argued that 'poetry' penetrates unaided through these *jointures* [90]. In support of this he cites "General de M…": "The great battles are nearly always begun at the intersection of the staff maps." [55] This elusive train of thought I interpret as meaning that the spectator is drawn into the film not by performance which is put centre stage in most film-making, but by the command to interpret shot A in relation to shot B in relation to shot C and so on. His is a paratactic method well suited to generating momentum, suspense even, as to what the next shot will show, and even an aura to each shot where it is 'less-ness' that stimulates the imagination rather than abundance. It is vital, Bresson is saying, that the spectator is undistracted in the way they receive the story by inappropriate expression, gesture, inflection and so on.

Yet it must be acknowledged that professional acting in which expression, gesture and inflection of the voice, the posture of the body even, can convey information about characters and situations, is a resource film-makers should use. There is then a separate debate to be touched on here – what acting style is appropriate in the cinema. Very briefly, one can identify three straightaway. First, the style of the trained theatre actor muted appropriately for the adjacent camera rather than projected to the back of the auditorium. Secondly, the 'psychological' style developed in partial reaction to the methods of the theatre which uses the closeness of the camera to communicate more subtly how the actor 'lives' in a role. Thirdly, there is the 'voluntary inexpressive' mentioned earlier, a method consciously pursued by actors aware that their presence is all that is required to communicate.

So, to square the circle: one can discern cinematic virtue in both the Bressonian aesthetic of modelling – or 'involuntary expressive' – and a style muted for the camera. What is alien is histrionics, a disproportion between performance and situation that is to be avoided at all costs, for then the risk that performance overwhelms the vital elements in film-making discussed in the next chapter may be avoided.

6   IT'S <u>NOT</u> IN THE ACTING

'Film as Film' was the snappy title given to a book by VF Perkins in 1972. If you purchased it thinking that you were getting a treatise on the nature of film as material and how films were true to a celluloidal essence of sprockets, of frames, of emulsions, encouraged in this view by the book's cover showing a film can and loose loops of film, frames and sprockets included, you were wrong. If instead you were drawn to the sober subtitle 'Understanding and Judging Movies' you got a much better guide to the contents. For a start "movies" sounds more generic, more abstract than "film". More to the point Perkins outlines an approach to appreciating film based on its mass popularity and its hybrid nature. In a polemical first chapter, "Sins of the Pioneers" – and like the best polemic, it works by using the words of their authors to attack their theories – Perkins seeks to demolish an earlier generation of British theorists who focused on editing as the essential aspect of film-making rather than (for example) the camera as a recorder of reality. Throughout the book he is unable to use the word "montage" without a certain distaste showing through.

It is true that the theorists he quotes tended to have lofty notions of the cinema as art, which found mass taste, and therefore popular cinema, unappealing, yet in attacking them, Perkins was attacking men of straw, because by the time of his writing the book, critical appreciation both in Europe and in America of the creative possibilities of popular cinema had begun to be widespread. On the other hand, his appreciation of directors like Otto Preminger, Nicholas Ray and Vincente Minelli is vigorously and refreshingly argued. His favourite value is "coherence" and he is particularly good on the way coherence can arise even from the hybrid nature of the creative process in film-making. As indicated by his attack on montage, he is not one to define the art of film as reducible to one particular technical process. Instead, he insists on the collaborative nature of commercial film-making in which there are many different contributions, although he does recognize that the director's role is *primus inter pares,* as a catalyst, as a coordinator in the creative process, as an "interpreting craftsman", all of which leads to him or her being the essential creator of the film ['Film as Film', pages 178-9]. But to reinforce his argument as to how collaboration can work, he comes up with an intriguing list of films in which "the meal has… proved more satisfying than the recipe would suggest": *Pillow Talk, Forbidden Planet, Gypsy, The Manchurian Candidate, North to Alaska, Them!, House of Wax, Foreign Intrigue, The Wonderful Country, Sweet Smell of Success.* [Perkins p. 175. All these films were released between 1953 and 1962 when Perkins was aged from 17 to 26. His response is a youthful one, open and perceptive.] To this list might be added the war film that I have argued in chapter 3 to be significantly greater than the sum of its parts, *A Walk in the Sun.*

In defining the nature of collaboration that goes into making commercial films, Perkins does not touch on the origins of many of them in the novel and in the theatre, despite their importance to the development of the medium. For the "hybridity" of film has another meaning, namely that it extends the popular novel and the theatre in its search for good stories, it extends painting and photography in the way it composes people, objects, interiors and exteriors within the frame, and it readily uses music to create mood or to signal significant moments. So the film director is at the opposite end of the spectrum to, say, a painter of watercolours, who is only a single person with a blank sheet of paper and a simple set of paints. It is true that other arts may require the contributions of more than one person but the process of time has distilled from them a single artist: Raphael may have had a studio of assistants to paint the "The School of Athens" but we think of it as due to the genius of Raphael alone; Shakespeare may have drawn on a story in the twelfth-century Danish History by Saxo Grammaticus in order to write 'Hamlet', and at the time others contributed to its performance, but Shakespeare's brilliance as a poet and dramatist is the essence of its greatness. And who would be a librettist to the composer of operas? Carlo Da Ponte is a most significant creator in the three operas Mozart made from his librettos, but it is Mozart who finally gets the applause; Stravinsky's 'Rake's Progress' should always be Stravinsky's and Auden's 'Rake's Progress' but usually isn't; in judging Harrison Birtwistle's 'Gawain' and 'Minotaur', we should be judging too David Harsent's librettos. Wagner, on the other hand, was the true operatic *auteur*, performing both roles himself. And for films too, this process of time is eroding any understanding of the cinema as a collaborative process. "Antonioni" is a single unifying imposing author of the films made in his name, when his cameramen, notably Gianni Di Venanzo, and his composers, especially Giovanni Fusco, should be included in the "idea" of Antonioni. Critical understanding of John Ford wrestles before everything else with the attitudes Ford, not his authors or script writers, expressed in his films and in how they changed over the decades, being modified to the point where late Ford virtually contradicts early Ford. [See Kitses, the essays in Studlar and Bernstein, and Cawkwell pp. 178-183.]

Perkins's book, over thirty years on, remains commendable both for its rationality and for his clear refusal to confuse that with objectivity. However, despite his scepticism, academic writing has continued to seek a defining essence for film. This may be in the invention of Grand Theory, "how signifying systems construct a subjectivity within society" [as defined by David Bordwell in 'Film Style' p. 140] or, being more reductive still, how a film as a "system of signs" brought to the surface hidden ideology in society and unconscious drives in individuals; while there are plenty of other sign systems, the commercial cinema – made by individuals, dealing with public concerns, catering for a mass even global audience – seemed a natural focus for such ideas. Or it may be Gilles Deleuze's 'movement-image' and 'time-image'. Or the grand theory may be that of postmodernism, the devotion to surfaces, the fascination of superficiality. Or the essence may be found in what film-makers were doing outside the commercial framework, for example in the American underground/avant-garde film and in structuralist film-making in the UK, which fed into the scholarly dissection of minutiae in film-making of the first decades. Without suggesting a direct causal connection, there is a link to be made between the following ideas:

that Warhol's films from 1963 up to *Chelsea Girls* (1966) and beyond reinvent the cinema; that Malcolm Legrice's *Berlin Horse* (1970) interrogates a single image; that Ken Jacobs' *Tom Tom the Piper's Son* (1969, and many of his subsequent films) interrogates a single silent short film from 1905, and his 'eternalisms' rejoice in forward cinematic motions being stuck in one place; that Noel Burch's *Correction, Please or how we got into pictures* (1979) arose from his participation in the screening of almost the entire corpus of extant film from the first years up to 1906; that Tom Gunning could write his PhD in 1986 on 'DW Griffith and the Narrator-system: narrative structure and industry organization in Biograph films 1908-9'; that the Pordenone Silent Film Festival starts in 1982 (and is still going). In the period film culture at the margins focusses on the camera (framing, spatial arrangement of sets, objects, people) and editing, as if to suggest that these were paramount above dialogue or music, in defining what the cinema should be. It seems the most natural thing in the world to seek to pin down some essence of the cinema, and the pleasure of doing so should not be denied to ourselves, even while we recognize Perkins's perception that while we can be rational in our quest, we cannot be objective. Another maxim can be added: even as we define the essence, actual film-making practice will open up other possibilities we had not taken on board, or even thought of.

So, one part of film's uniqueness is in its origins in photography and in giving photography motion. Right from the start, in the first films by the Lumière Brothers, audiences could see still photographs come to life. One of the pleasures in the recent discovery of the Mitchell and Kenyon films from Blackburn in the UK was the sense of the camera being wide-eyed at what it was capable of recording: from 1901 came a diagonal tracking shot from the open top of a tram as it travelled along the seafront at Morecambe Bay, capturing the waiting horse-drawn carriages, a form of motion that the internal combustion engine was making redundant, adults promenading in the sunshine (including a man swinging his umbrella in insouciant fashion) and children throwing their caps in the air in their own enthusiastic response to the cameraman atop the bus. "O brave new world That has such people in't." What is more, over a century later, the spectator can replay the shot again and again and feel the rapture of these flickering pictures, of the evanescent made permanent: time has broken these lives, but film has resurrected them and YouTube has made them subject to instant replay.

Coming to the present day, in *The Prestige* (2006), a film that wonderfully re-creates Victorian London, there is a street scene in which Angier follows Borden at a distance, a short sequence that forms a bridge passage in the narrative.

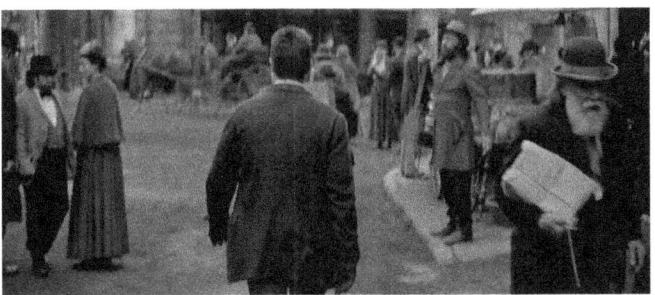

The director, Christopher Nolan, and his art director, have recreated a Mitchell & Kenyon scene of a busy London street, full of traffic and people, but the camerawork has changed: instead of a static viewpoint the camera pans and tracks, intercutting from separate shots of the two characters while a repeated ostinato in David Julyan's music gives a shape to the momentum of the camera. We continue to rejoice in camera movement. The 'panning' shot is so-called from the property of the camera to move across a panorama, whether it be the stately splendour of the slow pan across the landscape in Westerns, a film version of American Sublime, or Dreyer's interior pans across human faces: the ecclesiastical judges in *The Passion of Joan of Arc* and 200 years later the same scene, the judges of Marthe condemning her as a witch in *Day of Wrath*, and 300 years after that the little congregation during the service at Peter the Tailor's house in *Ordet*.

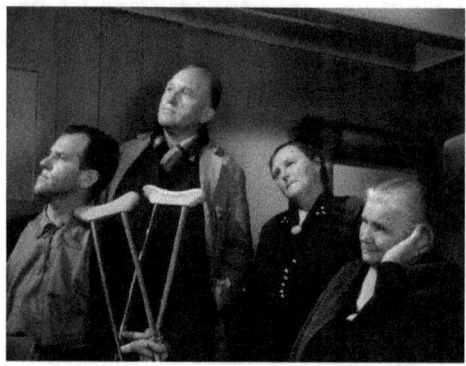

Tracking and panning can then be given a three-dimensional quality in the crane shot: in *On the Black Hill*, in order to mark the divide between England and Wales, the camera lifts into the air from the pastoral classical landscape of England into the rugged romantic landscape of Wales, the hill shrouded in mist. Models and computer-generated imagery have allowed further possibilities still: in the view from the spaceship coming into dock of the sprawling, heavily polluted city in *Blade Runner*; in the aerial shots of the gothic battles in *The Lord of the Rings*; or in *The Dark Knight*, Batman swooping among the night-time skyscrapers, in effect allowing the camera to adopt an "impossible" point of view suspended on skyhooks.

So, camera motion can make films into an exhilarating spectacle, unique to film because other arts cannot follow. Yet if there has to be more to this essence than photographed motion, it must be in the editing of strips of film and, *pace* Perkins and many other writers, it remains an intriguing question: was the advent of the talking picture detrimental to the development of film? There is an obvious yes to this, because it took several years for sound technology and some freedom for the camera to be reconciled. But there may be a subtler yes in the way the talking picture prevented film-makers from negotiating conventions with the audience that would have encouraged a more image-based language.

To refer to "language" in the silent cinema is to enter on slippery ground. In origin the word is about communication through the *lingua* or tongue, i.e.

through speaking, a very different thing from communicating through images. Nor in truth can language literally understood as words be escaped in the cinema. To watch a film of some length composed entirely of images without spoken words or music on the soundtrack is a bracing experience (although potentially rewarding in films, e.g. Stan Brakhage's *Dog Star Man* and Michael Snow's *La Région Centrale*). Aware of this the silent cinema quickly developed the use of inter titles to explain the images, or even in a way just to anchor them. Even at its purest zenith, the pure images of Dreyer's *The Passion of Joan of Arc*, he felt compelled to use titles based on the transcript of the trial in the Paris archives. The invention of sound could not come a moment too soon for the commercial cinema, for audiences were ready for it and when it came embraced it.

This immediately raises the hoary question of whether a film with a lot of dialogue can be regarded as filmic, i.e. as achieving something that a play or novel could not. Three names – Warhol, Pagnol and Rohmer - spring to mind as having done this successfully. When Andy Warhol began to use sound in his films [*Harlot* (1964) and *Kitchen* (1965) have scenarios by the playwright, Ronald Tavel; see Gidal p.100] he has hours of monologue or dialogue spoken to camera or for the camera. Their quality lies much less in what is said (and what is said is often not easy to hear because of the primitive sound) than in the appearance of Warhol's "stars" and in the way they speak, revealing an assertion or nakedness in performance and an unexpected compassion in the view that the camera takes. Nor do they contradict the idea of film's essence residing in giving photography motion. The camera is stationary, and the motion comes from the personalities, in the mobility of their faces, and in their gestures. This is subtly brought out in Warhol's *Screen Tests* already referred to previously. Individuals were filmed for the length of a reel of film at a speed of twenty-four frames per second, their eyes fixed on the camera, the camera returning their stare. When projected, the films were shown at sixteen f.p.s. which slowed them down marginally and in watching them, the time spent doing so is determined by the film-makers not by us, and eye-blinks, slight movements of the head, the smallest movement of face-muscles give these "photographs" a soul beyond mere carnal representation in a single photographic image. Intriguingly, this humanizing process was used by Philip Gröning in his long documentary on life in a Carthusian monastery, *Into Great Silence*. He punctuated the film with portraits of the monks, a frontal shot of the face lasting about 20 seconds.

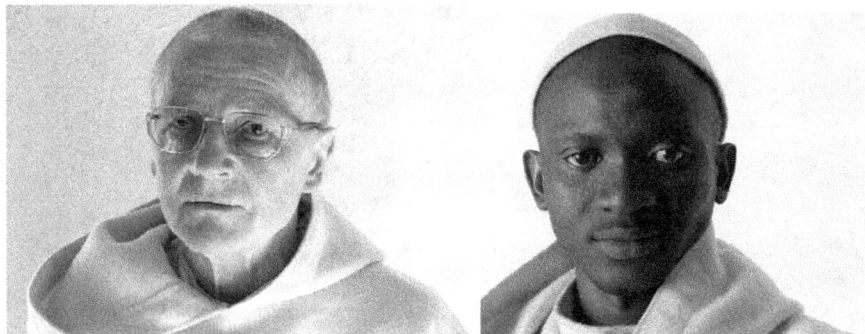

Secondly, take Marcel Pagnol who seems to have positively exulted in the advent of synchronized sound as an opportunity to film his plays and capture a particular time and a particular place, Provence in the early 1930s, so that the films, verbose in the extreme, have become a rich record: the passage of time has blessed them with greater significance still. Pagnol's films are ancestral fore-runners to those of the master of the conversation-piece, Eric Rohmer, who has specialised in the conversation film far beyond any other director: the six *Contes Moraux* between 1963 and 1972, six *Comédies et Proverbes* between 1981 and 1987, four *Contes des quatre saisons* between 1990 and 1998, and a striking list of single-tons throughout his career (not to mention shorts and works for television). Nearly all contain long passages of dialogue and the series films often focus on the vulnerability of a character as his or her illusions receive a jolt precipitated not

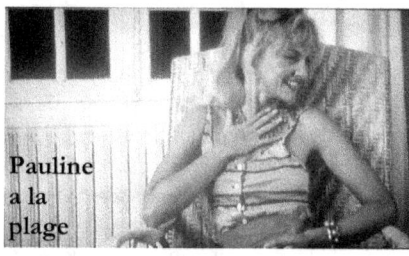

by an act so much as by what is said or by an attitude revealed. This could equally be done in a novel, but Rohmer's contemporary films now embody an astonish-ing visual chronicle of the French middle class over 40 years: how they behaved certainly, especially how they talked, but even more how they dressed and how they went about their daily work and leisure. This will be a mine for social histo-rians getting to grips with what has been in fact a documentary project, one better suited to the cinema than to any other medium. Furthermore, a Rohmerian in-heritance keeps cropping up: in Louis Malle's *My Dinner with André* (1981), a 110-minute conversation between two men in a New York restaurant, in Whit Still-man's *Metropolitan* (1989) a group of young socialites discuss their lives and their loves, the difficulties thereof, in the series of low-budget Hal Hartley films, and in Richard Linklater's trilogy, *Before Sunrise* (1995), *Before Sunset* (2004) and *Before Mid-night* (2013). In the first film Jesse and Céline meet by chance on the train to Vi-

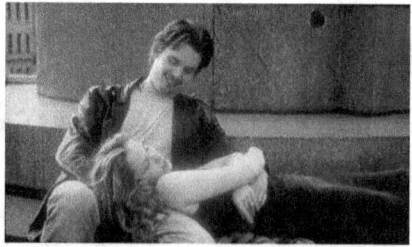

enna and then spend the evening and the night talking with all the openness to experience of youth as they wander around the city; in the second film five years later they meet again by chance in Paris and again their conversation extends itself, with their characters subtly matured and changed by time. By the time of the third film they are parents with middle-aged concerns – but still talking and talking. In all three cases, judgement of the film is not solely on the brilliance of the dialogue but as much on the non-verbal elements, the way a film can capture a particular time or place.

If there is a strand to the cinema which brings action to the fore, or places a premium on what is shown before what is said, these conversation films take us back to the recipe of Howard Hawks for film-making – 'good scenes'. As it happens, Hawks was a master of the action film and *Only Angels Have Wings* combines the two sides of his creativity perfectly: the film depicts the daily life of a small company in a tropical location in the Andes flying mail over the mountains to remote places, celebrating, like the French writer Antoine de St Exupéry, whose 'Vol de nuit' had been published in 1931, the hazardous but inspiring early days of aviation. It features not only a remarkable documentary sequence of one pilot landing and taking off on the rim of a crater in order to airlift to safety an injured man, but to depict a failed landing and the death of one of the company's precious pilots, Hawks capitalizes on the sparsity of the means at his disposal – model aeroplanes, a model landing strip, intercutting between pilot and ground as he is talked down in the fog, a crash conjured up by sound and the reaction of onlookers – to create a 'good scene' that a colourful ball of fire could only diminish (see overleaf). But these scenes are only part of the equation, since Hawks gives as much attention to the verbal sparring that goes on in the bar, especially between male and female. Electricity is not just in the action, it is in the dialogue, and the building of action by a simplicity of means provides a perfect analogue to the way the emotions of the film – the equivalent of the ball of fire – are suppressed under the laconic dialogue. Unlike the excessive plating of emotion from directors, actors and composers in recent cinema, the spectator has to discover their own inward tears. In a film like *Only Angels Have Wings*, Hawks exemplifies the complete classical film-maker in a production-line system that relied on good screen-writing (in this case Jules Furthman) and inspired improvisation on the set.

The role of screenwriters only serves to emphasize the essence of cinema as being a collaborative art and great films can arise from the sum of great contributions, a sum which quickly exceeds the parts. So a cinematic essence can then be found in film-makers like Robert Altman and Mike Leigh using their actors to create good dialogue and strong performance, in effect to create character on screen in a different way from how it is done in a novel or how it is done on stage. Nor is it solely to do with words, for what would be the effect of watching Altman or Leigh with the sound off? A loss of a whole dimension obviously, but it would draw attention to something visual, to character conveyed through expression, gesture and movement, to a more sophisticated version of the fundamental visual truths contained in Warhol's film portraits. This line of thought quietly draws us back to the 'cinematic purity' advocated by some as only truly to be found in the silent era. *The Passion of Joan of*

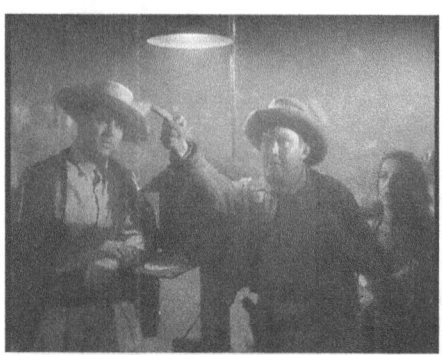
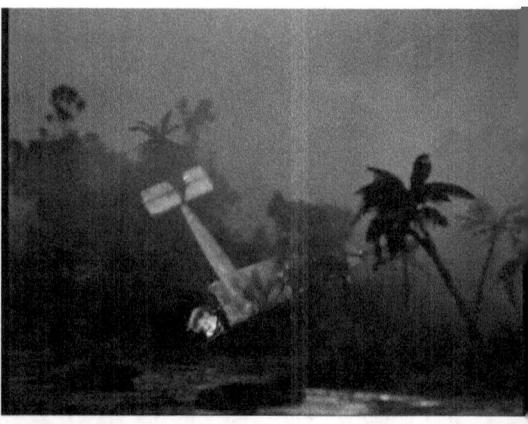

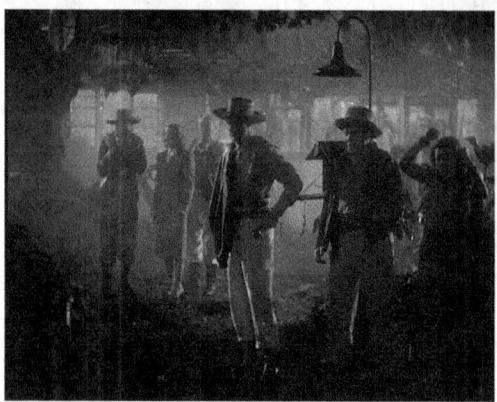
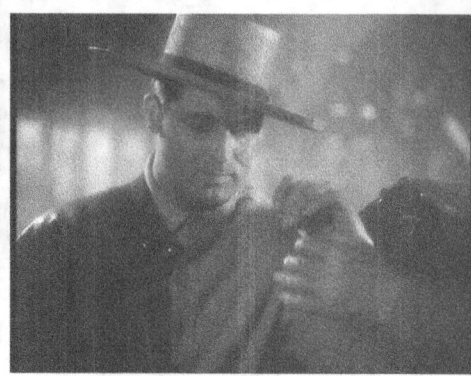

Only Angels Have Wings: sequence of Joe's death constructed on a sound stage and a documentary sequence with real planes in the Andes

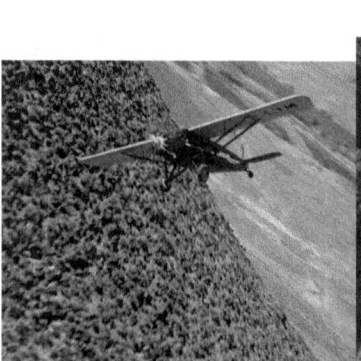
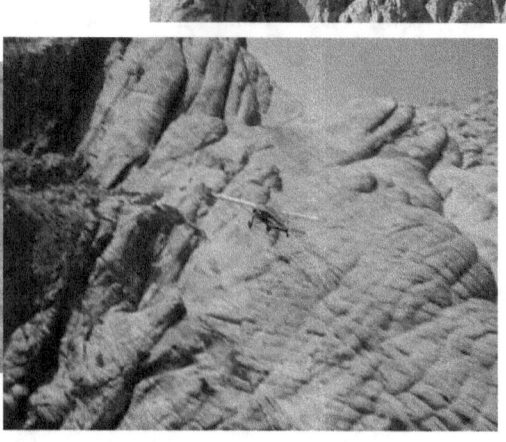

Arc, besides being a narrative of a trial, is a study of Joan's emotions as expressed in the close-ups on her face. Their wordlessness is their point.

And while there is a pleasure in dialogic brilliance, in actors speaking their lines so expressively, there is a risk as well of running the cinema up a cul-de-sac, of making it a servant of the theatre, second best to the theatre because verbal brilliance and performance skills in a theatre have an immediacy and resonance which film could never achieve. For a critic like Perkins, with whose views this chapter began, that secondary quality is no barrier to great film-making, but I believe it has exerted its own pressure on film-makers to explore the uniqueness of film. Furthermore, to rely solely on dialogue for the creation and exploration of character is to mistreat the potential of cinema to use visual clues for psychological illumination – just as to focus solely on photographed motion may be to underplay what speech, sound and music can bring to the finished artwork.

The lament still remains, now with a strong nostalgic tone: was embrace of the talkies, while helping to develop narrative film, also detrimental to the working methods of film-makers in the silent era such as Eisenstein, Dreyer, Chaplin, Keaton, Von Stroheim, Sjöström? Not all were able to adapt. Some did, notably John Ford in whose case formation in the silent era trained the way he looked through a lens and told the story through a sequence of images. The advent of sound only enhanced resources available to him in terms of the actor's performance, the development of character and the scope for improvising on set. In his case, the hybridity of the cinema was enormously valuable, and his idea of a good film was of a good story told in crisp, well-composed dialogue, judicious use of music, powerful acting, as well as a narrative rhythm imparted by a sequence of striking images, from the grandeur of the American landscape, to light falling on faces, to the framing of figures in a doorway.

So, with John Ford in mind, how can film capitalize on being a visual medium before it is a verbal one? The cinema died in 1928, but it promptly sprang to life again, and this reincarnation opened up new ways of creating a language for film. "Talking pictures" are pictures plus talk, pictures with sound effects, pictures with the music added in a more considered and significant way. All aspects went to increasing the resources of the cinema in opening up the picture people have of the world. Prior to it, literature had performed this task, supplemented by painting and illustration. The advent of photography in the nineteenth century had moved the process of understanding what other places and other people looked like into a higher gear, but it was the cinema that accelerated the process throughout the twentieth century contributing enormously to the global understanding we have of the world today. Nor is that understanding just of the present, film having drawn heavily on the past for many of its narratives, some of them highly celebrated. (Some examples: *Day of Wrath, Smiles of a Summer Night*, the Soviet *War and Peace, The Draughtman's Contract*, Rossellini's series of historical films such as *The Age of the Medici* and *Blaise Pascal*, Rivette's *Joan the Maid, The Fall of the Roman Empire, Gladiator, L'Anglaise et le Duc*, Mike Leigh's nineteenth-century trilogy (*Topsy-Turvy, Mr Turner* and *Peterloo*) and so on

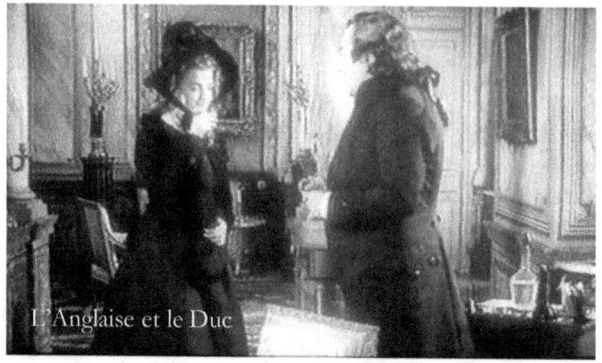

L'Anglaise et le Duc

according to taste.) But is it then an essence of the cinema that it can give us a window into the past? If so it needs to be heavily qualified, because historical authenticity on film has proved so elusive. It would be better to think of historical films as allegory, hugely extended similes, in which modern stories giving a contemporary of view of the world are dressed up as historical.

In describing historical films as essentially allegory, I use a literary figure of speech, and such figures (metaphor, simile, metonymy, hyperbole, asyndeton, litotes, aposiopesis etc) give particular qualities to writing. Are they reproducible in film? Can the cinema develop its own "figures of film"? The most obvious usage is hyperbole: at first this was signalled by histrionic performance and slow motion, to which ingredients have now been added a thick layer of music laid on film. Here are two more subtle examples of figures of film from the work of a master of narration, Robert Bresson. The first is a part standing for the whole (synecdoche): in *Pickpocket* the handcuffs being placed on Michel's arm stand in for the scene of his arrest, as they are sufficient to tell us all we need to know at this point in the story. The second figure is the significant breaking off from the narrative (aposiopesis). This is different from omitting words in order to stream-line writing (ellipsis), a figure of speech matched on film by the jump cut, a technique that likewise streamlines narrative. A good example of this breaking off is to be found in *A Man Escaped*: as he makes his slow and arduous escape from the cell to the outside wall of the prison, Fontaine finds he is obliged to murder a German guard barring his way. We see him pressed against a wall waiting to pounce on the guard as he patrols back and forth, and at the right moment he leaps out of sight behind the wall. We do not witness the murder itself, which is only indicated by the grunt of the guard as he is strangled, and by his boots sticking out from behind the wall. Until Fontaine re-emerges with the job done into the frame, we have to imagine the shock of the murder: Bresson uses the break in the narrative action, this aposiopesis, to underline its dramatic significance. Compare this with an effective instance of hyperbole on film which by using shock is cinematic at the opposite extreme: in *Torn Curtain* Professor Armstrong and Sarah Sherman murder the East German guard who has been following them, and find it to be a difficult and gruesome process requiring strangulation (a failure), a knife (which breaks), and finally stuffing the head into a gas oven (success at last). We are spared none of the details.

Literature extends its power to make the reader think more widely, more imaginatively about an action or feelings by the use of simile and metaphor. Simile allows comparisons to be made, especially effective when they are unexpected; metaphor in particular can jolt us into a different understanding that may be a widening. It is one of the frustrations of the cinema that it has not yet evolved an equivalent of "like" or "as" in the written word. Could there be a convention that a dissolve or a wipe could alert the spectator to the introduction of a shot or sequence that would be a comparison to an element in the main narrative? This has not happened, nor is it going to, because the convention would only be an arbitrary one, and would be quickly broken by a film-maker using a dissolve or wipe in a different way. Nevertheless, Eisenstein's use of cross-cutting in *Strike* to parallel the slaughter of the bull with the massacre of the workers, to show that

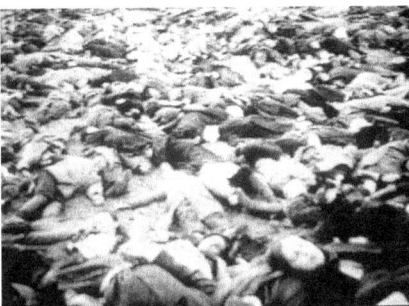 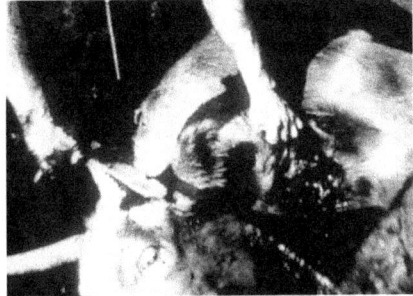

the latter is as brutal and bloody affair as killing and dismembering a bull in a slaughterhouse, remains suggestive. The spectator has a sense of the two things happening at different times and in different places, as happens with simile, but the rapid montage of the two elements has the power of metaphor: the soldiers carry out the lethal slaughter of the workers. Yet this sequence, for all its seeming potential, has not resulted in multiple examples of filmic simile for the reason that the obstacles are too great for the audience. The filmed image is too literal, so that the intercutting of the parallel images raises questions of what is happening and where it is happening. (Chapter 7 discusses the idea of simile/metaphor further.)

Because the filmed image conveys to us an immediate truth, narrative film makers have sought to use that quality to make thought and ideas concrete. To give an example, Powell and Pressburger's *A Canterbury Tale*, set in wartime, hinges its main story on whether Alison can come to terms with the loss of her fiancé, Geoffrey, who has been reported missing in action. The cardinal point in the film occurs when the news is brought to her that he is in fact alive. This "miracle" is made dramatically effective by the sequence leading up to it, showing Alison going to look at the caravan in which she had spent a blissful summer with Geoffrey in 1940. For a writer characterising Alison's clinging to this memory, the method would be to make explicit the thought processes, the actuality of the holiday played against her memory of it, into which would be introduced the risk that the memory was either an illusion in itself, or that the news of Geoffrey's death would turn the memory painful, and for the film maker there is the option of using a flashback to portray the innocent bliss of the holiday. Powell and Pressburger however do something much more striking: the caravan's condition becomes a metaphor for the process of disillusion that she is going to have

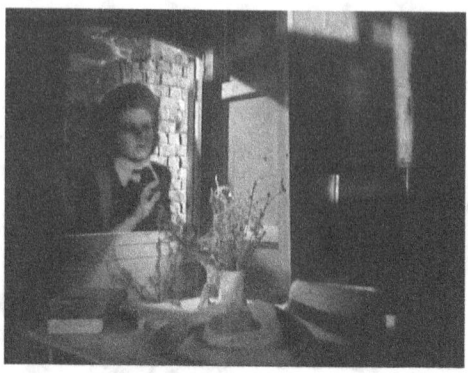

to face. When she opens up the caravan stored in the garage, the air is thick with dust, she finds the sun hats mouse-eaten, and moths fly out of Geoffrey's old coat. Its "weathering" in time is not just a concrete image we can witness, but a metaphor for the decay of memory. The tradition of story-telling in the cinema, in which Powell and Pressburger were masters, would not have allowed the caravan incident to be treated as a dream or introduced in an unexplained way as simile – a filmed version of someone saying to Alison: you are clinging to a decaying memory, as if it were a favourite object that you discover has lost its pristine quality and is now dusty and moth-eaten.

Powell and Pressburger were more adventurous in *The Small Back Room*, made four years later. In this story about a man fighting a drink problem

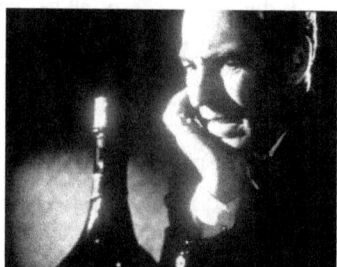
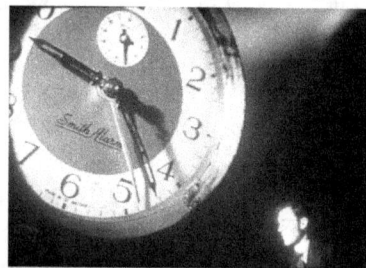

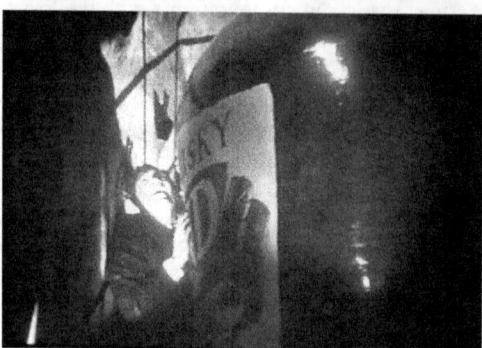

(among other things), there is a sequence of Sammy at home on his own, waiting for Susan to return. It is 1943 and because of the blackout he sits shrouded in darkness. A whisky bottle stands on the table; Sammy stares at it. Images follow of clocks accompanied by inexorable ticking, and of the bottle looming over Sammy. Are these metaphors for the difficulties of his life, or the interior images in his mind, less daydream than lived nightmare? The sequence may feel stilted, but it serves a dramatic purpose in darkening the mood of an already dark film, of breaking up the narrative, and of introducing a shock image: when Susan returns home and opens the door, light is thrown onto Sammy standing

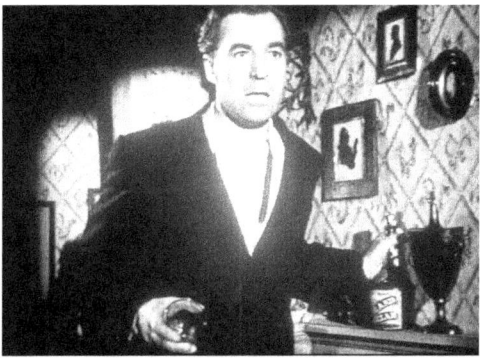

with the bottle and glass in hand – we see him as she sees him, we cut straight from his subjective nightmare to her objective view.

To pursue the idea of simile in film further, here is a famous one from St Matthew's gospel [Matthew c. 3 v.16]: "No sooner had Jesus been baptised and come up out of the water than the heavens were opened and he saw the Spirit of God descending like a dove to alight on him." The presence of the dove in the written account illuminates for us a mystical process, of how the spirit of God

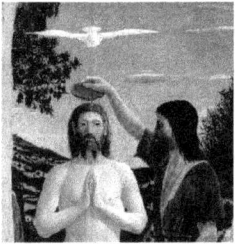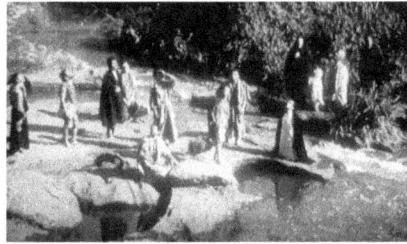

could enter a person, and provides a visual clue for Piero della Francesca to do the same. When he painted the scene ('The Baptism of Christ', 1450s, National Gallery, London), he placed a dove hovering above the central figure of Jesus, both to reflect this essential detail in the gospel account, and for formal purposes, for the dove in the painting emphasises the monumentality of the moment, like placing a pediment on a building in order to cap its proportion and harmony. [See also Drury p.88: "That dove is beautifully shaped to match the shapes of the clouds in the sky. This gives stillness and calm to the energy of its hovering . . . a mixture of activity . . . and rest."] However, this visualisation is not without its pitfalls, for the spectator needs to know the gospel accounts in order to be clear what the dove is doing in the picture. When Pasolini filmed the scene in *The Gospel According to St Matthew*, he films Jesus with John and the crowd from high up, as if from the heavens, giving the dove's or rather God's eye view of the event, suggesting a link between heaven and these persons on earth. If Pasolini had used a dove flying down to earth in order to illustrate this link it would have felt too elusive: unlike the clarity of the written account, the spectator would be struggling to connect the bird to the spirit of God.

Or is this being too literal? Is there scope for a more adventurous approach? One can see the dove in Piero's painting and without knowing it stood for the spirit of God, have a sense of a mysterious and blessed presence. Similarly in filming this incident from the Gospel, could one insert a sequence of a bird in flight, using cinematic virtuosity: frame-by-frame cutting, a vivid colour style, the presence of the bird in a vast landscape showing heaven and earth, and made arresting by being silent (avoiding the temptation for "holy" music)? Digital film-making would make such a sequence possible, its imaginativeness would extend the range of visual possibilities, and it would capitalize on current audience taste for fantasy in the cinema.

One possible reason why the example of simile in *Strike* has been barely pursued by other film-makers is that it occurs in a film that is narratively unconventional. *Strike* is a message film, a statement from the film-maker, not an interior isolation of the thoughts and feelings of a character or characters in a narrative: the people in the film are schematically drawn, and barely come across as individuals. In commercial cinema around the world, on the other hand, narratives concern the circumstances or predicaments of individuals: spectators are directed to see events through their eyes. Eisenstein's tendentious idea of how to use montage would therefore need to be adapted to such narratives.

So, how might the freedom of the resources of cinema be deployed, that could draw not just on the contributions made by script writers, composers and sound engineers, but also use photographed motion and editing (montage even, if we use that word to describe the early Soviets' visible editing as opposed to the invisible editing favoured by the French post-war *nouvelle critique*)? This introduces new terms for defining the unique quality of the cinema, namely the way it is able to manipulate time both in narrative and non-narrative films.

7   TIME'S LABYRINTH

"I like a film to have a beginning, a middle and an end but not necessarily in that order." [This quote is regularly attributed to Jean-Luc Godard, supposedly during a conversation with Georges Franju, but I cannot track down where this anecdote was first recorded.] In the days before narrative film, story-tellers would tell their stories from beginning to end, but then the retelling of the tale led to different ways of telling, so that they looked back before looking forwards, not necessarily in that order. By the time the cinema is invented, Marcel Proust is gestating his great novel, which will take the narrative of remembering to new levels just as the new art of film begins to explore the treatment of time, going backwards, forwards and sideways.

CROSS-CUTTING

Going sideways in narrative is not an invention of the cinema. With the growth of the novel, especially in the nineteenth century in writers like Dickens and Dostoevsky, the story shifts from character to character, from side to side as it were, in order to accommodate several points of view. In the theatre, melodrama prepared the way for the cinema by adopting dual box sets and area lighting. [See Vardac.] But one can go back earlier than that: a random search through Shakespeare's plays reveals him cutting in different scenes from character to character. Take 'Richard II' for example which starts with the two main protagonists, Richard and Bolingbroke, and several important supporting characters, sharing the stage; after Bolingbroke's banishment, the conflict between the two is developed through intercut scenes:

Act 2 scene 1   John of Gaunt, Duke of York, <u>Richard II</u>, <u>Queen</u>, others, when Gaunt upbraids Richard for his rule

2.2   <u>Queen</u>, York

2.3 & 3.1   <u>Bolingbroke</u> back in England from abroad, York, others (with brief inserted scene [2.4] of the Earl of Salisbury with a Welsh captain)

3.2   <u>Richard II</u> with others learns of desertions from his side

3.3   <u>Bolingbroke</u>, York & Northumberland meet <u>Richard II</u> to negotiate a settlement

3.4   <u>Queen</u> and the gardeners

4.1   <u>Richard II</u> meets <u>Bolingbroke</u>, Northumberland, York and others in order to hand over power

     and so on.

Now, it may be the case that the single point-of-view is a key ingredient in seducing an audience to identify with a heroic or tragic character, particularly on stage – and here Richard II proves this rule, for while character-changing does move the history along with great swiftness and clarity in explaining the struggle between Richard and Bolingbroke and in who is siding with whom (and who is deserting whom), its real greatness as a play derives from transcending this cross-cutting history by putting centre stage Richard's swivelling between despair and hope and his reflections on mortality and kingship, replacing a dual focus with a single one. We identify with his agony, his Passion almost [see Ure p.lxii], even while recognizing his shortcomings as a king. The play precedes the writing of Shakespeare's great tragedies with single haunted characters foremost – Macbeth, Hamlet, Lear, for example - and points to them. Yet by the time the cinema is invented, something has changed. There is still a place for the narrative with a central character in crisis, but narrative has developed as well to encompass stories with more than one viewpoint or narrative centre. Is this due to an awareness of the world gained through journalism in both written and visual form, through a less hierarchical understanding of society, through better literary technique? Have all these factors precipitated a move towards greater realism and thus greater narrative complexity?

Whatever the answer, when in the cinema DW Griffith began to build on the first tentative steps to create a language for story-telling, and to develop one narrative device particularly associated with his name, that of parallel editing or cross-cutting whereby the narrative is developed by shifting the story from one group of characters to another, he cites as precedent the novels of Charles Dickens. There is a story that Griffith encountered some resistance from his 'employers' to the idea of parallel editing, an idea which Griffiths cited as drawn from Dickens, who being a name to conjure with in early twentieth-century America could safely be cited as an authority for the practice. [See Eisenstein p. 205, quoting A.B. Walkley in 'The Times' of London for 16 April 1922 for this story. Walkley comments that the idea of a "break in the narrative, a shifting of the story from one group of characters to another group" was really "common to fiction at large" not just in Dickens.] Now this resistance from Griffith's employers reflects commercial necessity: will such experimentation turn people away because they cannot understand its purpose? In this instance, Griffith the showman knew he was on to something: part of his attraction for audiences in the 1910s derives from creating a new sense of excitement as he developed his rescue narratives leading up to the zenith of *Intolerance* in 1916, which not only featured one of his grandest of them but applied the technique of cross-cutting to four stories with a parallel theme. [See Gunning.]

These four stories are set in Babylon at the time of Belshazzar, in Jerusalem at the time of Jesus's crucifixion, in 1572 during the massacre of St Bartholomew's Eve, and in the modern era. The scenes with Jesus are fewer than for the others, Griffith appearing to assume his audience knows the Gospel story sufficiently, and the parallel editing is therefore focused on the other three stories, the crosscutting between which speeds up as the film reaches its climax, requiring considerable alertness on the part of the audience to remember the point at which each story had reached. Griffith was striving for the spectator to make a mental connection on the themes of hatred and intolerance versus love and forgiveness, but this method undermines the dynamism of each story, especially the modern one which concludes with a race between one group (the woman or the Dear One, the policeman helping her, and the woman who shot the Musketeer while he was in the act of raping the Dear One) to reach the state governor in time for him to issue a reprieve for the innocent Boy due to hang for the murder and then get it to the prison governor to stop the hanging. Racing cars, speeding trains, the telephone are all involved, and the melodramatic but highly effective image of three knives poised over the strings the cutting of which will cause the trap door to open underneath the Boy to be hanged. While the modern story (especially when watched as a separate story on dvd) gains enormously from its contemporary setting, with much of it having an intimacy and psychological detail denied to the other elements in which set and costume overwhelm the drama, especially in the Babylonian story, an additional virtue is its rescue narrative which has a see-saw quality between the accelerated movement in cars and trains and the decelerated motions of an innocent preparing for his death. Will the Dear One get there in time? The answer is yes, but the inter-

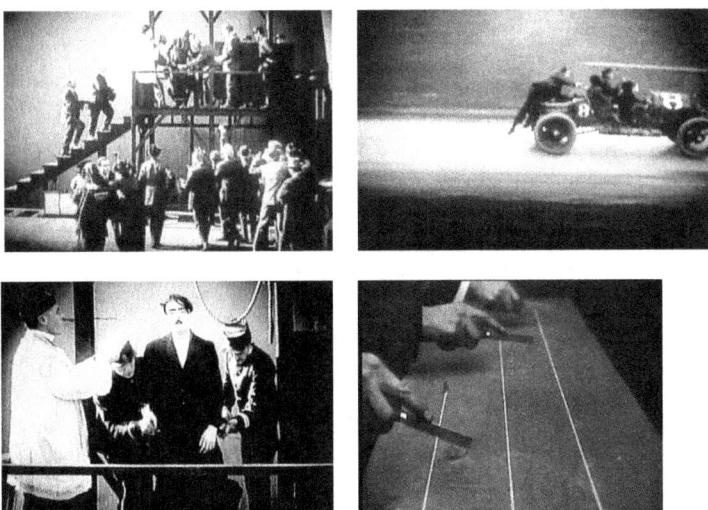

cutting with the Babylon and France stories suggest a different outcome because in both of these the Mountain Girl and Brown Eyes are killed before they can be rescued. Griffith ends his depiction of intolerance through the ages on an upbeat note, of justice and of reconciliation, of love finally triumphant in this world.

Despite its failings, *Intolerance* is a film of enormous ambition whose temporal sweep remains to be matched in subsequent film-making. There is one film that comes close, but is at present virtually unknown: Dreyer's *Leaves from Satan's Book* was made in 1919-21, a post-*Intolerance* production but by no means overshadowed by it. Shorter than *Intolerance* [in the dvd version from Grapevine in the USA the length is 131 minutes against the 197 minutes of the dvd version of *Intolerance*; in Sadoul the Dreyer film is given as 2000 m. approx against 5200

138

m. for the Griffith film] it has four parts, set in the time of Christ (again), of the Spanish Inquisition, of the French Revolution, and in Finland in 1918. Its theme is of human weakness in resisting temptation, so like *Intolerance* it has a moral purpose embedded in its story-telling, and since it is only in the last episode that resistance is upheld, it is like *Intolerance* in being pessimistic about human virtue until the last reel. Crucially Dreyer shows the four episodes in sequence not in parallel, with a gain in narrative power without detriment to the overarching theme of the film [see Cawkwell pp. 65-6].

What is the narrative force of these rescues, or chase sequences so beloved of Griffith and early cinema in general? The technique imparts a moral dynamism to the story: will wickedness be caught in time by the forces of good? At a personal level, will the hero save the heroine? In Griffith too, the screen comes alive kinetically, as rapid movement back and forth heightens the sense of spectacle and arouses the spectator physically, hence the phrase "I was on the edge of my seat" used to describe involvement in suspense narratives. Demands are particularly made on perception, for as the film speeds up, especially if the shot lengths reduce, the spectator needs to adjust, while at the same time using the brain to interpret where the different shots fit in time and space. As already argued in chapter 2, narrative suspense is not unique to the cinema, but it does it best.

This dynamism in the editing was an ingredient of the "revelation" that Eisenstein claimed Griffith represented to the new Soviet film-makers of the 1920s [Eisenstein, 'Film Form', p. 201], and manifested itself in ways well beyond Griffith's method. As mentioned in the previous chapter in a discussion of filmic simile and metaphor, Eisenstein's *Strike* cross-cuts the massacre of a body of workers fleeing from soldiers and being shot down with the killing of a bull in an abattoir from the delivery of the lethal blow to the head to the slitting of the body to release the blood. [See Eisenstein, 'Film Sense', appendix 3.] As narrative, the montage of bull and massacred crowd makes no temporal or spatial sense, instead it proposes a parallel in the mind between the bloody killing of the bull and the bloody mowing down of the crowd, an assault on the senses and understanding in order to give force to the final title, 'Never forget'. The version of the film in circulation has some thirty shots for the slaughter sequence, lasting about ninety seconds, and pummels the spectator visually, an illustration of Eisenstein's idea of the 'kino-fist' as a tool of revolutionary violence.

As with Griffith and Dreyer, crosscutting in *Strike* has a judgmental purpose, to condemn the perpetrators, to stir compassion for the victims and to provoke action on their behalf. Subsequently, audiences have responded much less to such moralising and much more to the excitement that crosscutting narrative can create. Fritz Lang made *M* with Griffith and *Strike* in the mind, but his focus is amoral: the child-murderer is pursued by the police, but Lang adds to the narrative excitement by having the underworld pursue the murderer as well in parallel to the police. Or, to take a much more recent example, a triple focus of a similar kind underpins *No Country for Old Men*: Sheriff Bell tracking Chigurh tracking Moss, and then trying to reach Moss before Chigurh does. Cormac

McCarthy's novel from which the film is taken is formally structured in chapters alternating between the ruminations of Sheriff Bell as he tries to engage with the case and the actions of Chigurh and Moss so that reading it gives a clear sense of a pendulum, between amoral action and moral reflection. The film version made by the Coen Brothers, being so much more action-centred, is more successful in handling the former than the latter. The drama of Chigurh's pursuit of Moss becomes a riveting example of cross-cutting in which the two characters are linked by the story, by the precision of their methods – Moss in hiding the money, Chigurh in locating Moss's whereabouts – and by the device of a transponder in the suitcase of money, used by Chigurh to get on Moss's trail; by the time it is discovered by Moss, the two men are close enough to engage in a tremendous firefight. McCarthy's novel is so remarkable because he finds a way of articulating the pounding relentlessness of the chase alongside reflections on the amorality driving the drug industry especially as it operates on the Texas-Mexico border, a thickening of his narrative that largely eludes the film version. [For a fuller exposition of this point, see the essay on the film on www. timcawk-well.co.uk.]

No Country for Old Men may have brought cross-cutting right up to date, but since the very early days, the cinema has marked out the manipulation of time as its own territory in particular, to the extent that by the time Andrey Tarkovsky, heir not just to the Soviet tradition but that of European art-house cinema as well, writes his artistic credo he makes this definition: "What is the essence of the director's work? We could define it as sculpting in time." He even uses the phrase to provide a title for his book on film aesthetics, 'Sculpting in Time'. He conceives an ideal piece of filming: "The author takes millions of metres of film, on which systematically, second by second, day by day and year by year, a man's life, for instance, from birth to death, is followed and recorded, and out of all that come two and a half thousand metres, or an hour and a half of screen time [Tarkovsky p.65]." The project is an apt description of Orson Welles's *Citizen Kane* (1941), central to film history for its treatment of time and truth. It may be described simply as the life of Charles Foster Kane, but that life is made complex by the way Welles uses (documentary) newsreel of Kane within the (fictional) film of his life and by the way Kane speaks for himself from youth to age, when this view is constantly altered by being filtered through the memories of others, those memories made concrete – as if objective – by being shown in flashback. This is surely Tarkovsky's 'sculpting in time', the patient assemblage of the significant fragments of a life to make a mystery story, using the precision of particular images and particular sequences to unfold the story for the spectator.

In his own work, the film that comes nearest to the idea of a life filmed is *Mirror* (1972) which is both biographical and autobiographical, layered in time over three generations with sequences from the mid-1930s, from the war in the early 1940s, and from around 1970, i.e. the present day. In the final long tracking shot in the field outside the dacha that has featured throughout the film as the repository of childhood memories and dreams, the elderly Maria who has been depicted earlier in the film as a young mother looks out over the landscape accompanied by her son and daughter, not as adults, but still as the very young children we saw them as when the boy Alexey was five. So, what year are we in? 1935, when the children are their real age and their mother has shifted mysteri-

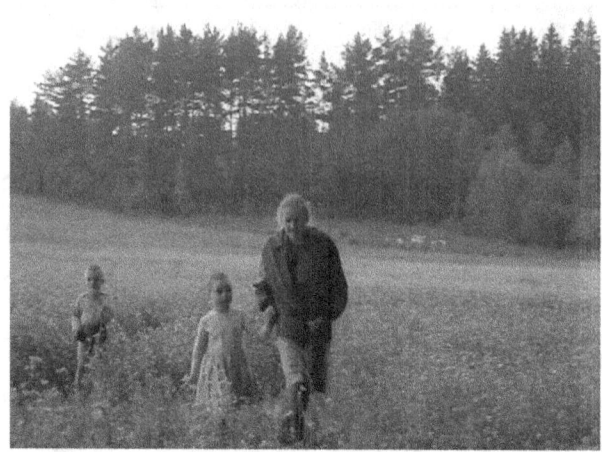

ously into old age? Or in 1970, when the mother is her real age and the son and daughter are somehow remembered as little children? The shot magically brings together past and present, childhood and old age, reality and memory. This celebrated moment asserts the supremacy of time and human love over family tensions; to the turbulence of the Soviet background – Stalin's terror, the Great Patriotic War with its enormous deprivations, the petrifaction of Communist rule in the 1960s and 70s – it offers a point of stillness, almost a counterpoint to the frenetic turbulence of *Strike*, a putting to rest of Leninist revolutionary violence as a motor of human existence which is to be more truly found in the patience of family love. [*Mirror's* layers of time are well analysed in Synessios.] Tarkovsky would have been immersed in the traditions of montage cinema that came out of the Soviet encounter with film before the coming of sound, when a visual language was a necessity for creating films. And this encounter brings the filmmaker face-to-face with time, in the form of strips of time, making them inside the camera, and then stitching them together on the editing table, losing a few seconds of a life here and there, and sometimes dumping whole sequences in the bin.

But it was not the commercial logic of capitalist film-making in Griffith and Hollywood, nor the ideological film-making of the newly created Soviet Union, but the arrival of Surrealism that most radically stretched the filmic possibilities of manipulating time and space. A profound assault on temporal and spatial logic is mounted in *Un Chien Andalou* (1927), puzzling the spectator about the relationships between the different spaces in the film (room, street, park, beach etc), the relationships between the different characters, and most absurdly the temporal relationships. Five inter-titles throw us into disarray: "once upon a time/8 years later/towards three in the morning/16 years before/In the spring."

Yet this overturning of logic, this disobedience to the rules of 'grammar', allows the images to take on a potency, and an aura of 'meaning'. *Un Chien Andalou* was too limited in circulation to have an immediate influence, but in the long term it is prophetic in the way it stakes out the possibilities for inverting concepts of time and space in the cinema, for turning narrative on its head, and for cinematic dreaming, even if the prophecy is yet to be properly realized in terms of films made under its influence.

The dominance of Hollywood narrative cinema in the first half of the twentieth century meant that audiences became settled in a comfortable familiarity with the treatment of time and space in narrative. When Alain Resnais' *Last Year in Marienbad* won the Golden Lion at the Venice Film Festival in 1961, it was nothing like the first film to treat time in a radically different way, but it had a more significant impact than what had gone before. This is a story about. . . except that in trying even to outline the story uncertainty sets in. It features a man (X) and a woman (Y) and a third party (M) who may be the husband of Y. X seems to be trying to persuade Y that they met a year ago and fell in love. This penny-plain situation is given colour by the sight of M shooting Y, and by X sitting on a balustrade which then breaks so that he falls, possibly with the broken parts of the balustrade on top of him. But neither point is clear: in the context of the story, they are more plausibly explained as dreams or unrealized alternatives rather than what really happened. It is certainly uncertain whether what we are watching is the present or the past, or even the future.

This story may be so trivial as to be meaningless, which is a criticism frequently made of the film. But if the story is truly meaningless – not just without importance but without direction or even intention – then it may be said to take on validity and purpose. It is a depiction of people lost in time, made with a bravura quality: the conception of a world of elegant people who seem never to move forward or back, or inhabit any other space than this grand hotel, is an audacious narrative concept; Sacha Vierny's camera work is luminous; the setting of baroque chateau, of gravel paths, of clipped hedges is visually stylish, matched by the stylishness of the clothes, especially those of Y, embodied in the stellar presence of Delphine Seyrig; above all, there is the disembodied voice ("un fois de plus le longeur de ces couloirs . . . immense, luxure, baroque . . . salons deserts . . . salles silencieuses . . . marbres, glaces noirs . . . ces tapis, si lourds, si épais") intoning and repeating Alain Robbe-Grillet's hypnotic words, fading in and out of Francis Seyrig's interminable organ-piece on the soundtrack, with its echoes of cathedral music in praise of space, in praise of grandeur, on the threshold of praising God, but which then, one realizes, is going nowhere except to echo the emptiness of these human lives, to embody the *ennui* of being lost in space and time. That the story is as much about thwarted desire as anything links it to the world of Luis Buñuel, not just the assault on logic of *Un Chien Andalou*, but his later work dissecting the cruelties of prosperity: wealth buys an escape from the misery of poverty, but it only reveals more starkly the tragedy of human inability to find happiness, to experience only the constant thwarting of desire.

It also makes sense of the re-release of *Un Chien Andalou* in 1960, about the same time as *Last Year in Marienbad* was being made, with the 'Liebestod' from Wagner's 'Tristan und Isolde' and an Argentinian tango added to it as a musical accompaniment (more dislocation, this time of cultural sensibility), as if between them the two films could capitalize on the creation of a new sophisticated audience for temporal mysteriousness. Even Hollywood, the home of no-nonsense narrative, is not immune: David Lynch's *Lost Highway* (1997) runs with one story for half an hour, full of anxiety leading to an unexplained and unrevealed terror, then replaces its protagonist Fred Madison, now in prison, with Pete Dayton, without explanation to the characters, to the prison guards, let alone to the audience. The main story of Pete's infatuation with Alice then begins, reworking the doomed fascination of Walter Neff with Phyllis Dietrichson in *Double Indemnity* of fifty years earlier, until near the end, Fred replaces Pete again: the film ends with Fred being chased through the night desert by patrol cars, pursued and pursuers lost on the highway. Despite this narrative farrago the film remains engrossing: we may not care for or about the characters, but the depiction of suburban America, the empty but threatening space of interiors, the spying with a video camera, the reworking of motifs in colour of the black and white crime thrillers of the 1940s, the beach cabin 'imploding' from ball of fire and smoke to cabin (by running the film backwards) make the whole seducing – in a way that engages with our sense of dreaming where spatial and temporal switches seem perfectly logical. Dreams are visual and re-created in the cinema can have a conviction that make written versions feel laboured.

In making *Lost Highway*, David Lynch must have consciously drawn on Maya Deren and Alexander Hammid's surrealist masterpiece, *Meshes of the Afternoon* (1943), which in turn echoes *Un Chien Andalou* in several ways: in dislocating space and time, in the camera gazing at the stock-in-trade objects of psychoanalysis – knife, telephone, key – in slow-motion movement, in the use of highly arresting music (Teiji Ito's classical Japanese music to parallel the tango intercut with Wagner's 'Liebestod'), even in a jump cut from room to sea shore. In the first half of *Lost Highway* Lynch uses the same suburban setting as Deren and Hammid, namely Hollywood Hills in Los Angeles, and his doubling of character with Fred / Pete / Fred again is paralleled with the woman in *Meshes of the Afternoon* both being herself and seeing herself as a double. Its subject insofar as it is discernible feels laboured now, but the visual brilliance which is sustained throughout its thirteen minutes lifts the story out of its time and place, Deren and Hammid instinctively using the camera to relish both the illusion it can produce such as eyes or lips in close-up, and the 'dis-illusion' too: the spatial disorientation the woman feels as she seems to fall down the stairs, or the way the camera rocks the stairs from side to side as she ascends them being thrown from side to side. What is happening in the film is elusive. Its true narrative is in its intermingling of images drawn from everyday vision, dream vision and nightmare vision.

For many people, the narrative labyrinth of *Meshes of the Afternoon* and of *Un Chien Andalou*, and of *Lost Highway* and *Marienbad*, for that matter, is an offence, against reason but also against the purposes of narrative, to involve, to illuminate, to give meaning. So, the cinema was, and is, faced with the challenge of using the way film can manipulate time – an inherent quality in it as an art form, its own 'truth to material' – while at the same time building narrative coherence. I have therefore divided the possible narrative strategies of manipulating time into four: first, **flashbacks**; second, **remembering things past**; thirdly, **conditional or 'what if?' cinema**; and finally **repeated narratives**.

FLASHBACKS

The natural place to start is the flashback, which by the time the cinema came into being, was already a long established literary device, for example providing a significant part of the framework for Homer's 'Odyssey'. A notable example of its use occurs in *Le Jour se lève* of 1939, which starts with François locked in his room being besieged by the police while the story of how he came to be in that situation is told in three flashbacks: the film observes faithfully a three-act dramatic structure. Some ten years later *Sunset Boulevard* is more startling: the retelling of the past is done by a corpse so that the story explains how he comes to be a dead body floating face downwards in a swimming pool.

In Japan, to take a very different culture, *The Life of Oharu* begins with a melancholy tracking shot at night following the prostitute Oharu, heavily made up to disguise her age, as she gathers with other women around a fire. Drawn by the sound of drums and bells in the temple, she enters and gazes at the statues of Buddha's disciples. In one of them she sees the face of the man with whom she had had an affair at court, doomed because it cut across class and

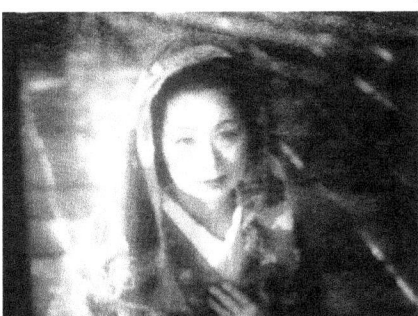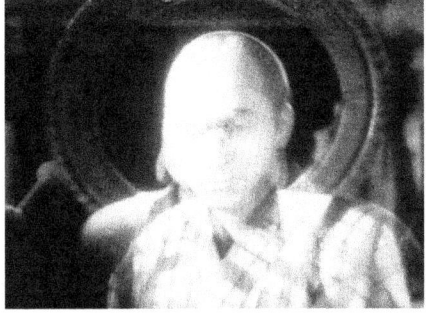

was therefore illicit, which causes a long flashback recounting a relentless sequence of incidents marking her decline in which Oharu is always the victim, usually of conventions and attitudes determined by men. Towards the end the opening tracking shot is repeated and the scene in the temple leads to Oharu's final humiliation as she watches her son, now a clan lord, from afar but is prevented from getting near to him. In the final shot, we see her going from house to house at night seeking alms. When she exits left, the camera holds on the temple buildings in the background. A 'retro-narrative' like this lends the story a deeply pessimistic quality. We start with a view of the protagonist *in extremis*; the flashback then portrays them in the past as happy or prosperous. The narrative drive is then in tracing this fall: we know the ending, the unknown is how it is reached. To give another example, in Max Ophuls' *Letter from an Unknown Woman* (1948), this pessimism is explicit from the outset: the woman of the title dies of an illness at the end, but we are told this in the opening scene when the pianist she loves returns home to read her letter which begins: "By the time you read this

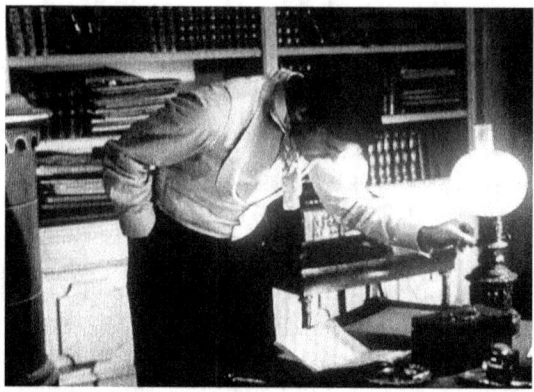

I shall be dead." The retro-narrative appears to make her death an inevitable consequence of his heartlessness. For *Le Jour se lève*, the music linking the main sequences contains a muffled drum, as if to underline the march to the scaffold that François must undertake. The drama is in how the main character got to this point of crisis, challenging any member of the audience rebelling against this inexorability to pinpoint some decision or action taken earlier that could have prevented this conclusion. In essence these structures allow for a version of tragedy specific to the cinema.

These films all go backwards to then go forwards. The next step is to go backwards to the beginning, which then becomes the ending of the film, to tell the story not from A to Z, but from Z to A. Such is the device of Christopher Nolan's *Memento* (2000), essentially a revenge melodrama: a man loses his wife when she is raped and murdered, so he vows to find the killer. So far, so ultra-conventional, but Nolan sets the story in motel rooms, diners, industrial sites, that is to say the bleak landscape of modern America, and creates not the black and white era of film noir of the 1940s, where shadows and pools of light create their own illusions, but a polychrome world somehow emptied of colour. Furthermore he makes sure that the details of the story leave as many questions unanswered as present the viewer with incontrovertible truths. This is to echo a long tradition of Hollywood detective fiction in which the how is of more importance than the what, atmosphere coming before fact: this is *Maltese Falcon* (1941) and *Big Sleep* (1946) territory. But in order to lift the whole project out of the run of the mill, he tells the story backwards by making the man bent on revenge the victim of short-term memory loss, a fatal condition for revenge which is fuelled by the vividness of memory and needs concentrated effort on the details involved in identifying the murderer. This is the premise of *Memento*, an ordinary story turned into something gripping by using film to lead the spectator to 'watch backwards'.

The hero, Leonard, copes with his condition by taking polaroids of peo-

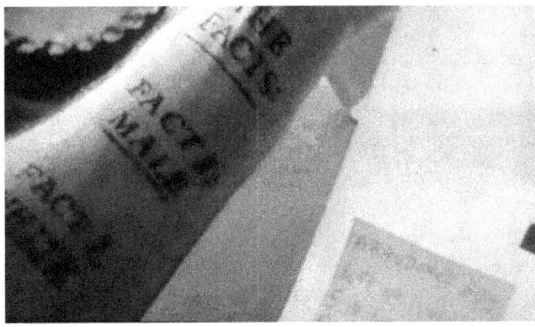

ple and places, writing notes to himself, keeping a file of papers, and in particular tattooing the vital facts on his body as constant reminders. In order for us to understand the nature of his problem, the film is told in just over twenty segments or slices of action, each just long enough for Leonard to remember what is happening. The audience needs to exercise its faculty of memory if it is to understand the whole sequence of events, so the film becomes a test of its capacity to string the segments together in a coherent fashion.

As if this wasn't enough to cope with, in between each segment (filmed in colour) there is a black and white sequence which explains more fully the nature of Leonard's condition, and in particular the case of Sammy Jankis, another victim of memory loss, whom Leonard, a professional loss adjuster, meets as a result of an insurance claim. If Jankis is deemed to have a physical illness, then the insurance company must pay out; if a mental illness, they can wash their hands of the case. Leonard is successful in getting it judged a mental condition. When he is afflicted himself, he realizes that the condition affects him physically, it is not a mental condition out of which he can awake. This back story emerges in the twenty or so alternate sequences from the colour ones, and while it does not go backwards, it reinforces the complexity of the time layers in the film. The two sequences merge at the end, when Leonard leaves the motel room to meet Teddy/ John Gemmell/ Jimmy Grants. The film ends in a maze of shifting identities, including that of Leonard, and in a time warp: Leonard has moved forward to what is the start of the film, when we learn that the black and white sequences all precede the plot unfolded in the colour ones.

This time labyrinth generates a proper suspense, because the viewer has to work to match up visual beginnings and ends, i.e. you need to get the hang of it to make sense of it, only to find that this does not create a way out of the labyrinth, only a clear understanding of where you are in it.

REMEMBERING THINGS PAST

The second category of film narrative relies on triggers to make sense of what has gone before. This recovery of the past is a potent source for dramatic tension, a re-working of the convention of *anagnōrisis* (recognition) in ancient drama, when (for example) two people separated in the past and thrown together discover they are twins. Shakespeare's 'Comedy of Errors' reworks Plautus's 'Menaechmi' so that the moment when the twins are revealed to each other is the moment of relief for the audience – and the moment the comedy ends. In the first act of Wagner's 'Die Walküre', on the other hand, the mutual recognition of Siegmund and Sieglinde that they are brother and sister redoubles the dramatic power of their falling in love. In the cinema, the moment of recognition is most naturally triggered by a visual memory: the protagonist sees, hears, feels something which we as spectators recognize has a significant past. Once again, literature has paved the way in the form of Marcel Proust's 'In Search of Lost Time', published as eight volumes between 1913 and 1927. Its remarkable visual quality and layering of memory make it a natural subject for a film, even if its immensity and philosophical sophistication are beyond the present resources of commercial cinema. The version of the whole made by Raul Ruiz in 1999 as *Time Regained*, strictly the title of only the last volume in the sequence, has an admirable weight in its length of 162 minutes, and achieves a *coup de cinéma* in its handling of Proust's *coup d'écriture* towards the end of the book, when Marcel stumbles on the pavement, the stumble which brings the past world of the Guermantes back to him. In the film, Marcel is in a public garden in Paris, and we see his feet walking on gravel. The film then cuts to his feet on the pavement in Venice and his stumbling against a protruding paving stone. Marcel freezes in the pose of falling forward and after memories of Venice he becomes a frozen figure at the exterior of a reception at the Guermantes' palace. Becoming reanimated, he enters and is shown to a place in the library while a concert is in progress. There he is assailed by a sequence of memories evoked by the sound of the sugar spoon in the cup, the napkin with which he wipes his lips, and a book drawn from the shelf, each of which triggers a visual recollection of the relevant scene: the engineer tapping the wheels of the little train as it halts in the countryside, the nap of the adolescent Marcel's towel on holiday at Balbec, and his mother reading the book to the boy Marcel because he is afflicted with insomnia and longing for her. In a voice-over Marcel reflects on how this process of memory restores his faith in writing, because it stops his fear of death, and takes him outside of time. Although it is arguable that the stateliness of the film, its series of tableaux almost, cannot do justice to the fluidity of Proust's description of these events, and proper understanding of their import requires prior knowledge of the book, the film intriguingly and successfully uses four Marcels, as boy, as adolescent, as mature man, and in old age, in certain shots encountering each other in a *Mirror*-like collapsing of time, all of which requires particular alertness on the part of the viewer. The film is bolder in departing from the novel with certain purely visual dreamlike conceits such as the mature Marcel wandering among top hats on a chequerboard floor, and three Marcels wandering among what seem to be gigantic tombs, conceits which indefinably but successfully indicate the labyrinth of time in which Marcel is placed.

Another story of remembrance in an aristocratic setting, made four decades earlier and possibly unconscious of any Proustian influence, is Satyajit Ray's *Jalsaghar* in which the master of the great house, destitute of wife and son, stripped of his land and his wealth, suddenly arouses himself from his lassitude to stage a final 'jalsa', or musical performance, in his music room, scene of many such performances in his younger days. The film has a Q-type structure: it goes in a circle but a tail leads off at the end in order to complete the story. It begins with the master alone on the roof of his great house, who, stirred by the sound of the Sacred Thread ceremony in Mahim Ganguly's house nearby, recalls the one he had arranged for his own son. This is a memory triggered by music, which is a common human experience. In a flashback, we learn how the master of the house has reached his position of destitution, coming full circle to the beginning. There follows the tail of the narrative: the sound of Krishnabai, the Kathak dancer, performing at Ganguly's stirs him back to life and moves him to go down to the music room, closed off and untouched for several years. When

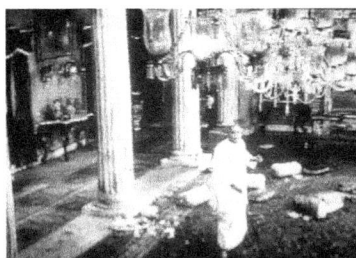 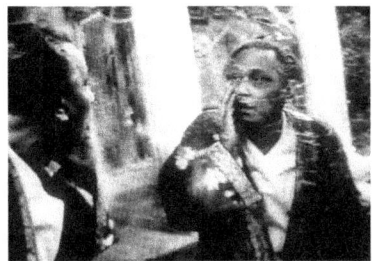

he enters, Ray uses the sight of the tinkling chandelier, of the ancestral portraits on the wall, of the dusty mirror, as the camera explores the room anew, to jolt the master into life and order his own performance by Krishnabai. The penultimate climax of the film therefore starts with this stirring of memory, the preparation of the room by one of his two remaining servants, and the performance itself, as if the room had been drained of its past and had to be refilled with music. This is a visual sequence, going from decay to life, matched by the sound of instruments tuning up, and then in full performance.

From these examples we see how the cinema can naturally weave together present and past. The achievement of Antonioni's *L'Eclisse* is to weave present and future, to realize the future in a way that invests it with a sense of atmosphere and meaning far beyond what a description of the images, a sequence of sense impressions, would suggest. At the end of the film, Vittoria and Piero, mutually attracted to each other, she on the rebound from a failed relationship, he in refuge from the pressured life of the Rome stock exchange, agree to meet in their 'usual place', which we have been shown in a previous sequence, a corner of a new suburb of Rome. It is with this understanding that the spectator is then asked to view the limpid procession of pictures, almost each containing movement of some kind, from the brisk trotting of a horse across the screen to the microscopic ants crawling along the bark of a tree-trunk. At the same time, each image is like a still photograph conveying some specific information about the physical space, the time of day or the passage of time, and in several cases echoing appearances from earlier in the film, such as the trotting horse, the pram, the water in the oil drum. We watch in the expectation that either Vittoria or Piero, or both, will appear at their meeting, that is to say we sit in anticipation of a development in the story, perhaps a climax of some kind between the two, a row leading to a break-up, or a passionate clinch after their tentative moves. Antonioni eschews such melodrama in favour of something apparently empty, but which in fact is its own climax, made dramatic by being unexpected, and made terrifying by being undesired, the fact that Vittoria and Piero can only choose an unmotivated separation, only social emptiness. And this emptiness is underscored by being linked to a larger spatial and physical emptiness, because the setting is the new planned architecture – building, roads, trees – of EUR, the suburb to the south of Rome begun in 1935 by Mussolini, and developed after the war. Gianni di Venanzo's cinematography brings out the visual qualities of the place in verticals and horizontals, in textures, in the evening sun whose Mediterranean light lends a *douceur* to all things. And yet the mood is one of spiritual terror. The final image is of a street lamp that has come on, its harsh light dominating the screen and symbolizing the eclipse of the title, which Antonioni inverts: instead of light obscured by a dark object, the falling darkness is obliterated in the glare of artificial light.

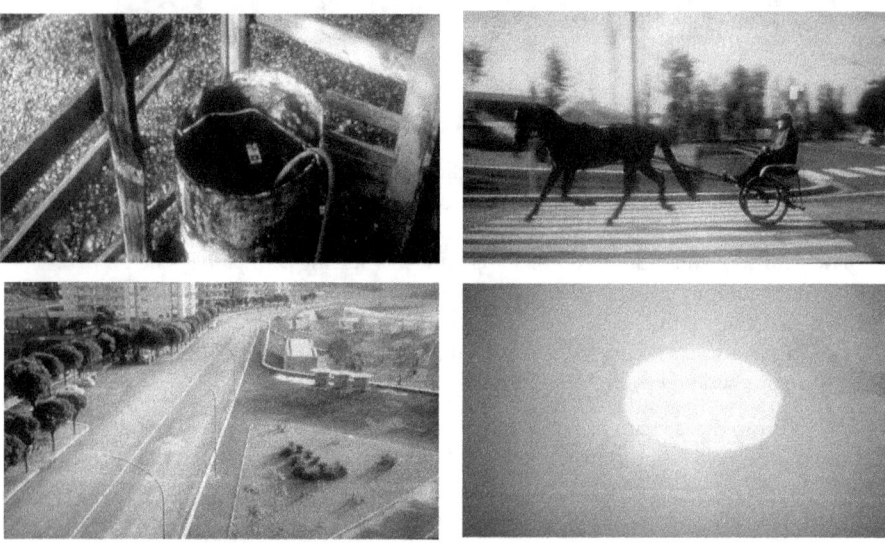

Only the cinema can give the necessary precision to this picture: the cumulative passage of images and their echo of earlier moments in the film take the sequence far beyond a series of photographs; words would risk getting bogged down in describing the two levels of ordinary appearance and extraordinary overtone. For once cinema's literalness allows the act of transcending imagination, as the greatest written poetry so often achieves. 'Fled is that music' (from the last line of Keats's 'Ode to a Nightingale') aptly describes the sequence's meaning.

Can one therefore speak of a conditional cinema? *L'Eclisse* has a protasis (the 'if' clause in a conditional sentence) – "if Vittoria and Piero are characterized as these sort of people in this sort of setting" – then the apodosis (the main clause in a conditional sentence) – "they break their promise to meet up" – is the seven-minute sequence that completes the film. Although as a main clause on its own it is banal, as the second half of a sentence beginning with 'if', it gains in excitement, but requires the preceding 115 minutes to create its potency. For a moment in the narrative the spectator desires a happy ending, a resolution of the tension in the relationship between the two lovers, but when it dawns that the apodosis is coming to pass – they will not meet up – a sense of the inevitability of this conclusion replaces the initial feeling of bewilderment. On the face of it we are watching a conditional narrative, but it turns out to be closed. Genuine conditional cinema on the other hand explores narrative openness.

So, the third type of narrative is a literal conditional cinema. *The Terminator* was released in 1984, a science-fiction story set in the present with flash forwards to the future (alternatively, set in the future but mostly taking place in the present). The wicked machines of the future, opposed by an underground movement of freedom fighters, use time travel to send back a 'terminator' to kill the woman who is to be the mother of the virtuous leader of the freedom fighters; at the same time the freedom fighters send a 'protector' back to prevent this happening. The idea is, 'If such and such can be prevented from happening in the past, then this would not be happening now.' This simple idea is played for thrills and for suspense: will our hero be saved, even though he's not been born yet? This is the realm of pure speculation: "Suppose George III, King of England, had said to himself, 'If only George Washington had never been born, there would be no rebellion in the colonies, so troublesome to the Empire,' and then instructed his villainous generals to send someone back in time to erase Washington's mother before his birth, and suppose the colonists had sent their own freedom fighter back in time to prevent this happening." This realm of fantasy starts to take on absurd trappings, suggesting time travel is a better device for comedy than the portentous.

The same thought seems to have occurred to the makers of the *Back to the Future* trilogy, the first of which was made very close in time to the first of the *Terminator* series. The trilogy shifts between 1985 and 1955 in part one, 1985, 2015 and the 1950s in part two, and 1985 and 1885 in part three. The plot hinges therefore on a number of hypotheses cast in a comic light: when he goes back to 1955, Marty is faced with the disturbing prospect of not being born; in part two the story hinges on how he prevents Biff Tannen becoming richer still and despoiling the home town by using knowledge of sports results in the future to make himself rich and powerful; and then in part three, Marty goes back to the old West of 1885 to ensure that Doc survives, and thus their future adventures can take place. In this context, the comic figure of Doc is more enduring than the heartless cyborgs of the *Terminator* series, and the technology of a time-travelling DeLorean car is more subversive than the picture of machines taking over the planet. The film is in tune not just with the home-town picture of Frank Capra's *It's A Wonderful Life* (1946) in which Clarence the Angel uses the apodosis of loss that flows from the protasis of Stewart's committing suicide in order to prevent it, but also with the subversive comedy of Preston Sturges' *Unfaithfully Yours* (1948): the conductor imagines the murder of his wife for (imagined) infidelity, but his murderous thoughts are thrown into disarray by the comic incompetence of his attempts to realize them.

It is the comic possibilities of 'What if?' cinema (and its commercial success in the *Back to the Future* and *Terminator* series) that created the brilliant premise of *Groundhog Day* – what if you woke up anew each day at the same time in the same place, with a choice before you of how you were going to conduct it? Given a second chance, what would you do differently? Given an umpteenth chance, how would you seek to escape from the tedium of yourself and your limitations? The film is at first anarchic, faced with all the possible variations that can be played on a theme, but becomes serious: it could be heading for the territory of Samuel Beckett's 'Waiting for Godot', of Vladimir and Estragon stuck in time as it were, but for the sake of happiness, it chooses to become moral: only by becoming a 'better person' can Phil Connors climb out of the vicious circle he finds himself in. It is thus a film about the exercise of free will, American in its optimism on that score (against the pessimism of Beckett's stripped-down despair), and giving us a version of what Purgatory might look like, metamorphosing ourselves from sinful to virtuous in preparation for entry into Paradise.

Yet it can be tragic. In the psychological thriller, *The Woman in the Fifth* (2011), the director, Pawel Pawlikowski, leaves the viewer adrift as to whether the film is a realistic account of Tom's life – full of puzzles, impossibility even – or a paranoid construct of his imagination, whether as a result of mental illness, or from the narrative of the new novel squirrelling destructively away in his head. The 'what if' element derives from what he imagines, except that it is never signalled as such so that it is impossible to reach the objective truth. For this version of time's labyrinth there is no way out, whether for Tom or the viewer. Film is good at dreams – and nightmares too.

REPEATED ACTION

The Woman in the Fifth reflects the bleak despair of modernist literature, Kafka-esque, unredeemed, which found a fertile labyrinth in the idea of repeated action. If you take this idea but deny the option of a moral way out, then you end up with a film like Akira Kurosawa's *Rashomon*. This is the story of the murder of a samurai and the rape of his wife by a bandit in the forest, a story that gets thoroughly entangled in the various variations enacted in the forest, told in court, and retold by the three characters of woodcutter, commoner and priest, who reflect on the crime at a city gate, dressed in tatters and sheltering from the rain – a stage-set image of Japan in time of war that contrasts with but echoes the documentary depiction of a ruined Berlin in Rossellini's *Germany Year Zero*. The film unfolds as a series of flashbacks recounting the same event but contradicting each other, as if the truth of what happened can never be definitively told, as if it were impossible to escape the condition of deceit. It works by using the same setting and the same persons in the same clothes to vary the events. The contradictions become a visual conundrum. [This tangle is expertly analysed by Fleishman.]

Rashomon was made in 1951 in the shadow of Japan's defeat in the war, and reflects a seriousness about who is to blame: who is guilty? Or, more to the point, who is not guilty? Two more recent versions of the narrative structure – *Run Lola Run* by Tom Tykwer and Zhang Yimou's *Hero* – exist in the territory of fantasy. *Hero* recalls *Rashomon* in its retelling of stories in front of an audience, the King of Qin, who then reinterprets them for us. The conditional element (what if Nameless is not telling the whole truth?) becomes a key to the ending of the film. The audience needs their critical faculties to assess the versions. A similar demand is made in *Run Lola Run*: Lola must find 100,000 marks if she is to save her boyfriend Manni, who has managed to lose 100,000 marks he is delivering to the master criminal running a smuggling ring, and who must die unless he can deliver them. There then follow three versions of how Lola tries to get the money, the third of which involves winning 100,000 marks in a casino. Thus Lola saves Manni and, in a satisfying twist, they recover the original 100,000 that was stolen (although there is something dissatisfying in the fact that the inept Manni does not deserve the resourceful Lola). A similar relentlessness – Lola pounds the streets of Berlin in tune with the techno soundtrack – informs the superficiality of the story, but Tykwer makes it a platform for something cleverer: in the three versions, we keep encountering the same characters and learn more about them each time, as if the three stories were unpeeling them.

Run Lola Run inhabits a post-Cold War emptiness: the modern condition is concerned not with political systems, but with how we gain money and how we spend it. This narrative cleverness is also used in the romantic comedy *Sliding Doors* which shows in its first half how Helen's life develops following her catching the underground train in time, while in the second she misses the train with the result that her life turns out very differently. The idea has been plagiarized from Kieślowski's remarkable *Blind Chance*, made less than twenty years earlier, which provides a context to the rise of the Solidarity trade union which precipitated the end of Soviet communism in Poland. In this case there are three versions of the story and they reflect much more serious options for the main protagonist, Witek. All three start with him running for a train. In the first, he just catches it and ends up joining the Communist party where he is brought face to face with the dishonesty required to be a good Communist. In the second and third, he just misses the train: in the second scenario he becomes a member of the opposition to the Communist regime, while in the third, he becomes a doctor and settles down to the peaceful life, but when he takes a plane flight abroad, he dies in a mid-air explosion. The running for the train is followed in each case by Witek taking a decision as to his future. The film plays with the idea of chance and fate being complimentary images of each other: in the third story, in fact, chance and fate clash, for it is chance that Witek dies in the plane explosion, but it is suggested as well that it is his destiny, a moral judgement of a kind on the choices he has made. In the first two, it is chance that determines wheth-

BLIND CHANCE: three outcomes

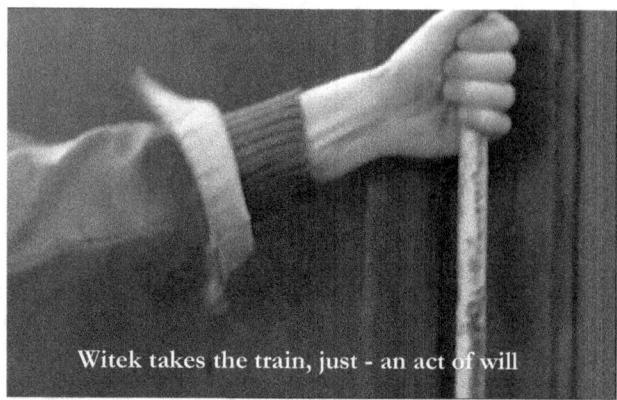

Witek takes the train, just - an act of will

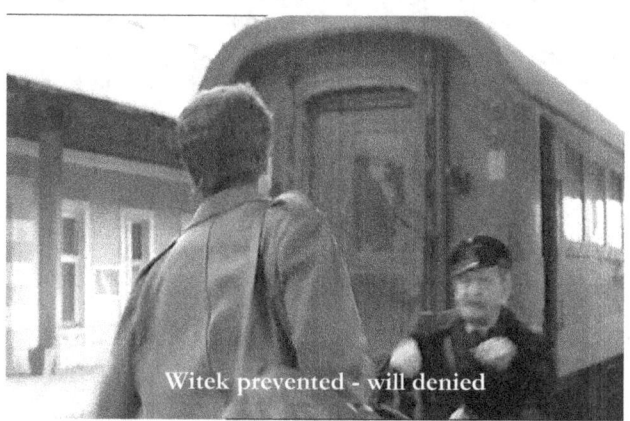

Witek prevented - will denied

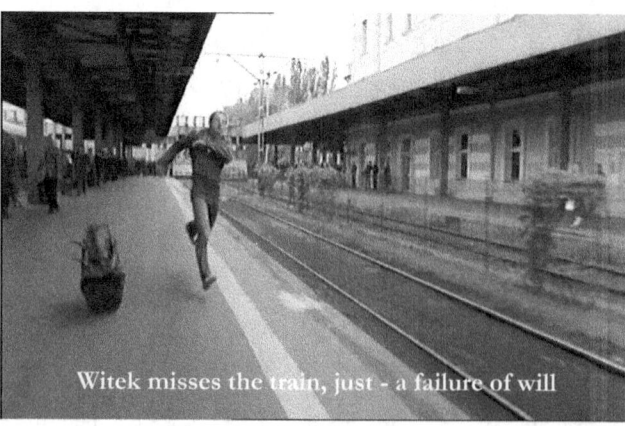

Witek misses the train, just - a failure of will

er he becomes a Communist or a dissident; once this occurs, it is fate, or the historical circumstances in which Witek finds himself, that determine how he is to behave. Witek's character remains the same in each story as a decent, likeable young citizen, but our perception of him in the first story is overtaken by how we perceive him in the second and third. Kieślowski must have juggled with the question of which order to show them in. He liked stories that 'hinge' and thereby intrigue, even discomfort the spectator: in the two best-known episodes in *Dekalog*, we feel repulsed at the young man voyeuristically gazing at the woman in the flat opposite (*Dekalog 6* – also known as *A Short Film about Love*), or at the young punk murdering the taxi driver (*Dekalog 5* – also known as *A Short Film about Killing*), only in the second half of each film to sympathize with the young man who has fallen in love with Magda on whom he has been spying, and with the murderer as he is taken to be hanged by the state. So, in *Blind Chance*, should he show Witek becoming a communist in the first story, then an oppositionist in the second – or the other way round? For the order affects how we judge Witek: the second version allows us to judge him more comfortably as a good person, not just decent but right-thinking, only for the third version to discomfort us again: for the choice of career as an uncommitted doctor may mean he contributes to society at one level, but fails to do so at a deeper one. Because in each story we see and hear Witek as real human flesh and blood on screen, the distance between the three versions of his character is all the more stark than it would be in a written version.

SO WHAT?

When Tarkovsky conceived of a life being filmed from beginning to end, elements from which are then spliced together to give the life significance, he makes use of two essences of the cinema. First, it is an art in which duration is a vital building block. Secondly, this element of linearity in time, going from point A to point B in time, can be manipulated.

Film shares the durational element with music: both put an audience in a room, the film or music begins, and the audience stays to the end (since it takes a particular act of willpower to abandon the music or film unfolding before them). If written literature is derived from the public art of story-telling, then it too was once a durational art: once the story-teller started, the audience felt a collective compulsion to listen to the end. However, in its written form, when the reader can take up or abandon the book at any point without losing the thread, or go back to check a particular passage, narrative is experienced in portions, for continuous reading requires great concentration and can dull inattentive readers to the virtues of what they read, whereas resuming a book can sometimes renew appreciation – in two ways: the novelty is renewed, and in the interval between reading we allow the mind to absorb what has been read so far. Films of narrative could develop in the same way as a result of being able to be consumed privately on a dvd, establishing an intimate link between artwork and spectator in which a pause in the film, or abandoning it altogether, is easy. Indeed the benefits of reading a book and then returning to it can now be extended to filmed narrative: appreciation of the work can be renewed.

Music on the other hand, despite its availability away from the concert platform in all sorts of media, surely needs to be absorbed in a single act of attention. As the musical argument of a symphony unfolds, to abandon it in the middle risks the attention being broken, the listener's absorption being diluted. However, this can be true as well of filmed narrative and even of literary narrative. I have concentrated in this essay on films that can be watched at a single sitting and given the necessary attention to appreciate their manipulation of time. 'Attention' may be too mild a word: the ability of film experienced in the cinema to hypnotise the spectator by obliterating all surroundings can mean that time is experienced as suspended, that awareness of clock time is destroyed.

Such temporal dislocation may come from the story being so absorbing. But it can also be an aspect of a visual fascination trumping the narrative, as is the case with *Un Chien Andalou* and *Last Year in Marienbad*. In the latter, as already explained, the narrative intrigue comes not from the story (which is exasperating) but from the stylishness of its world and the sense of being in a labyrinth. *Un Chien Andalou* also creates a time labyrinth but it does so in satirical fashion, with the film being short enough to avoid encroaching on the area of being painful to watch. But this comic element (the tango element) sits side-by-side with the metaphors of desire (the 'Liebestod' element): the man gazing at the moon, the blood congealing on the face, the woman at first resisting then yielding, the hand covered in ants mesmerising the man. To this ingredient is added shock and strangeness: the shock of the eyeball sliced, the strangeness of hair in the armpit becoming a spiny sea urchin.

To take a more downmarket example, the *Back to the Future* trilogy, which has already been mentioned as an example of 'what if?' cinema, positively revels in the way it shifts backwards and forwards in time. The spatial centre of the film is the small town of Hill Valley, the site where the main characters – Doc, Marty and Biff – encounter each other. In part one, the clock tower is at the centre of a caricature of a suspense sequence, with vertical shots exaggerating visual space, and time being seen as stretched out as the long hand on the clock approaches 10.04 p.m., when Marty knows that it will be struck by lightning and Doc proposes to harness that electrical energy to send the DeLorean back into the future. An understanding of its role in part one then is necessary to invest the construction of the clock tower, and the dance to mark the starting of the clock, with more significance than merely a small-town ritual. Its witticisms – the knowledge in 1955 that Ronald Reagan would become president, the DeLorean car as a time machine – are trumped by the way the three films hinge their drama on the consequences of 'disrupting the space-time continuum', something that films do all the time. The potential darkness of manipulating our past to change the future is overcome by American lightness, Doc's blithe assertion that the future "is what you make of it".

If it is the case that cinema's weakness is an inability to match the way literature can imagine the interior life of people, could 'what if?' film open up new ways of exploring thought and feeling? *Blind Chance* is suggestive. Because the three parts are shot as observed narrative, the film does not characterise the episodes as Witek's own projections of what he might do with his life. But it would surely be possible to use a similar set of circumstances to allow characters to imagine for themselves how they might behave in a particular situation, whether as a flashback to a past event in which they imagine different responses (as in hindsight we can say to ourselves, "I wish I had done that differently") or in the wish to respond to a set of circumstances that might arise in the future, where we think to ourselves, "If that happens, I'm going to do this." And then such future behaviour can be imagined differently when someone says to us, "Well, if you do that, such and such will happen, not what you think will happen and want to happen." These ideas bring us to how narrative film handles or might handle 'interiority' but before coming to this, a final reflection can be made about the filmic manipulation of time that takes us back to the beginning of this chapter and reference to the way cinema began to float free from the conventions of literary and theatrical narrative by the use of cross-cutting. Such parallel narratives were always resolved by the protagonists in each parallel story coming together or in the way the parallel stories were linked to each other in terms of narrative. This has now been taken to a very sophisticated level in Altman's *Short Cuts*, which weaves some eleven stories (although it is hard to count them as they begin to mesh with each other) to satirize the nature of human relationships – whether in marriage or out of it, in the family or out of it, whether as a couple or single. As the different stories unfold in a bravura composition using intercutting to intrigue the audience without losing them, connections across them begin to be made, thickening the portrait, whether one takes it of general humanity, or merely of Los Angeles society to which special rules apply (although judging for example by Altman's other films, such as *Nashville, Pret-à-porter* and *Gosford Park*, all of which use his trademark of narrating a story through an ensemble of characters, they do not).

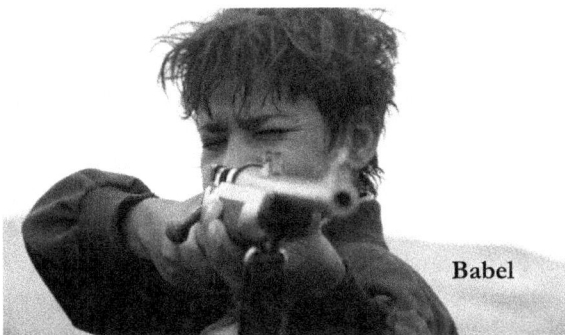

Babel

The same strategy is used by Iñárritu (as director) and Arriaga (as screenwriter) in their loose trilogy of films (*Amores Perros, 21 Grams, Babel*) but is characterized by much greater spatial boldness. The first two films interwove stories of different people inhabiting the same city, while in *Babel* three contemporaneous stories feature different characters in three different parts of the globe: California/ Mexico, Morocco and Japan. The connections between the three stories are revealed glancingly as they progress, and what really links the three situations is the highly strung nature of the modern world, where the pursuit of pleasure – tourism in Morocco/a wedding party in Mexico/the seeking of sexual satisfaction in Japan – leads to tragic or near-tragic outcomes. This audacious geography reflects the globalized nature of society. What is more this narrative strategy in using the globe to make a big statement about human behaviour neatly takes us back to Griffith's *Intolerance*, discussed at the beginning of this chapter, which is similarly audacious in its use of time, interweaving four stories from very different periods of history in order to make a large point about the consistency of human behaviour. As the cinema begins to realize the possibilities of huge narratives, an idea explored in the final chapter, this idea will surely be given a new dimension.

The manipulation of time in the cinema is therefore rich in possibilities, which perhaps film-makers have only begun to exploit in the first century of the cinema. These narrative strategies can be used to counterpoint realism with fantasy, tragedy with comedy, the surface of daily life with a moral or metaphysical dimension. They have formal structures but they are used as ways to reinvent storytelling. Furthermore, in the experimental arena, unconstrained by the straitjacket of the 90/120-minute feature, film-makers have explored the more formal possibilities yet of treating time in the cinema. These are covered in the next chapter.

8   THE MÉLIÈS WAY

Film, like music, has mathematics built into it. Think of the way the height and width of the frame have proportion, which has varied over cinema's history. Think of the way it uses individual images run at speed in order to capitalize on the capacity of the human brain to achieve persistence of vision and thus cinematic motion: twenty-four images per second does the trick. A film-maker of a formalist bent can find fruitful stratagems to create with these tools, and manipulation of time becomes less to do with manipulation of meaning through successive shots and more to do with manipulation of form, the way we perceive more than what we perceive.

Right from cinema's year one, there was a divide between a cinema of observation and a cinema of manipulation. By a nice symmetry, within a year of the use of the camera by the Lumière Brothers to observe the world around them, Méliès the magician saw the camera as a means of cutting up and reassembling reality for magical effects. Auguste and Louis Lumière saw the possibilities for mimicking real-time; Georges Méliès saw the possibilities for illusion, of showing that the impossible had occurred, in effect reinventing what we see. The Lumières were fascinated by the camera as machine, Méliès by the film strip as a series of still frames which could be magicked into movement. In honour of their contemporary and fellow countryman, Marcel Proust, whose promenades along Swann's Way and the Guermantes' Way were used as metaphors for the course of his adult life, these two poles of film aesthetics may be described as the Lumière Way and the Méliès Way.

When in the New-Frontier America of the early 1960s, a cult of the new and experimental found heroism in the creative individual, a cultural movement that had its roots in the previous decade especially among the Abstract Expressionist painters, a different kind of film-making from that of Hollywood rose to the surface, one that strove to map quite different territory, both in subject matter and method. At the centre of this movement was Stan Brakhage, who although only twenty-seven in 1960 had made several short films, the first in 1953 (when he was only twenty). A particular milestone in his development was *The Wonder Ring* (1955), in which he used documentary to transform mundane steel structures (the Third Avenue elevated railway in New York) into patterns of sunlight and shadow, in effect a celebration of light, to transform a banal reality into a place of wonder. The light flashing through the window frames shuttling through the station became a metaphor for the projector light flashing through the celluloid frames. The film also eliminated depth in the image or 'de-emphasized' perspective [Arthur p.43] and the use of this tactic began to mark Brakhage's retreat from Western perspective, which is another link with the Méliès Way, at least in Brakhage's eyes. In his lecture on Méliès from 1970 he claimed that Méliès "was obsessed to attack the whole of Western painterly trappings – Renaissance perspective in itself: he therefore began to conceive his movie scenes as a series of movable 'flats', offering a minimal 'vanishing point' and maximal relationship to the screen against which they would be projected [Brakhage p.22]." *The Wonder Ring* creates a private experience seen through the mind's eye, more open on the inside in a way than to the reality on the outside. This inner vision is characterized by a nervous intensity as images merge and jump into one another, assembling the hundreds of pieces of film into a visionary whole.

All this work from the 1950s has a radically experimental feel, as if Brakhage experienced no fears in trying to reveal what the camera was capable of, now that smaller and lighter models were on the market. By the end of the 1950s, he had achieved a technical mastery of the equipment needed to make films without sound, having concluded that sound was a dispensable element of film-making. Also, he had learnt to engage with the film in its most physical form: a strip of polyester with sprocket-holes at the side, and composed of individual frames. His most radical idea, being explored by others at the time, was to think not in terms of shots but of individual frames lasting 1/24th of a second, and to explore the minimal threshold at which images on the screen registered on the spectator's consciousness. Brakhage's head was stuffed with visual ideas and personal experiences which he wanted to realize on film, while both his employment in film laboratories and his private film-making saw him bent over the editing table, handling film, seeing frames in close up, feeling the emulsion on the strip of film. Film he concluded was physical matter, an idea very consonant with contemporary American painting, for example the work of Jackson Pollock whose studio Brakhage visited as an awestruck young man. He must have been impressed by the raw intensity of Pollock's work when paint was dripped, dribbled and flung at the canvas. An interesting link can be made to the painter Francis Bacon who achieved a marvellous vitality in his handling of paint, and who contrasted texture in a photograph which "seems to go through an illustrational process" with that of a painting which "seems to come immediately onto the nervous system." [Bacon p.58.] Brakhage's empathy with Pollock's surfaces "coming onto the nervous system" is partly behind his wanting to transform observational cinema into something that would engage the optic nerve by reproducing the way his own nervous system reacted to what he saw. In defining the ability to manipulate time as one of the essential attributes of film, it is necessary not just to recognize what can be achieved in terms of narrative (as described in the previous chapter), but to grasp the ability of film to 'explode' onto the consciousness in bursts of a fraction of a second.

By 1960 Brakhage was ready to pour his learning into a big work of art, one that stepped away from his private world onto a cosmic stage. At the time, P. Adams Sitney used the neologism 'mythopoeia' to describe its ambitions: the making of myth in order to make the world anew [Brakhage 'Metaphors on Vision' introduction]. *Prelude: Dog Star Man* is in five parts. A long opening, called the Prelude (25 minutes) is a film about creation both of the world and of consciousness. Part 1 (30 minutes) is of a man struggling up a slope with an axe; Parts 2, 3 and 4 (5, 7 and 6 minutes each) complete the narrative; respectively, they feature a birth, a 'sexual daydream' and the woodman chopping at a dead tree. The man struggling up the hill is mythic in recalling Sisyphus, as his efforts seem fruitless and endless, but the film does in fact reach a climax, as he wrestles with the tree. That the man is played by Brakhage himself is an important index of his Romanticism, in which the artist is at the centre of the world, and creation is a heroic and subjective process which would not allow anyone else to play the central role. He is an artist in the mould of the Nietzschean superman, like Pollock and Bacon, whose visionary gift takes him outside conventional society and mainstream art, challenging that mainstream to follow.

The film is elemental, with the primary element being light, light shining through the transparent celluloid that creates the images, their forms and colours. Brakhage sets out to recapture that primal quality of the first appearance of the world, in swirls of colour, in half-envisioned shapes and pictures, in the rearing-up majesty of the Colorado landscape (where Brakhage was living). The seminal image is of solar flares, footage which he obtained from Boulder Observatory, the rim of the sun seen during a solar eclipse showing great globules of fire hurled into the atmosphere and falling back again. The film is therefore of public visible creation, and like the Book of Genesis in the Bible, Brakhage couples this with individual private creation. It is therefore a hymn to the nuclear family – to Brakhage himself and his wife Jane and a new-born baby – the entry into consciousness of new human life, to match the creation of the world. To see this film for the first time is to experience an epic revelation of a created universe extending from the macrocosm to the microcosm.

At the same time as Brakhage's whole-hearted journey down the Méliès Way is a journey in counterpoint, the rediscovery of the virtues of early observant cinema – the Lumière Way – by Andy Warhol, only a year or two older than Brakhage, who came to film via Pop Art. Warhol had already come to notice by the time he took up film-making, having had his first one-man show in 1962. From the beginning, like Brakhage he wanted to make cinema anew, in a way that could be described in direct opposition to Brakhage's aspirations. By running the camera uninterrupted and immobile, pointed at individuals who barely seemed to move, Warhol threw down a crude challenge to the spectator. Many hours of film were shot in this way and seen as a whole, some development of technique is discernible, as if he were reinventing the history of the cinema. This history may be summed up in the distance travelled from his first phase with films such as *Sleep* (1963), which uses a fixed camera and "shows a man sleeping for six hours. (It is actually three hours of ten-minute segments that were shot over a six-week period. Each segment is shown twice.)" [Gidal p.84.] In the next phase, Warhol added sound to the fixed camera in order to film scenarios written by Ronald Tavel, although because the sound was optically recorded directly on film during shooting, the words are, if not inaudible, certainly inexactly audible. The third phase used scenarios and were co-directed by Chuck Wein, culminating in the radical complexity of *The Chelsea Girls* (1966), a series of half-hour takes of individual portraits and conversations shot at the Chelsea Hotel in New York and made up into a 3 ½ hour film, making extensive use of the zoom lens and much of which is split-screen, i.e. showing two takes side by side, a combination of the compelling as we catch some of what is said, the frustrating because of the poor sound quality, and the impossibility of taking in two screens simultaneously. A fourth phase saw Warhol moving to a more commercial cinema by the use of colour and clear soundtracks. The complete trajectory is a version in miniature of cinema's development: fixed images/black-and-white/no sound through to camera movement/edited images/colour/sound.

Both Brakhage's and Warhol's films contain the possibilities of a different kind of cinema from the commercial narrative film. Although this led to a reaction from other experimental film-makers against the unbounded quality of the films in order to reassert a classical rigour in the way their own films were structured and assembled, it is hard to imagine Michael Snow's *Wavelength* (1967) and Hollis Frampton's *Zorns Lemma* (1972) without them, to take two classics of the avant-garde film. In their own way they synthesized the 'spiritual' or metaphysical impulse implicit in Brakhage's films and the cool fascination with humanity in Warhol's world.

While the conventional description of *Wavelength*, that it is a zoom from one end of a room to another, makes it sound as if nothing happens, in fact it is constantly giving us new information and things <u>do</u> happen. Most obviously, there are four incidents in the film: first of all, two people move a bookcase into the room; secondly, two women enter, and while one sits on the prominent yellow chair at the end of the room, the other stands by the window and plays the Beatles song 'Strawberry Fields'. The first woman then leaves, and at the end of the song, the other one leaves; thirdly, in one of the night periods, a man staggers into the room at the bottom of the frame (the zoom is now closing in on the window), and falls to the floor; fourthly, again at night, a woman enters and uses the phone to tell someone that there is someone lying on the floor; "What shall I do?" she says and then leaves. This elliptical and unexplained narrative might be thought to be the content of the film, but it is overwhelmed by the 'narrative' of the zoom in space. The room itself is sparsely furnished, and uncarpeted. The film starts in daylight, then the day becomes night, and then it is daylight again, but only as long as the windows are visible in the frame, for when they pass out of our visibility, the film's timeframe begins to vanish completely.

The soundtrack is very important in cementing the film into a whole. For the first fifth of the film, we hear traffic outside the window. It is then taken over by an electronic sine wave that starts at 50 cycles and increases to 12,000 cycles over the bulk of the film, although right at the end it disintegrates into a rising and falling sound. It is this decelerated crescendo that gives tension, for you think it is building to a climax, that it cannot get any higher or harsher, but then it does and you never get to a climax. It is the sound that provides the film's real minimalism, since compared to the sound the image is very impure. Not only does the film have the series of incidents described, but it changes colour and flickers, and every now and then images appear in superimposition as a result of the readjustment of the camera as new spools of film are loaded:

the camera has in effect taken a small step backwards and that bit of the zoom has to be repeated.

If the sound does not in the end obtain closure, the image does. At the beginning of the film we remark (if we have seen the film before) on the pictures pinned to the wall between the windows, and that we cannot decipher them, i.e. they are out of our mental focus. Tension is given at the end by the way the camera moves closer to them so that we can start to decipher them. One image eludes decipherment, a second is of Michael Snow's walking woman silhouette (a signature image from his work as a sculptor), the third is the image that might give meaning to the whole as it is the one on which the camera finally rests: it shows a surface, possibly of water, possibly of a desert, possibly of the moon. We assume it is probably water (hence the film's title) and in the closing minute or two, the showing of this picture, bleeding off the frame, as a still photograph, takes over from the zoom. It has its own emptiness, but also its own mystery.

Like *The Wonder Ring*, Snow starts with something documentary – a room, especially the yellow chair, and the traffic audible through the windows; we can even make out the store signs above the shops over the road – but then moves to reflect on the photographic process in its clever use of the negative and positive: in the daylight scenes, the windows are light, while the room is comparatively dark; but at night, the room is light, while the windows are dark. Ultimately, the film is a metaphysical experience. It is a film about perception, and demands a different kind of perception from what we are used to. It takes the long-attention span cinema of Warhol, and gives it a philosophical dimension. We are not just witnessing everyday reality but scrutinising it, interrogating it. It is appropriate that the film concludes with the image on the wall. This has its own air of intrigue (like the narrative incidents) but this part of the process is also a metaphor for perception. When like the prisoners in the cave in Plato's *Republic* we emerge from darkness into light, can we interpret the new reality beyond the reality we are used to? Is there another existence more eternal than the mere human life-span?

Wavelength takes the Lumière Way to new extremes, spilling the act of observation into the area of forced attention that metamorphoses into undisturbed contemplation. Hollis Frampton who was a film-maker himself when he played a small part in *Wavelength*, was stimulated by the film, and, as we shall see, the works of Brakhage as well, to create his own major statement a year or two later in *Zorns Lemma*, which poses the same questions about how the mind engages with what it sees on the screen in front of it. This is a sixty-minute film in three parts. The first, quite short, consists of a black screen while on the soundtrack a woman recites from an alphabetical primer, as if reading to a child. It puts us on our mettle for part two, which requires immense concentration: Frampton strings together shots of words captured in the everyday world in alphabetical order of their initial letter, and runs through that alphabet again and again, while finding new words drawn from the signs around him in the street, the alphabet of the Bay State Primer used in part one made demotic image in part two. The game then truly begins because the spectator quickly realizes that words beginning with particular letters are being replaced by images.

Wanda Bershen describes this section as follows: "Section II (47 minutes, 9 seconds) begins with a silent run through a 24-letter Roman alphabet (no J or V) composed of large silver letters in relief on a black field. A word beginning with letter 'A' (in this case the word is 'a') appears, and is followed by a word beginning with 'B', and so on through the alphabet at a speed of one second per letter-word. The words all occur in the urban environment, on store fronts and other kinds of signs and notices. Each run through the alphabet preserves the same rhythm while the words and their contexts vary: on the 5th round the letter 'X' is replaced by a shot of a bonfire at night. On the 7th round 'Z' is replaced by an ocean wave advancing and receding down the beach, and on the 12th round a horizontally trucking shot of sea grasses blowing in the wind replaces the letter 'Y'. The film proceeds with the gradual replacement of each alphabet-word by an image until at the end of the section the final run-through is composed entirely of these replacement images." [Bershen pp.42-3.]

The concentration comes not just from following where Frampton is so playfully leading us, but also from the fact that each image lasts one second – so in this section of the film, 47 minutes and 9 seconds long, there are 60 images in each minute, making a total of some 2,900 images. While these 2,900 images are separate, there are multiple repetitions allowing us to cling onto how the formula is working itself out, like some mathematical theorem. Herein lies its sophistication, as it offers us the opportunity to participate in the structure of the film, to follow the argument, to recognize what is happening in advance of it happening: to realize that ultimately all the words will be replaced by images, and that as we watch we can learn to memorize the sequence of images, as if we were learning a melody, and learn to anticipate how the film might change as if we were taken up in a game.

The third part, eleven minutes long, shows a couple walking away from the camera across a snowy field, into the woods at the other side and out of sight. It is a literal let-down, letting our eyes down to rest after the relentless sequence of part two, and an anti-climax too: after the triumphant climax of all the filmed words in part two being replaced by images signifying reality in a quite different way from words, we are faced with a virtually static image of virtually no meaning. The soundtrack comes back into play as it did in part one. Six voices recite a text about light written in the thirteenth century by Bishop Grosseteste, but the atomizing of the text into its separate words prevents us from recognizing the shape of sentences and paragraphs through the intonations and inflections of a single voice. We are in effect denied the chance to participate in assembling the text's meaning in our own minds, just opposite to the way part two encouraged us to participate. The film therefore trickles away, as if the excitement of the central section must be followed by stasis, an intellectual exercise without meaning, an emptiness that constitutes a rejection almost of what has gone before. For what has gone before is a description in its way of the whole world, or what Frampton sees around him, in essence an autobiography.

Initially, Frampton was fascinated by poetry, but a polymathic streak in him led him via sculpture to photography and film, the realm of images, and only with films did he find the voice he was looking for, that gave adequate scope to his interest in words and in pictures, and to his erudition. An essay of his on the photographs of Paul Strand [Frampton 'Meditations' p.57] ends with a quotation from Jorge Luis Borges: "Through the years, a man peoples a space with images of provinces, kingdoms, mountains, bays, ships, islands, fishes, rooms, tools, stars, horses, and people. Shortly before his death, he discovers that the patient labyrinth of lines traces the image of his own face." At first sight, Borges is the perfect writer for Frampton: his elegant description, in 'The Library of Babel', of the infinite library as the labyrinth in which humans find themselves finds its echo in *Zorns Lemma*. But there is also in Frampton a humorous overtone: as he put it, "*Zorns Lemma* . . . is an optimistic work, it skips happily up the street, reciting the alphabet and counting [Frampton interview p.72]." More than that, he asks the spectator to join in, to participate in discovering a trajectory. To quote from his Strand essay again: "The ambition of this activity can amount to nothing less than the systematic recording of the whole visible world, with a view to its entire comprehension." This optimism, if it can be called that, finds its echo less in Borges than in JS Bach's 'Goldberg Variations', a piece which works the bass harmonies of a sarabande in thirty variations, marked by increasing elaboration, nine canons with the musical interval in each one taken from unison to 'alla ottava' exactly spaced through the work, creating an encyclopaedic effect and demanding no less concentration than *Zorns Lemma* in order to comprehend its structure.

The idea of the series appealed deeply to Frampton. Hence too his admiration for Eadward Muybridge whose heroic and obsessive venture in 'Animals in Motion' to use the camera to record movement – by animals and by humans – has exercised such fascination in the twentieth century. This demystification has revealed how inventive the eye linked to the brain is, the brain elaborating the data that sight gives us [as Paul Valéry commented on what the photographs proved, quoted by Frampton in 'Eadward Muybridge' p.51]. From a scientific point-of-view Muybridge's fame relates to the fact that his photographs settled the question of whether a horse in motion ever had all its hooves off the ground, but from an artistic point of view his multiple series not only shed light on all manner of movement but opened up new ways of seeing movement. And there is a larger impact, which the photograph in general makes, especially the photography of the first hundred years, that seems particularly to have engaged Frampton, in that the still camera produces statements of what the world looks like.

Frampton carried that preoccupation into his films. For example, *Lemon* (1969) shows a lemon in close-up with a light slowly moving over it for the length of the film (7½ minutes). As we gaze at it, we may "stay the eye" on it as a lemon, or "through it pass", to use phrases taken from George Herbert's poem 'The Elixir', and see the moon in its phases: we elaborate the data that sight gives us. Part two of *Zorns Lemma* then can be interpreted as a much more elaborate exercise in how a series of sense data can be perceived merely as such or, to make them much more interesting, interpreted as they are perceived in order to create our own encyclopaedia. To spice it up, Frampton chooses not to make each image last say five seconds, making this 47-minute section five times as long, but by confining the images to one second each to put the spectator to work, barraged by this relentless succession, the turbulence of which turns out to be illusory because while virtually none of the images is completely still (it is true that a static tree in a snowy landscape does get included), we perceive them like frozen photographs to which the motion-picture camera/projector has given the illusion of movement. For some of his films Frampton looked in the direction of the Lumières – for example, in *Lemon,* and in his later *Magellan: Drafts and Fragments,* which has been described as remaking "the cinema of the Lumières in fifty-one 1-minute films" [from entry for Hollis Frampton in Wikipedia]. But in the second part of *Zorns Lemma,* he works firmly in Méliès territory, assembling the observed but dismembered images into some magical construction. It is striking how this endeavour harmonises, mysteriously in its way, with what Brakhage was doing in his films. Frampton's films may feel different: cool, rigorous, methodical, at root classical, against the warm, free-flowing romanticism of Brakhage, but the record of a conversation between them shows a remarkable meeting of minds [Brakhage/Frampton in 'Artforum'].

While Frampton's autobiography has to be excavated from *Zorns Lemma,* in Brakhage's films, it is right on the surface: Stan and Jane's children, Stan and Jane making love, the death of their dog, Jane giving birth, all very private subjects, and then more private still, Brakhage pouring his 'closed-eye visions' onto film, about which he continued to speak throughout his life in an autobiographical fashion. Take *Rage Net,* a short film of fifty-two seconds made in 1988, one of the many hand-painted films he made. The images are pure abstraction, using the strong light from the projector to intensify the colours on the screen. The patterns are smears, jagged marks, blotches etc. made stained-glass vivid by their colour, by the vigour of the mark-making, and above all by the fact that they are made frame by frame so that this tiny film contains over 1200 images in all (52 seconds, 24 frames a second). This is sufficient in itself, but Brakhage, when asked, spoke of the film as a result of the divorce he was going through at the time, a meditation upon rage "rather than being trapped psychologically by rage". None of this seems relevant to an appreciation of the film, although these extraneous facts and comments help in stringing together a narrative for the huge corpus of films Brakhage left behind, almost 400 in total by the time he died in 2003. While some of these are very short (the shortest is nine seconds long), their closely edited texture and the large amount of handmade film indicate a truly heroic level of effort. They <u>seem</u> to be all inspiration, but are also in large measure the result of perspiration.

And yet inspiration is a key factor in Brakhage's oeuvre, with its explicit origin in the Latin for 'to breathe' ('spirare') – making films gave Brakhage oxygen – but implicitly too, for his films celebrate the 'breath of life', and suggest some supernatural 'spirit' as his creative source. Thus, in describing one of his most famous films, *Mothlight,* Brakhage spoke in a letter to Robert Kelly how it came into being as "the film's simple passage through me" [Brakhage to Kelly in 'Metaphors']. He liked also to refer to the Muses, which I suspect he did in no casual sense, but as a proper way of speaking of himself, or more exactly his eye collaborating with the mind as creator: "I became instrument for the passage of inner vision, thru all my sensibilities, into its external form." [Brakhage to Sitney in 'Metaphors'.] As Socrates puts it in Plato's 'Ion': "In like manner the Muse first of all inspires men herself; and from these inspired persons a chain of other persons is suspended, who take the inspiration. For all good poets, epic as well as lyric, compose their beautiful poems not by art, but because they are inspired and possessed. . . . For the poet is a light and a winged and holy thing, and there is no intervention in him until he has been inspired and is out of his senses, and the mind is no longer in him"[Plato, 'Ion' 533d-534b, trs B. Jowett].

The excitement of the process of making *Mothlight* gives his description of it an unusual tension, of how in a situation of economic desperation for him personally, the sight of a kamikaze moth meeting its end in the candle flame gave the idea of sticking moth's wings, body fragments, leaves, grasses and petals in between strips of transparent film and then running them through the printer, creating a film in the cheapest possible manner, cruellest necessity mothering profoundest inspiration. Technical problems then became an obstacle, because these strips were destabilising the printer, until Brakhage had the idea of interspersing them with plain leader which allowed the printer to adjust periodically in the film's rollercoaster passage through the printing gate. The resultant material could then be edited to make a 3¼-minute masterpiece, a hymn to the microcosm of nature: "What is the moth that thou art mindful of him?" Now that the film is on dvd [included in *By Brakhage: an anthology* in The Criterion Collection (USA) 2003], it can be watched slowed down, in order to admire the detail, just as the film strip when reproduced in photographs gives some idea of the marvellous intricacies of the image. Yet - like *Zorns Lemma* - it needs to be watched at twenty-four frames per second, so that the images tear through the brain and explode against each other. This freneticism re-creates out of tranquillity the purest participation in the wonders of the film.

For Brakhage, the imagination is an internal realm of the mind, not an externality, and his life was spent in celebrating this fact. In recognition that an extraordinary body of work was being created in the cinema, in 1963 the magazine Film Culture published an interview with Brakhage and an assemblage of his writings, statements and letters in 'Metaphors on Vision', in which he expounded his call for a new visionary cinema. The opening paragraphs, written on the threshold of his creative maturity, bring to mind the impassioned prose of Thomas Traherne in their extolling of the virtue of vision before the advent of the Word. 'Silence' is a vital part of appreciating the films (not that all his films are silent but the majority are), best appreciated accompanied by the sound of the projector in the room providing a rolling thunder, an elemental background to the act of visual perception.

It was an accident of birth that seems to have given him a different eyesight from the rest of humanity. In an interview published in 1973, he spoke of his childhood as a time when "I'm not sharing the world of vision that I'm supposed to in order to exist in the general air with all the people around me." [Brakhage/Frampton p.74. At the beginning of this interview Brakhage talks about his childhood, "when the glasses . . . were a solid manifestation of my own removal from everything around me" (p. 73). Release from this isolation came with throwing away his glasses.] In an interview towards the end of his life Brakhage continued to maintain it as a crucial fact about him when he refers to the way the physiological weakness of his eyes led to developing vision [from 'Encounter with Stan Brakhage' on the first DVD in *By Brakhage: an anthology*]. This awareness led not to 'correcting' spectacles but to transferring this myopia from himself to others, a feeling that he was "seeing all kinds of things that other people don't see or don't admit they see" [Brakhage/Frampton p.78]. If Frampton's interest in series and arithmetics links him to JS Bach, the condition of Brakhage's eyes link him to Beethoven. The composer's increasing deafness as he grew older could have led to silence or madness, but as it was, it created the conditions for his most original compositions, allowing him to live as he did in a musical sound world of his own imagining, undistracted by extraneous music. Something similarly single-minded seems to have occurred with Brakhage, since he became alert to how he saw things, with eyes open or eyes closed, in a manner different from others, but transferring that private, subjective vision to the public medium of film.

There may also be a narrative of Brakhage being motivated to become an artist because of the isolation caused by the nature of his eyesight, and because of an urge to find a way of expressing himself. In his writing, he evinces a quirky liking for words, their rhythm, their origins, and their capacity for double meaning, expressed through distracting, even irritating puns. He might therefore have become a writer but it is film that seduces Brakhage, film that gives body to his dreams, night-dreams or day-dreams, and to visions. He and Frampton shared an awareness that the glass lens being invented at the time the Renaissance helped to formulate the laws of perspective and how to render chiaroscuro and light on surfaces. For Frampton this was an intellectual point, while for Brakhage it was a polemical one, providing further grounds for arguing that there was another way of seeing, different from that of the Renaissance. In 'Metaphors on Vision' he catalogues how this 'objective' vision may be subverted: by spitting on the lens, by speeding up the motor for slow motion, by holding the camera in the hand rather than mounting it on a tripod (and thus "inherit worlds of space"), by over- or under-exposing the film, by using the "filters of the world" such as fog and downpours, or glass that was never designed for the camera [in the statement 'Camera Eye' in 'Metaphors']. Thus *Text of Light* (1974), a 71-minute film made by photographing glass objects in a sun-drenched office on a macro lens, in order to fragment the light and images of his surroundings. [The film started out as a portrait of a friend in business, and became an examination of light under a microscope, as it were. See Brakhage 'Seen'.]

If Brakhage's work is described as 'documentary' this is not true in its commonest sense of filming the world in order to inform, but only true as documenting his surroundings and his concerns. He is closest to being a documentary film-maker in the conventional sense in his three Pittsburgh films (1971), *eyes* chronicling the work of the police, *Deus Ex* showing a doctor performing heart surgery, and *The Act of Seeing with One's Own Eyes* filmed in a mortuary and showing the autopsies being carried out on dead bodies. All three could be described as extreme subjects, in particular the last which is so extreme as to be taboo. But Brakhage still makes it highly personal, preoccupied as he was with "birth, sex, death and the search for God", as he puts it in the last sentence of the opening statement in 'Metaphors on Vision'. Birth and sex had been explored ten years earlier in *Wedlock House: An Intercourse* and *Window Water Baby Moving* (both 1959) and in *Dog Star Man* (1961-64). *The Act of Seeing with One's Own Eyes* is the arena of death: to see a mortuary worker make an incision along the top of the head of a corpse, loosen the flesh from the skull, fold it back over the face covering the nose, and then carefully cut the skull away to reveal the brain, is to come face to face with our own raw, lifeless carnality, all soul and spirit removed, to confront the factual brutality of fleshly existence. The 'brutality of fact' was an expression coined by Francis Bacon, one of of whose earliest paintings, 'Crucifixion' of 1933, has been linked both to Rembrandt's painting 'Slaughtered Ox' of 1655, showing a raw carcass mounted on a frame, and two photographs by Eli Lotar of the slaughterhouses at La Villette in Paris [Harrison p.21]. Inspired by the scene from *Strike* described previously, Georges Franju had made a notable documentary in 1949 on the Paris slaughterhouses (La Villette again and Vaugirard), *Le Sang des Bêtes*, and with *The Act of Seeing*, Brakhage without any known reference to Lotar, Bacon or Franju is making his own exploration of a human activity which, until the arrival of the camera, still and film, remained quite beyond the bounds of ordinary experience. The most obvious way is just to observe, but while Brakhage's film is superficially observational, he eschews a voice-over describing what is happening and musing on the scene before us, for his deeper purpose is to engage us directly with understanding his subject through the way we perceive it, a mental process purified by the silence of the images.

Brakhage was very taken with the etymology of the word autopsy from the Greek αυτο- or 'one's own' and the stem word οπ- at the root of the Greek verb for seeing, a word which before it came to mean dissection of a dead body, especially to ascertain the cause of death, meant 'seeing with one's own eyes'. The film therefore allows us to <u>see</u> what death means for ourselves, but the phrase has a much larger resonance in Brakhage's own work because he spoke frequently of his experience of 'closed-eye vision', or the abstract patterns that could be seen when the eyelids were closed and rubbed with the fingers, a literal interpretation of seeing with one's own eyes. This preoccupation was the clearest expression of a desire to create another kind of vision at a distance from Renaissance and Rationalist modes of thought, one that synthesised the operations of mind and body. It led him especially to the hand-painted film, where the film strip was worked on directly without the mediation of a camera, for which there were precedents (in the films of Len Lye, Norman McLaren, Harry Smith), but Brakhage took it to quite different levels, non-narrative and dense with pattern. Right from the beginning of his film-making, he had scratched his name on black leader as an initial title to the film, "eye-sharpeners" as he called it, and it was with *Mothlight* of 1963 that Brakhage discovers most truly how he can realise an obsession as he puts it in the opening of 'Metaphors': "Imagine an eye unruled by man-made laws of perspective". Other films followed but it seems that it was in the last twenty years of his film-making – the 1980s and 1990s – that he used this technique most persistently and most creatively, e.g. *The Garden of Earthly Delights* (1981), *The Dante Quartet* (1987), *Rage Net* (1988), *Untitled (for Marilyn)* (1992), *Three Homerics* (1993), *The Dark Tower* (199), *Love Song* (2001). Often, as has been said, he superimposed his own autobiographical dimension, either in the titles or in his comments on the film, that without these explanations will elude the viewer. Not in the long run that this will matter, for Brakhage's genius will be recognised firstly in his taking of film-making into a wholly new area, and secondly in his superb technique, equivalent to the way the great painters enhance their greatness by the way they handle paint.

After 'birth', 'sex' and 'death' Brakhage's other preoccupation was with the 'search for God'. Among the short hand-made films made in his sixties is *Chartres Series* of 1994, which came out of a visit to Chartres Cathedral "which surely transformed my aesthetics more than any other single experience" [from Brakhage's notes to the film for Re:Voir Video editions 1995] and out also of the news of the death of his wife's sister, one an aesthetic experience and the other an emotional experience, ones that open up transcendence. There had been plenty of indications earlier, wonder at the sacrament of birth (*Window Water Baby Moving*), at creation (*Dog Star Man*) and at the glories of the microcosm (*Mothlight*). There was too the feeling of a 'muse', or something divine, however it may be described, making passage through him. *Chartres Series* connects his vision with a religious space, appropriately through the Cathedral's stained glass, pre-Renaissance, dense, intensely coloured and demanding on the eyes – all qualities of Brakhage's film-making.

For all his career as a film-maker, Brakhage was charting new frontiers, either discovering them, as with *Anticipation of the Night* or *Mothlight*, or, subsequent to their discovery, pushing them into further territory. This career extended over fifty years, during which time the technology of cinema changed as much as it had between Méliès' day and when Brakhage first started filming. Most significant has been the switch from celluloid to video as the basis for filming, a change largely driven by the observational Lumière aesthetic, of making pointing the camera and shooting easier to do. However, this technological shift has not been sympathetic to a film-maker working with very short segments of film, with the frame even, or who is excited by the chemistry of taking two physical pieces of film and putting them together. I doubt if it was true in any way that Brakhage's huge output was motivated by a desire to use the technology available to him as a young film-maker before new inventions made it obsolete, since his motivation was derived from an inner self. And it is not the case that his films look or feel dated; only a small proportion of the whole is available us (and what is has come about through dvd technology), but it is likely that as other films are released, Brakhage's originality will be recognized all the more. We are only just beginning to appreciate his achievement, and to move him from the periphery to the centre.

*

If I have dwelt at length on a film-maker who is largely unfamiliar to many people who know about the major milestones in the history of the cinema, this is to underline a particular point, that there is a way of making films that concentrates solely on the soundless image, or more precisely, on the single frame or small groups of frames. This makes them hard to watch, but there are rewards in persisting, and they may open the cinema to a new syntax. Innovative film where it is made by a single person, or a very small crew, has begun to explore how subjectivity can work in images. There is an analogy with poetry here. Poetry, while it does have a public form for example in epic, for the most part is used to convey the private and the personal, to portray the intimacy of personal thought, feeling and imagination. In the next chapter, 'Interiority', I discuss how the cinema might develop the 'soliloquy', when the resources of poetry are deployed in the middle of theatrical narrative. If it does so, the subjective cinema of the experimental film-makers could suggest ways of doing it. This style produces intensely personal work, one that gets us inside the mind as it were. As I have noted elsewhere in this book, fictional dreams have long been a staple of the cinema and have produced some particularly intense visual passages. But there needs to be a greater adventurousness in this area that applies the idea of 'coming onto the nervous system' to the narrative cinema.

The other impact of formalist film-making on narrative could be in devising more complex and more interesting narrative structures. Kieślowski's *Blind Chance*, discussed in the previous chapter, uses the idea of variation to tell three different stories about Witek, envisaging three different outcomes from him running for a train. This is particularly fruitful: one can envisage the variation idea being used much more, and extending such formalism, one can envisage not just an $A - A_1 - A_2 - A_3$ etc. structure, but the use of $A - B - A$ form (or $A - B - A - C - A$ etc. form, or $A - B - A - B$ resulting in C, and so on); or formalized slow-fast rhythms; or cross-cutting being taken further still. These devices can be used to enrich the story, but they can also be used to develop interior thought, how an individual visualizes his or her options, and how what is imagined squares up with what actually happens.

It is worth turning attention then to what can and cannot be achieved on film in terms of interior thoughts and feelings and to what has (and has not) been achieved so far.

9   INTERIORITY

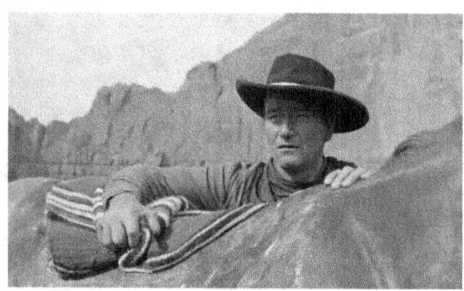

There are three notable close-ups in John Ford's *The Searchers*. The first is when Ethan rubs his sweating horse (above) as he watches Marty rush back to the ranch they have set out from in order to chase the Indians only to find it was a ruse to draw them away. His expression shows that he has put his brother's family in mortal danger of a cruel death. The second is in the cavalry fort where Ethan is shown the white woman 'rescued' from a life with the Indians: the camera tracks into his darkening face. The third is when he emerges from the tent having just scalped Scar, his enemy, his nemesis, his doppelgänger. What is registered on his face in these three shots? Fear, anxiety, hatred – any of these and much more besides: their common essence is a glimpse of some deep mental anguish, but only a glimpse, no more, for how we as spectators interpret them is a key to our understanding of what happens in the story, and judging by how the critical litera-ture, virtually since the film's appearance in 1956, has wrestled to pin down Ethan's character, revisiting and revisiting the film, we can only begin to under-stand this through multiple viewings.

Ethan is played by John Wayne. Was he, to quote Ingmar Bergman's de-fence of professional actors [see chapter 5], an actor 'trained to express complexi-ty'? Not trained (as we would understand it today) but with long experience of acting before the camera by the time he made *The Searchers*. Nor is he an actor associated with expressing complexity, yet this is to under-rate him, and it is cer-tainly to belittle the contribution he brings to the film under Ford's direction. In the second close-up described above, while several creative decisions have been made - that his face be grizzled, that his dark hat almost cover his eyes, that the interior feel cold and unlit – and these belong to the director and cameraman, the look in the eyes and the set of the mouth belong to Wayne, bringing a lifetime of knowledge about how his face will appear on screen. Their aim is to use appear-ance as a window onto the man's interior life, an obvious way for the camera to portray interiority.

In the last chapter, the history of cinema was structured in terms of a po-larity between observation and manipulation, and if Warhol was at the former pole, then Brakhage like his hero Georges Méliès was at the latter. This polarity can be developed further between that of exteriority, a mode in which the cinema since its inception has excelled, revelling in all the richness and diversity of the world being globalized by modern communications, a process of which the camera is itself a part. Literature, on the other hand, turning away from the newcomer, has found new worlds of its own, in particular interior mental states; painting, relinquishing to the camera its capacity to illustrate, has used painterliness to explore the formal, to depict dream, to open the door to abstraction, in other words to delve inside appearance. Cinema is left holding the high ground, but as it occupies the field, its next campaign is to address how it portrays interior states, and how it might do it better. To develop this idea, I start by focussing on a story fundamental to humans, the drama inherent in father and son relationships. In *The Road to Perdition*, when Michael Sullivan the father asks Michael Sullivan the son what subjects he had liked at school he says, 'Bible studies, because of the stories', the story of Abraham and Isaac hanging in the air unspoken. That reply rhymes with the heroic quality of a story about how a gangster father, Michael Sullivan, on the royal road to perdition, might save his innocent son Michael from a life of crime and necessary damnation.

The Road to Perdition (2002) is a classic Hollywood product – big stars, big sets, big music, in Sam Mendes a circus-master director of terrific ambition for his film, and a big budget of $80 million (2002 prices). The film enrols two veterans, Paul Newman as John Rooney, and the cinematographer Conrad Hall whose career had begun in the early 1960s. The composer was Thomas Newman who appears to be almost as prolific and successful as his father, Alfred Newman, as a composer of film scores. The designer Dennis Gassner is a leading figure in his field. On the other hand the scriptwriter David Self was fairly new, and it was only the second film for the director. It was released in July 2002, got strong reviews, did well at the box office and in the penultimate imprimatur of success received six nominations for an Oscar (but only got the actual award for its cinematography). By coincidence, within twelve months another film on the father-son relationship came out, this time in Russia. *Vozvrashcheniye* or *The Return*, released in June 2003, seems to have been made on a modest budget – no figures are available – by a largely untried team of producer, director, cameraman and actors. If fewer dollars were at stake with *The Return*, a more intangible risk was being taken with the careers of those Russians involved, a risk that paid off handsomely when the film won the Golden Lion at the Venice Film Festival, a prize that underlies its arthouse credentials. In style it feels palpably close not just to Tarkovsky (see below) but to Polanski's *Knife in the Water*, which similarly plays out the tensions of its three characters on a holiday on a boat on a lake.

A comparison between the two films is fascinating. Both come out of the cinema of excess: *The Return* is shadowed by the long-take cinema of Tarkovsky, *The Road to Perdition* by the *Godfather* films and the aspiration to make of the gangster film a revenge tragedy, rather than some nugget of criminal grittiness. In 1950, *The Road to Perdition* would have been an 89-minute gem whose larger themes would be confined within the conventions of the genre and the iron dictates of B-movie production, but in 2002 it is a 112-minute film the serious credentials of which are manifest for all to see. What is more, there are some unexpected shared details in the two stories, for example Michael learning to drive in *The Road to Perdition*, Andrey, the elder brother in *The Return*, doing the driving both at the end and earlier when his father (who is never named, which only increases the mystery surrounding him) pushes the car out of the mud. Then, both young Michael (in *The Road to Perdition*) and Ivan (in *The Return*) join the battle of wills with their father by not eating in a restaurant even when hungry. Thirdly, to signify release from the burden of being a son, Michael puts his head out of the car window, while Ivan does the same, urging his brother to photograph him as he does so.

There is a much more significant connection in that both use religious themes to shape the big story. The Catholic context of *The Road to Perdition* is overt, featuring as it does churches, candles, communion, rosary beads, plaster Maries etc. as the necessary context for the story of rescuing young Michael from damnation. *The Return* is unspecific, although numinous in its filming of the landscape, and striving to uncover depths of human feeling. Gratuitously perhaps, it films the father sleeping from the foot of the bed in apparent deliber-

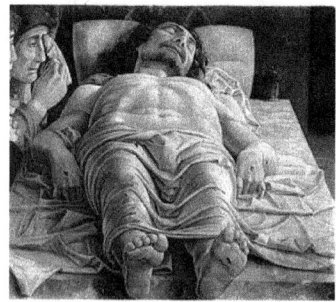 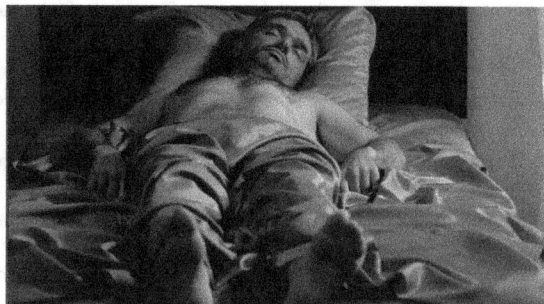

ate homage to Mantegna's 'Lamentation over the Dead Christ' [in the Pinacoteca di Brera in Milan]. If there really were any doubt whether its subject has a Biblical resonance, the film answers it by deftly juxtaposing a photograph of the very young family – father, mother, Andrey, Ivan – with an engraving of Abraham at the moment of being stayed from slaughtering his son by the presence of the angel. Most significantly, the climax of the story strikes a note of redemption as if the father's death is an act of self-sacrifice that brings Ivan to understand him and as a way of making sense of all the friction that has gone before. Both films turn the father into a mythical figure, *The Road to Perdition* because Michael Sullivan makes his way with the gun like any Western hero, especially when he is getting the upper hand on those pursuing him, *The Return* because when the boat sinks in the lake carrying the father's corpse with it, it is filmed like a Victorian painting of the dead hero going to Valhalla, the face sinking slowly into the water. Young Michael Sullivan's sentiment expressed as a voice-over at the end of *The Road to Perdition* that he asks for judgement to be suspended on whether his father was a bad man, adding 'He was my father,' is a truth that young Ivan has had painfully to discover for himself.

The point raises a matter of taste. The Russian film has the virtue of creeping up on its audience, surprising the spectator into the largeness of its theme, while *The Road to Perdition* cannot resist labouring the point from early on. And it is on matters of taste that the two films diverge. Both use large spaces in which to pitch the action, but the open horizons of *The Return* are the more arresting and more formally deployed, intentionally so because the film-makers

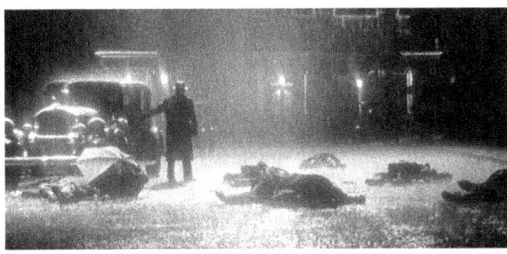

tried to begin and end each episode with a wide shot [as explained in the feature on the making of the film, on the dvd, Twentieth Century Fox 2004]. Secondly, the climaxes of each film – when Sullivan guns down Rooney's bodyguards and then Rooney himself, and when Ivan's father tries to reach Ivan frozen at the top of the tower but falls to his death – are both done in a bravura manner, but it is *The Return* which causes the spectator to gasp. In *The Road to Perdition*, the scene is soundstage-bound, even though the rain machines, the shadowy city street and the blazing light of the machine gun in the dark are all technically superb, never done better even. In *The Return*, the shot of the father's face in medium close-up appearing at the top of the tower and then, when the plank breaks, disappearing followed by the camera craning over the top to see his dead body sprawled on the ground is technically remarkable, and utterly breathtaking. The contrast underlies the way the religious dimension is handled in both films. In *The Road to Perdition*, the Catholicism feels historical, abstract, a hook for the story, whereas the *peripeteia* in *The Return* is acutely real to the audience, experienced as pure feeling.

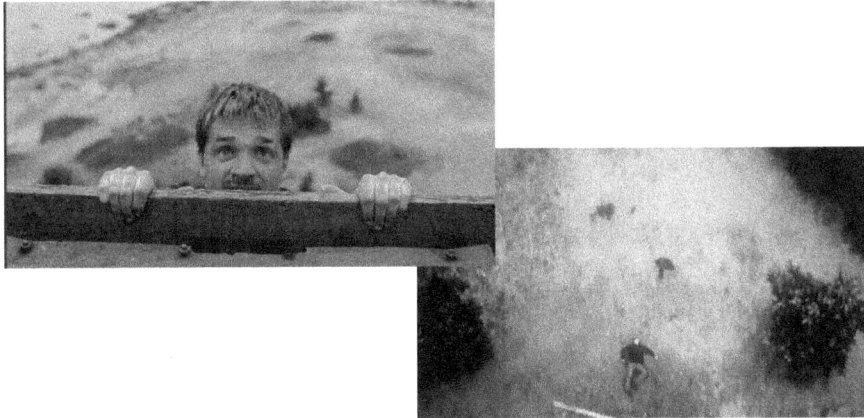

As mentioned Tarkovsky's shadow is on *The Return*. If there is a criticism of the film it is that the influence approaches the slavish. When we see the father sleeping on the bed in medium close-up, near the beginning, a feather sinks gently onto his pillow as if it had broken loose from Tarkovsky's *Nostalgia*. The director, Andrey Zvyagintsev, is as enamoured as his master of water and rain, of wind in the bushes, of disused buildings, of the family treasure in the form of a book of Old Master reproductions with transparent interleavings (Leonardo in Tarkovsky's *Mirror*, of engravings in *The Return*). The bravura crane shot at the climax is surely inspired by the one in Tarkovsky's *Andrey Roublev* to film the hoisting of the newly cast bell, although Zvyagintsev breaks new ground in using it to mark the tragic turning-point of his story, and to echo formally the view at the film's beginning of Ivan frozen at the top of the tower too frightened to jump from it into the lake. This particular shot was so difficult that an experienced technician, Astakhov, was brought in to assist the filmmakers with finding a technical solution to how to create it [as explained in the feature on the dvd].

Why should *The Return* be the more compelling film? Surprisingly, it scores over the Hollywood film by virtue of having a better constructed script, when it might be thought that the great tradition of script-writing in Hollywood would win this match. *The Return*'s two experienced script writers, Vladimir Moiseenko and Alexander Novototsky, produced a classic three-act structure, with the slow ratcheting of dramatic tension, while *The Road to Perdition* suffers from being much more plot-driven. For example, when Ivan battles with his father over whether he is hungry or not, this is a wrestling match of wills. When young Michael Sullivan refuses to eat and stays in the car, a point is being made about the father-son relationship, but it is also a plot device to ensure young Michael is out of sight in the car when McGuire goes into the diner to kill Sullivan (but fails). Wonderment at young Michael's unwillingness to eat is dissipated instead of being channelled into increasing the tenseness of the relationship, as it is in *The Return*. It may be that *The Return* scores higher because in its own way it observes the Hawks formula of 'make good scenes'. A price to pay in making good scenes can be that the details of the plot get lost or invested with uncertainty, but there is a large gain in putting character and the relationship between characters constantly at the forefront.

The father-son theme in *The Road to Perdition* is more complex, because it concerns three relationships: Sullivan father and Sullivan son, John Rooney and Connor Rooney, John Rooney and Michael Sullivan (the son that Rooney never had). The emergence of 'fraternal' hatred between Sullivan and Connor Rooney is something Anthony Mann, with his classical training, would have made the steely backbone of the film. Instead, the focus is primarily on a portrayal of the two Sullivans, quite soft-centred by comparison with the ambiguities and mysteries of how Andrey and Ivan come to know and love their father in *The Return*.

In effect, the challenge taken up by the makers of both films is how to express in dramatic and visual terms the core relationship of father and son, of the transition from innocence to experience, and to do so with a lot more than mere recourse to words. This conveying of interior thought and feeling is natural in literature, but present-day cinema surely suffers from unrealized possibilities. In written fiction, it is a matter of not just describing what happens, what things look like, what people say, but articulating their thoughts and emotions with extraordinary precision and range. It is as if the publication of the twin pillars of interior literature, Proust's 'In Search of Lost Time' and Joyce's 'Ulysses', were intended to show the upstart narrative form how far it had to travel if it was to equal written fiction. Two decades later Joyce writes 'Finnegan's Wake' as if to leave the field of describing external appearance entirely to film, whether still or motion.

The complex and poetic articulation of private thought found a zenith in Shakespeare's soliloquies: characters step outside the time and space of the play to speak their wishes and fears and dilemmas to the audience, to unveil a larger person behind the masks of costume and of public style, and behind the mechanics of the unfolding drama. The soliloquy as a dramatic device is taken to new heights in opera: in Act One of Verdi's 'La Traviata', the courtesan Violetta is entertaining in her house, putting on a public face for the singing and dancing, while privately racked physically by consumption and mentally by the unhappiness of her situation. She is comforted by Alfredo, and after he has left she expresses the deeper truth of her circumstances in a double aria imagining loving Alfredo ('Ah, fors'è lui') and then persisting with a life of pleasure ('Sempre libera degg'io'). It is the force of this music that sucks the audience into sharing her feelings. Another example: in Tchaikovsky's 'Eugene Onegin', Lensky must fight a duel with Onegin, a duel that is unnecessary and ill-advised but demanded by convention. The audience senses Lensky's foolishness and rushes to the judgement that if he is killed, it is by his own foolishness. It is at this point that Tchaikovsky allows Lensky, waiting for Onegin to arrive, to express a heartfelt farewell to Olga, over whom the duel is being fought, and in so doing to humanise his character and enlarge our sympathies for him.

There is barely anything comparable to the soliloquy or private aria in the cinema, the bold sequencing of images to inform the viewer of character. One can illustrate this by comparing an episode from Pushkin's 'Eugene Onegin' and the way it is shown in the film directed by Martha Fiennes in 1999. Since it primarily concerns visual details expressive of Onegin's character, it is not suitable for opera and it therefore does not feature in Tchaikovsky's version of the story – music is as limited in showing externals as cinema is in expressing interiority – but the passage does read in Pushkin as if it has cinematic potential.

The episode occurs in Book 7. Onegin and Lensky have fought their duel and Onegin has killed Lensky. After a description of Lensky's grave and Olga's rather too swift period of mourning followed by betrothal to a lancer and her departure, Tatyana now alone wanders the countryside and finds herself on Onegin's estate. Onegin's servant Anisya lets her into the house. Tatyana observes a cue on the snooker table, a riding crop on the sofa; Anisya shows her the study – Tatyana sees the desk and lamp, a heap of books, Byron's portrait upon the wall, a bust of Napoleon. Pushkin calls it a 'modish bachelor cell' [Pushkin 'Eugene Onegin' 7.20, line 2, translation by James Falen.] She leaves but asks to be allowed to come back on her own. She does so early the next day and in the study she first weeps, then is fascinated by Onegin's books. Stanza 22 is given over to Onegin's taste in reading, and in stanza 23 Tatyana concentrates on the passages he has marked:

> 'And in the margins she inspected
> his pencil marks with special care;
> and in those pages everywhere
> she found Onegin's soul reflected.' [7.23, lines 9-12]

The passage is an opportunity for the film-maker to give the viewer an insight into both Onegin's way of life and the character of his intellect. Fiennes's film version does do something clever by ending the sequence with Tatyana finding some sketches by Onegin on the snooker table, which include one of herself (below left). This is not in the book, but we learn immediately of Onegin's artistic sensibility and his admirable skill at draughtsmanship, and more importantly still that Tatyana has meant something to him after all – pointing the way forward to the story's climax. But there is a missed opportunity of sketching more details – there is no sight of the bust of Napoleon (except

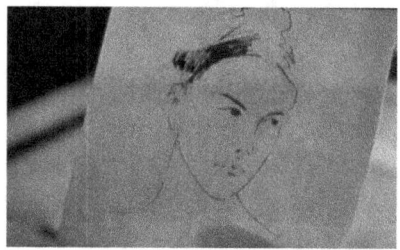 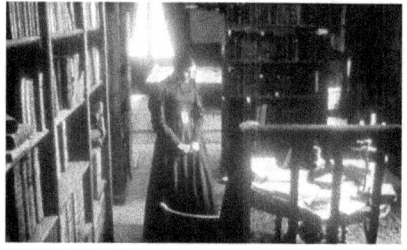

in a long shot), no portrait of Lord Byron or glimpse of his books on the shelves, and while we do get some close-ups of book illustrations, on the whole indecipherable, the glimpse of the marked passage is elusive. There is a wooden quality to the scene as if awe of the splendid room used for it had paralysed any attempt to use appearance to get behind appearance (above right).

It can be done. Take a different set of circumstances, but again someone is exploring a room from which we learn its owner's character. In Powell and Pressburger's *A Canterbury Tale*, Sgt Peter Gibbs is in pursuit of the man suspected of putting glue in women's hair, and he and his friends are beginning to think it is the local squire, Thomas Colpepper. Gibbs has cleverly got himself into Colpepper's study on the pretext of talking about history, since Colpepper is an antiquarian, as Colpepper's mother (the equivalent of Anisya) has let him in while she goes to fetch her son. She is elderly, while he is middle-aged, unmarried, living with his mother. A shot down the hall conveys something precise about the sort of house Colpepper lives in, one which is old and well-furnished with a fine set of stairs. In this study Gibbs looks round and the camera pans across the walls to reveal fishing gear, skis, a gun, walking boots, pictures of mountains, a bookcase. We strain for more detail and the film gives it, a close-up of Colpepper's desk strewn with papers, pamphlets and books, notably Fraser Darling's 'The Island Years' and a book called 'Soil and Sense'.

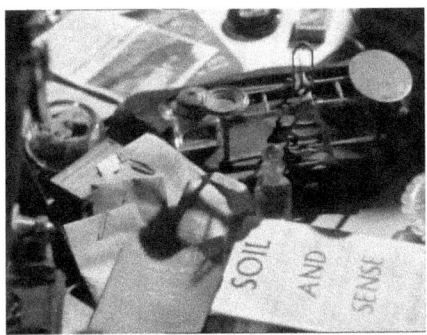

[See Christie pp. 79-93. Darling's 'Island Years' was about his experience as a farmer in Scotland; Michael Graham's 'Soil and Sense' argued for grassland farming without inputs of fertiliser. Both were pioneer thinkers on the subject of ecology.] Despite the scene being marred by the addition of jaunty music when the moment cries out for ambient sound only or even silence with all sound dropped away, in sixty seconds we are told a great deal about Colpepper's social position, his life as a bachelor, the nature of his recreations and his character as a thinker without a word being spoken. It is a small but significant moment in the story whose trajectory works by revealing Colpepper's God-like role against a narrative of unmasking him as the nasty glueman. Gibbs is like a terrier in doing the unmasking, but dense in his appreciation of Colpepper's qualities. The scene in the house does something that opera achieves naturally, when the characters miss what the music tells the audience.

Alfred Hitchcock, ever the intelligent thinker in pictures, uses the exploration of a room to tell us about a character right at the beginning of *Rear Window*. In a ninety-second camera shot, involving intricate pans, travels, moves in and moves out, he shows us the place where LB Jefferies lives with its view over the rear of an apartment block, some of his neighbours, his predicament – immobile in a chair with one leg in plaster – and then his profession as cameraman, but also more than his profession because by continuing his intricate camera movement, now in close-up, he shows us in effect the story so far: his smashed camera, explained by a photograph of colliding racing cars heading towards him holding the camera and taking the pictures, and then images of a fireball at a racetrack, an ambiguous image of someone being hit by a car, a war photo (Korea?), and the mushroom cloud from an atomic explosion. The shot does not end there because the camera travels left to a framed negative of a woman, and then left again to the same picture as a photograph, this time as a positive, on the cover of a magazine ('Paris Fashions'). From this sequence we not only learn that Jefferies' leg was broken in the racing-car crash, and that he is a man who likes danger especially of an explosive kind, but that he also does fashion

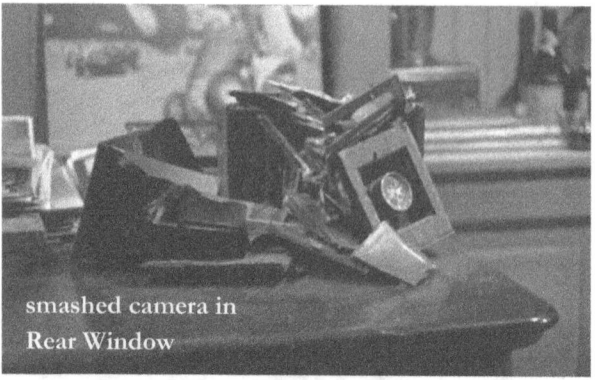

smashed camera in
Rear Window

photography, presumably to earn a living, and presumably because he likes beautiful women.

But this sequence is for the benefit of the omniscient spectator. A better parallel in Hitchcock's work to the Pushkin example is a noted sequence in *Psycho*, which combines in remarkable fashion the revelation of character as seen through the eyes of the intruder in the house, and an advance of the narrative by giving clues as to the revelations that are about to occur. While Sam engages Norman Bates in conversation at the motel, Lila Crane, sister of the murdered Marion, goes to explore Norman's house which stands looming behind the motel, a dark Gothic other half to its bland normality. The sequence with Lila exploring the house is purely visual, but Hitchcock cleverly intercuts Sam and Norman's conversation both to counterpoint sound and silence – to remind the audience of the two different worlds of motel and house, and to increase the tension: at what point will Norman realize that Lila is trespassing on his private world? It is that private world which is finally revealed to us through Lila's eyes as she explores first the bedroom of Norman's mother, with its heavy furnishings and its pastness – oval portraits on the wall, the *fin-de-siècle* basin, the bronze sculpture of a pair of folded hands on the dressing table, frozen in repose like the whole room and surreally unsettling. Norman's bedroom is more revealing still as Hitchcock intercuts gaze and object: a child's toys, a crumpled quilt, the old records on the gramophone (Beethoven's 'Eroica Symphony'), and – again the Magrittean touch – a book whose spine bears no title nor indication of which

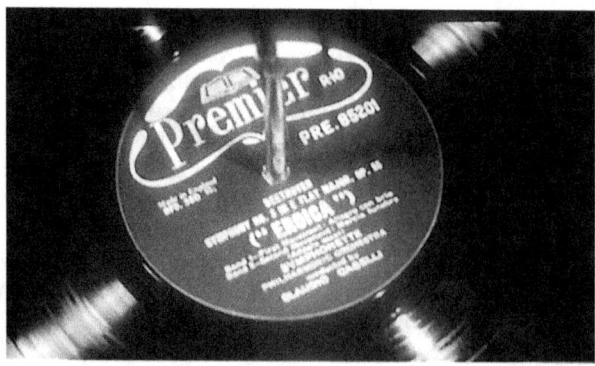

way up it should be read. At this point, we return to Sam and Norman conversing until Norman realizes something is wrong . . .

The sequence uses images not only to reveal the nature of Norman's obsessions but to hint at the horrifying *bizarrerie* of the relationship with his mother. Through Lila, we intrude on Norman's subconscious, which returns us to the question of what resources the cinema uses at present to express interiority. Here are six: voice-over; acting and facial close-ups; music; interiors coupled with set design; place whether interior or exterior; close-up; and dreams.

First of all, 'Voice-over' is a loose term that needs more precise definition. It is to be distinguished from 'voice off' when a character or characters hear a voice coming from a speaker not visible on the screen. This device allows the spectator to focus on the reaction of others to what is being said and enables the director to give priority to the interiority of those characters. It is also different from 'interior monologue', i.e. words heard by the audience and understood as coming from a particular individual, but not heard by others on the screen. The third type is voice-over proper, commonly heard during a flashback, when a character, already identified to the audience, or to be identified during the course of the film, gives a context to a flashback, or comments on it as it unfolds. [See Doane pp. 33-50, and Fleishman c.4. Both add a fourth category of voices that are heard but not seen – Doane cites documentary practice, Fleishman the sinister voice in *The Testament of Dr Mabuse*.] Such voice-over during a flashback enjoyed a particular vogue during the 1940s detective film in Hollywood, a vogue surely triggered by the fatalistic commentary in *Le Jour se lève* of 1939 spoken by Jean Gabin's *bon gars* worker: this demoralised first-person narrative not only told the story but revealed an individual struggling ineffectually against fate, at a stroke inventing the core of *film noir*.

Via Hollywood the use of voice-over in this way then influenced Godard in *Le Petit Soldat*: Bruno is a reporter in Geneva investigating the vicious atrocities of some obscure Franco-Arab conflict. The film's first words are a voice-over: "For me, the time for action is over – I have aged. The time for reflection begins." The narrative then interweaves Bruno's story, including that of his affair with Véronique, with his comments seemingly made as a voice off – except they turn out to be voice-overs, made at a temporal distance from the events on screen. Analysis is complicated because at a different level the film is an autobiographical one of Godard falling in love with Anna Karina, who plays Véronique, a fact which lends a further dimension to the pattern of Bruno's thoughts in the film. As an aside, it should be added that voice-overs have really only been used for a single character and not for several. This raises the question why not, and the answer may be that too much is being asked of the audience in terms of following who is thinking or explaining or imagining what.

Voice-over is very close to interior monologue. As was shown in the discussion of *The Thin Red Line*, it is used in the opening sequence: Witt's musings beginning 'Why this war at the heart of nature?' means that the film seizes our attention with a soliloquy, and we find a battle movie opening with a private vision of the absence of war. This characterization of Witt then risks being drowned as a result of the flaccid use of a musical sequence comprising the 'In Paradisum' from Fauré's 'Requiem', chanting by the islanders and Hans Zimmer's main theme for the film, shifting the focus from Witt to the much larger picture of mankind living in harmony with nature.

The **second** resource, and as discussed in chapter 5, for many directors the primary one, are actors. It is they who must use expression to convey a character's private feelings, even thoughts. It is invidious to select any one performance from the myriad on offer, but here are four, one from the early period, one from the middle, and two more recent. Possibly the most famous cinematic study of inner emotion is Dreyer's direction of Marie Falconetti in *The Passion of Joan of Arc* (1928), already referred to, where the facial close-up has never been more effectively used. [But see also Emily Watson's performance as Bess in *Breaking the Waves*. For this see Cawkwell p. 143: "Just as Falconetti allows the whole gamut of emotions to cross her face, Watson's expressions and in particular her voice reveal feelings of joy, hysteria, torment and serenity to the limit." The director Lars Von Trier got Watson to watch Falconetti's performance as preparation for the role of Bess.]

From the middle period, one can single out Marlon Brando's portrayal of Terry Molloy in *On the Waterfront*. Kazan was an actor's director and he elicits from Brando a performance that capitalises on repressed energy, and mute wrestling with what he should do and what he should be. Brando is helped by the sharpness of Schulberg's script, but he is as revealing when he doesn't speak as when he does. From the last twenty years might be chosen Clint Eastwood in *Unforgiven*, on whose face, voluntarily inexpressive, can be read the ravages of time and experience, or Imelda Staunton's moment in *Vera Drake* when she realises the police are onto her practice as a backstreet abortionist (for closer analysis see chapter 5). But good film acting, and good direction of actors, is commonplace: a glance here, a gaze there, a lifted eyebrow, a sneer or grimace, all are used to flesh out a character's role in the story.

Thirdly, of all the hybrid elements in the cinema, music has most readily been turned to in order to add an extra dimension of feeling to the way we experience films, as if film was a cold medium that needed unfreezing by the warmth of music. No film-maker has shown more awareness, although wariness might be a better word, of the impact of that extra dimension, than Stan Brakhage, since only a handful of his films have a musical accompaniment. Adding music is like hanging a mirror: you always risk dropping it and breaking it. It is too common an experience now for films to be awash with music for the greater part of their length, an excess which often diminishes even the coherent qualities a film score might have.

In itself, the history of film music has become almost as large a subject as the history of the cinema so that making some general points about the way it characterises individuals and situations in films is beyond the scope of this book. [See Cooke, who is able to draw on the valuable groundwork of others.] It often works best as an indicator of character when it derives from something played within the film itself. When the sexual predator Tom Frank, played by Keith Carradine, sings 'I'm easy' in Altman's *Nashville* and each of the three women scattered among the audience think it is written for them personally, the moment is operatic, a fusion of feeling in the four characters with the irony of the situation, a revelation and a cover-up at the same time. In Bresson's *L'Argent*, the old man in the house where Yvon takes refuge is shown both to be cruelly egotistical, and when he plays Bach's 'Chromatic Fantasy' on the piano in thrall

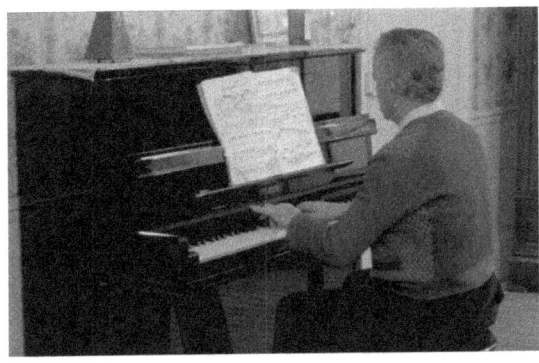

to Bach's dazzling invention. The ultimate pianist film is about a pianist, Wladek Szpilman. In *The Pianist*, his performance of Chopin's first Ballade for the good Nazi Hosenfeld and an orchestration of the Grande Polonaise Brillante when the war which he has survived by extraordinary chance is over not only define his character as a gifted musician, but as someone who expresses himself more completely through the music of Chopin than through anything else he says in the film, or even does, for by and large the whole of his war is spent having things done to him.

The **fourth** resource is the space in which the characters live and move, whether it be artificially lit interiors or the environment outside, built or natural. Early on German Expressionism used set design to say something about the unbalanced mental state of characters, an idea exploited cleverly and brutally five decades later by Samuel Fuller in *Shock Corridor*: when Johnny B the journalist seeking a Pulitzer, and therefore investigating a murder in an asylum for the mentally ill, pretends himself to be mad, he ends up losing his own mind. We are given a shot of Johnny in the corridor drenched by a thunderstorm and struck by lightning, a glimpse of his interior turmoil expressed in hard rain and

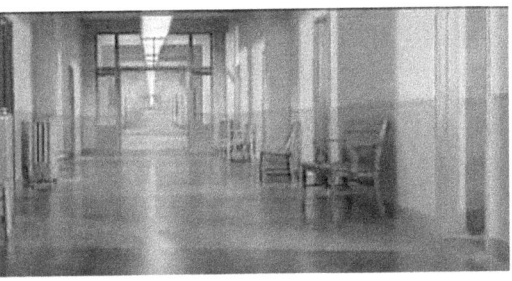 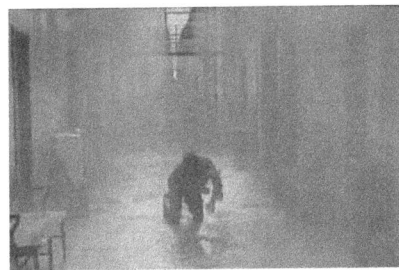

182

blinding flashes. Similarly, in the first half of *Lost Highway*, the apartment inhabited by Fred and Renée is austerely furnished and darkly lit, and its sinister presence stands out in the mysterious video recordings sent to Fred: are these an objective record of Renée's murder by Fred, or do these interiors project the imaginings of Fred's mind?

No director has more brilliantly connected the built landscape with human states of mind than Antonioni. In his first feature film made in 1950, *Cronaca di un amore*, bleak buildings and empty landscape form the backdrop to the alienation of the characters from each other. The final shot, at night, shows a taxi travelling away from the camera down the road. Inside it sits Guido who has just left Paola. She has asked him to phone in the morning, to which he has unconvincingly replied yes, and on leaving tells the taxi to take him to the station. The night shot expresses an interior emptiness in Guido's and Paola's feelings towards each other, an emptiness Antonioni was then to express twelve years later by a much more elaborate use of the built environment at the end of *L'Eclisse* (see chapter 7). *L'Eclisse* is then followed by *Red Desert*, in which he not only poses his characters yet more starkly in the street and among towering factory buildings but he paints elements in the landscape to convey the neurosis of Giuliana, as if the environment does not just mirror human confusion but oppresses the characters so much that their alienation is a product of it, a suitable visual metaphor for the sense of environmental crisis that was beginning to emerge in the 1960s.

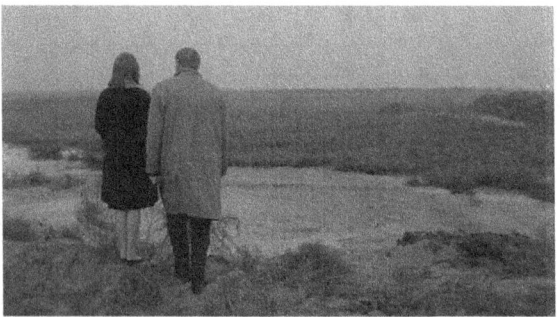

So, voice-over, acting, music and environment can all be used to express something of the inner lives of people on the screen. But only the last capitalises on the purely visual, without words or music. How else might 'purely visual' means be used? Here the **fifth** resource, the close-up, is crucial. A particularly interesting example for our purposes occurs in *Blackmail* because it was made in both a silent and a sound version. [I am indebted here to Barr pp.93-4.] Alice the heroine has murdered with a breadknife the man bent on raping her. After a sequence showing her walking the streets of London at night that uses dark and fog to express the blankness and horror in her mind – a visual soliloquy of a sort – she appears at her parents' breakfast table in the normal way. They keep a shop and a customer appears talking about the murder in the news. In the silent version, just before she appears, a close-up of Alice and a close-up of the breadknife are linked in order to indicate her anxiety. As she cuts the bread, there is a close-up of the doorbell sounding to herald the customer's entrance, at which Alice takes fright and jerks the knife into the air. In the sound version, the customer is talking when Alice's father asks her to cut a slice of bread. While she does so in close-up, the word 'knife' is subjectively distorted as if it was sounding in her ears – a 'voice off' which she hears in her own particular way – and as it sounds fortissimo, it causes Alice to jerk the knife in the air. Both versions are extremely effective, and indicate the mastery with which Hitchcock, trained in the silent era and very much drawn to the visual modes of German Expressionism (he had spent time in Berlin in 1925), managed to make the transition from the one film language to the other while drawing narrative ideas from both.

The close-up had been used from early on in the history of the cinema, especially in the films of DW Griffith, to develop a means of 'signalling' desires and fears through matching looks to objects or people, an idea richly exploited in the two great surrealist films, *Un Chien Andalou* and *L'Age d'or*, to convey the cruelty of thwarted desire. Buñuel had collaborated with Salvador Dali in making both films and using the shock of the surrealist image to reveal desire never left him. For example in *Tristana*, made four decades after *Chien Andalou*, Tristana has a vision of her guardian's severed head acting as the clapper tolling the church bell, wish being mother to the dream.

Indeed, as well as the close-up, the **sixth** resource, cinematic dreams, which had their vogue in the 1940s, open up the minds of characters. Three examples are Pedro's dream in *Los Olvidados* (1950, Buñuel again),the Edwardes/Ballantyne dream in Hitchcock's *Spellbound* (1945, Dali again) and Sammy Rice's nightmare in Powell and Pressburger's *Small Back Room* (1949) (see chapter 7, 'It's not in the acting'). An example using distorted sound to accompany images, as Hitchcock had done in the sound version of the breadknife sequence in *Blackmail*, comes from another 1940s melodrama, *Possessed*. In one sequence a woman, alone and distraught, is in her room on a rainy night. As David Bordwell comments, sound devices enable the narration to achieve subjective depth as well. The ticking of a clock and the dripping of raindrops magnified in volume mark the movement of the character into a hallucinatory state [Bordwell and Thompson p. 330]. Regrettably such unleashings of the imagination have gone out of fashion, perhaps because psychoanalytic theory has moved on, or because the first flush of surrealism is long gone, or because audiences were thought to dislike them since they disrupt their understanding of space and time. For a period Tarkovsky gave it magnificent new life – all his seven features have dream sequences in them – and it is time to exploit this crude but intensely visual device more. Nor should we necessarily despair, since a recent blockbuster like *Inception* (2010) takes as its sci-fi premise that you can become skilled at hacking into someone's dreams and wreaking havoc by stealing or planting an idea. The narrative then layers itself by going into deeper and deeper dream levels so that we seem to spend the whole film in a dream state. Furthermore, the Coen Brothers with their acute visual flair have inserted an intriguing nightmare into *A Serious Man* (2009): Larry Gopnik dreams of being out in the wild on the US-Canada border to send his brother Arthur to a new life, only to see him shot by the neighbour who goes hunting with his young son. As the boy's rifle is trained on Larry himself, he hears the father exhorting him, "There's another Jew, son." Having experienced Arthur's death in a style that visually is no different from the rest of the film, we see Larry jerk bolt upright in a sweat to find that his brother still with him. This is a terrifying 'what if?' sequence – how else might a nightmare be conceived?

But cinema needs as well to devise a more mundane form of visualising thought, and some of the narratives explored in chapter 7 show already how this could be done. As already discussed, Kieślowski's *Blind Chance* about the alternative futures facing a young medical student indicates how a different course of action might be imagined for Witek. All three futures are presented as possibilities, but suppose one is the actual option he took, then he might be shown as imagining one of the others, rather as if he were to say to himself, 'What would have happened if I had decided not to do such and such?' This 'what if?' idea is, as we have seen, beautifully exploited in *Groundhog Day*, in order to make both a comedy about what, given a second chance, we would say or do differently to gain advantage – such as boning up on French poetry in order to impress the woman you keep meeting afresh each day – and a moral tale about how the relearning of innocent behaviour can get us out of the cynical, self-serving rut in which we sink afresh each day.

The problem is the lack of a narrative convention to signal that the train of thought in a character is being visualised rather than actually happening, i.e. to signal the subjunctive rather than the indicative mood. The dreams referred to in the Buñuel/Hitchcock/Powell and Pressburger films of the 1940s are all clearly marked as such, so that there can be no doubt that the spectator is viewing weird private imaginings. To cue a visualisation of a thought which may be itself quite matter-of-fact and no different from the matter-of-fact tenor of the rest of the narrative, there might be a close-up of the eye followed by the sequence, or the use of black and white for such scenes in a colour film, or a sequence shown in a portion of the screen rather like the 'thinks bubble' in a cartoon, or by introducing the sequence with dissolves, fading in and out, irising in and out, or by some other way yet to be conceived.

Whatever method is created, the narrative would be disrupted, but as discussed already, judging by the power of soliloquies in plays and private arias in opera to thicken the dramatic quality of a story on the stage, this should be used and valued in the cinema as well. Take a hypothetical example: a man is on his way to a woman's house. He has slept with her before, and knows she is attracted to him. If he were to propose marriage, he knows she would say yes, but he is temperamentally indecisive, caught between the wish to love her, and the fear of being constricted. As he travels in the car, he has three 'what if?' visions to represent the possible futures he is thinking of. The first is an image of the two of them twenty years on that expresses a frozen relationship; the second is an image of himself in old age sitting alone in his house; the third is of the two of them in bed together. When he arrives at her house, the two converse lightly; she is pleased he's come while he is both glad to be there and at the same time wishes he wasn't. By allowing us to see the possible futures he has been thinking of, the film colours the conversation between the two. The images could be repeated as flashes in the conversation, in effect flashbacks to the flash forwards he has imagined in the car. The sophistication of time shifts which film-makers now use and audiences understand should mean that films do not always have to be watched as showing the present, the here-and-now, but mapping out futures as well. And there is a precedent. That bold experimenter with time, Alain Resnais, opens *La Guerre est finie* with Diego arriving at the border between France and Spain and envisaging a course of events taking place caused by X. But X does not take place and the narrative proceeds in a different way. The sequence works particularly well as an opening because it immediately makes real for the viewer the risks inherent in the old socialist Diego's clandestine return to Francoist Spain [Bordwell, 'Narrative in the Fiction Film' pp. 213 sq.], but it is also noteworthy for the way Resnais' construction of narrative possibilities could be fruitfully used in other films.

The idea surfaces in an unexpected place that predates Resnais' film, David Lean's *The Passionate Friends*. Mary is married to Howard Justin and the film recounts the passionate but unconsummated relationship she has enjoyed with Stephen Stratton in the past before her marriage to Howard, and which she enjoys again when she re-encounters him after her marriage, although 'enjoy' is a curious word to describe the pleasure she feels in his presence and the anguish she feels in his absence. In one scene Mary and Stephen have a picnic in the Swiss Alps. As Stephen prepares it Mary 'dreams' a flashback to their conversation in the cable car. She asks whether he is married to which he replies, "I'm not married; I couldn't marry anyone but you," following which they go into a romantic clinch. But this is a 'what if?' scene, because in the actual conversation

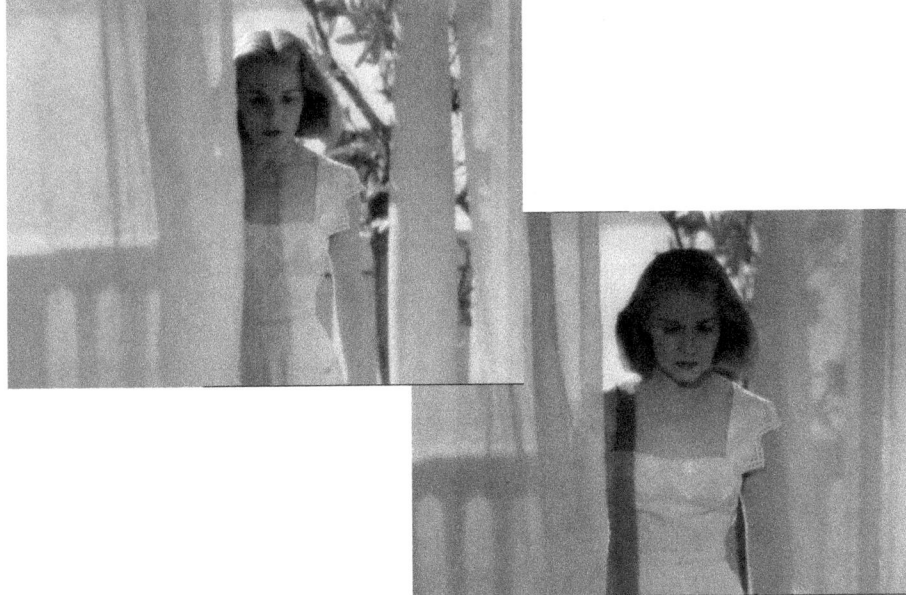

in the cable car, when she asks whether he is married, he explains, "Yes, during the war."

The Passionate Friends is outstanding in the way it explores Mary's interior thoughts and feelings, a narrative device given special force as a way of dissecting English politeness in which words mask rather than reveal thoughts, against the grain of expression on faces, and in the sparing use of Richard Adinsell's music. What is more, Lean is unafraid to use silence to heighten our sense of Mary's feelings. After the picnic, Steven brings Mary back to her hotel by boat, watched by Howard through by binoculars. Mary runs to her room to wave Stephen goodbye from the balcony. The wave is vigorous, but as she turns back into the room her head is bent, her figure veiled and unveiled by a billowing gauze curtain (previous page), an image that closely attunes the audience to a sense of the lost opportunities, but in a master touch Lean reinforces it by making the soundtrack go quite silent: even the ambient sound is lost, as if to connect us even more strongly with Mary's desolation. The moment marks a climax to the drama because when she comes fully into the room she finally learns what the audience already knows – that all this while her husband has been watching her.

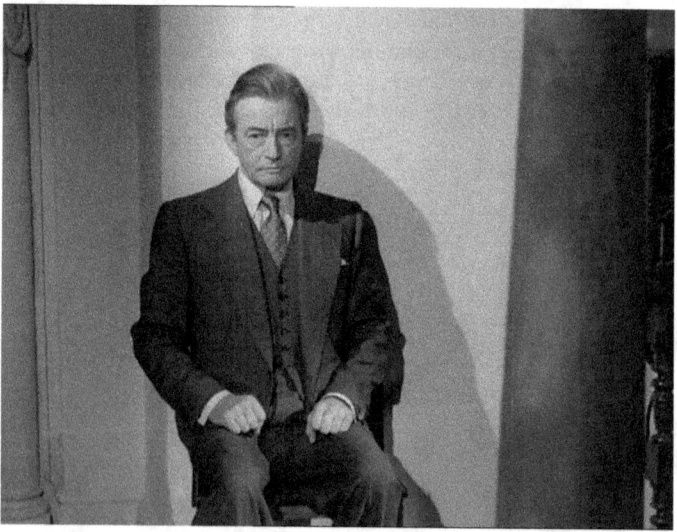

This economy of expression feels foreign in today's cinema, which brings us back to the two films discussed at the beginning of this chapter, The Road to Perdition and The Return. Both make full use of the blankness of the human face to hint at underlying thought and emotion. When Michael Sullivan shoots John Rooney, his adopted father, The Road to Perdition underplays the emotion, relying on the ambiguity of Sullivan's moistened face to convey it: we think that this is rain at first then understand that the wetness comes from tears. In The Return, after the gruelling boat journey to the island as a result of the outboard motor breaking down (not the best start to a fishing trip), the father sits with Andrey and Ivan by a fire on the beach. He takes a swig from his hip flask, and makes the two boys drink, bullying Ivan into doing so. The boys then retire, leaving him alone by the fire staring downwards, a shot which is held for fourteen seconds. What is he thinking? Imagination has to supply the answer, which is a virtue: he is baffled as to how to get them to recognize his paternal authority, he is in despair at himself, the loneliness of his life seeps into him, his inability to connect floors him. The film virtuously eschews musical accompaniment in order to tell the audience what to feel.

The sequence not only dispenses with music but at this moment refrains from using the Kuleshov effect, i.e. the juxtaposition of different pieces of film that convey meaning with a specific emotional impact. In such a sequence, instead of the father looking down, we might have seen him looking blankly out, followed by a shot of the darkened lake as a way of conveying his inarticulacy. This is an unsophisticated idea, yet with a more sophisticated film language, a 'film soliloquy' could have revealed the profundity of this human moment in still more interesting ways.

10   IMAGINING THE POSSIBILITIES

Pursuing the idea of interiority further, an excellent example of current practice, beautifully executed but an indication of how much further we could go if only film-makers were bold enough, is provided by *Band of Brothers* [see chapter 3]. In episode 5 entitled 'Crossroads' the focus is on Richard Winters, now promoted to Commander of Second Battalion. Because Damien Lewis plays the role with a wide-eyed blankness when he is not speaking, and says little about what he is thinking, he makes himself hard to read both for the other characters and for us.

It starts with him running up an embankment, shot from his point-of-view so that the ground seems to lurch about him, and we hear his heavy panting on the soundtrack, and when he tops it he shoots a surprised young German soldier. Is this a dream? The next shot shows him pulling the curtains to let the dawn light in, so it might be – but it does turn out to be a real memory. Two

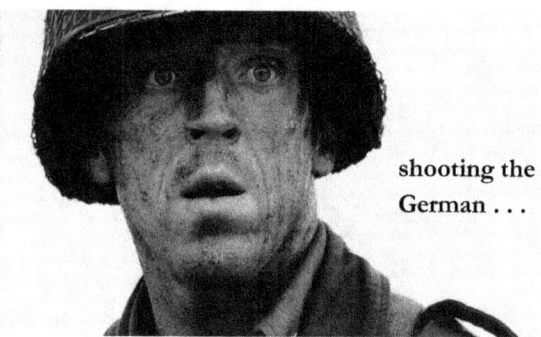

shooting the German . . .

weeks after the event shown in the dream he is ordered to write a report of the ambush by Easy Company of a German gun post on 5 October 1944, an ambush led by Winters and the chief action of which begins with him running up the embankment. We are shown the events in desaturated colours signalling a flashback, while the present tense is conveyed in more normal, albeit muted colours: battle-brown as opposed to battle-grey for the flashbacks. The events filter through his memory as he wrestles with the task of writing the report. In-

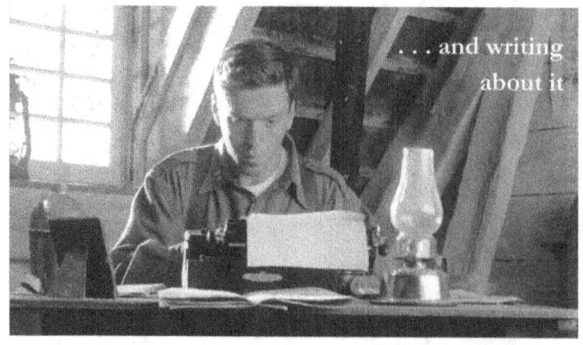

. . . and writing about it

deed Winters gives the impression that conducting the actual ambush is easier than writing about it. We get a sense of how his mind struggles to compose the report but not what those struggles consist of. We conclude that he cannot find the words to match the details of the engagement and certainly not to describe the complexity of the moment when he shoots what is in effect a German offering no defence. We learn instead how it has come to bother him, for on leave later in Paris, the sight of a young Frenchman on the metro triggers the memory of the young German he has shot. The episode is replayed in his mind in a slowed-down version that obliterates his sense of his present surroundings. When he comes to, he finds himself in the terminus station: like his memory of the event, the metro has come to a stop.

The whole incident neatly encapsulates the difficulty of revealing interiority: a more complex exploration of what Winters thought, both in voice-over and images – the memory of events, their sequence, their detail – would be out of key with the commercial demands of the television channel, but more significantly would appear to lack the necessary film grammar to depict it. While Lewis de-dramatizes the part (the events portrayed are dramatic enough), Tom Hanks, who directed the episode, does not over-direct the role, and above all there is virtually no attempt to 'psychologize' the role in the performance: we are faced with the 'voluntary inexpressive', while the spectator is given no insight into the state of Winters' memory. Yet might we be on the threshold of going much further in this area: how much more might be achieved?

Part One of this book explored how the invention of film led to the opening up of our visual imagination to the point that the medium has not flinched from the horrific such as the depiction of war and even bringing home the human capacity for cruelty – 'evil' might be a better word – in the pursuit of genocide. This has led to a widening of experience which, when absorbed uncritically, could be argued to have created a debilitating pessimism. But film has also enriched human lives by its portrayal of dreams, fantasies and idealised realities, not to mention its rich body of comedy, all of which can offer a counterpoint, a counterweight even, to pessimism.

Part Two then discussed the means used by film-makers to explore experience by deploying artistic imagination and technical skill in all the aspects that relate to the making of moving images: performance by actors, camerawork simple and elaborate, the use of music, sound and silence, and the sequencing of images on the editing table; it showed how the manipulation of time is an essential attribute of both narrative and non-narrative film. Yet to make film work to greatest effect, the spectator needs to bring their own mental capacity and imagination to watching it. It may be said that to document the world or to create stories about it is to express sufficient meaning about how we live, but there has to be more: the fullest appreciation, and thus enrichment, is brought about by our own imaginative engagement with the medium, just as is required for literature, music and all other artistic expressions, whether made in the past or made in the present. This chapter tries to explore how that engagement might be deepened in the future.

DREAMING OF A GOLDEN AGE

Making pictures is as old as civilisation but the making of moving pictures is synonymous with modernity. It is synchronous too, sparked by the invention of photography in the 1830s from which a technological impetus was given to creating a mechanism for sequencing photographs to create the illusion of movement. The cinema remains a stupendous novelty. Over its history, the human race has quickened its sense of time: the fact that in the present day seconds count is a suitable mirror to all those photographs flickering through the projector gate. We are overwhelmed. By comparison, in literature, music, painting, sculpture, the dross has succumbed to the oblivion of time, leaving a residue of gold, while the cinema is still an invention without a past, preoccupied very often only with the most recent success. What is more, the air of the showground novelty continues to envelop it so that no sooner has one technological advance been absorbed than another has come along to excite audiences: first sound, then colour, then widescreen, now digital imagery. The excitement shows no sign of diminishing, because our present expectation is of yet further technological advance. Is 3-D the next Eldorado, for example?

Has this voyage on the open swell, ascending one wave, then coming down the other side ready to face the next, distracted attention from stylistic developments, as if to recognize a changing art as much as a changing craft were more than we can manage? We may be aroused by the desire for novelty yet we are indifferent to what the film might achieve in form and style. There is a history of the cinema that sees it as a triumph of word over image, but when it seems as if it might burst forth in offering visual experiences beyond our present knowledge – in the silent cinema of the 1920s, or in the underground cinema of the 1960s, or with the discovery of digital manipulation of the image in the 1980s – the idea that film is best served as a hybridised version of theatre and literature, with the music added often indiscriminately, still prevails.

On the other hand, this version of film history is too simplified, and the way we appreciate films is a lot more complex. The use of sophisticated editing to manipulate time and space has allowed much more challenging narratives to emerge. Secondly, the desire for novelty has driven the sophistication of special effects; they produced a wondrous *King Kong* in 1933, but have been developed so much that the remake in 2005 was equally wondrous, a compelling and breathtaking version of mythopoeic cinema. Thirdly, the increasing rapidity of cutting in action films is recreating that visceral cinema, that assault on the optic nerves inherent in the initial discovery of pictures that moved.

A thread through this history has been the counterpoint of documenting reality, the Lumière Way, with the idea of manipulating reality, the Méliès Way. One might think more broadly still of impressionism seeking to pinpoint and describe the reality before our eyes, versus expressionism using the medium to express new visions of what the world looks like, both externally through the naked eye and internally through the naked imagination. Yet these oppositions hide a myriad of others that make any single polarity inadequate. Consider, for an example, an opposition between the **formalist** film and the **icon-making** film. The attraction of the formalist film showed itself early on. In 1904 Billy Bitzer (who was to become cameraman to DW Griffith) filmed the *Street Car Motor Room of the Westinghouse Works* by mounting the camera on a ceiling gantry and moving it over the whole length of the works, giving an aerial view of the assembly lines and the manifold human action they required. The effect is to take all that human effort and subject it to the all-seeing, all-enduring camera. The men have gone, the works have gone; only the film remains, the formal perfection of which foreshadows Michael Snow's 70-minute zoom across a room in *Wavelength*, and throughout the history of the cinema, film-makers have been mesmerised by what the camera (to take only one formal aspect of cinema) can achieve in its panning, dollying, tracking, gliding, craning, careering. For the icon-making film-makers, on the other hand, such formal concerns are a distraction. For them the main attraction is the showground, the populist recognition of all crude desires and fears. Some ninety years in time separate *Les Vampires* (1915) – in which journalist Philippe Guérande and his sidekick, Mazamette, are engaged in a Manichaean struggle with Irma Vep and her band of *vampires*, led by *un grand vampire*, symbolizing the criminal underworld threatening to take over Paris – and *The Dark Knight* (2008) in which Batman is engaged in a cosmic wrestling match with the Joker for rule of Gotham City: at stake once again is the fragile orderliness of ordinary living and working; only Batman can keep chaos at bay. This opposition, between formalism and icon-making, is one between asceticism and exuberance. Even if the latter strain may make use of formal inventiveness in the way the camera or editing is used, it still subordinates that use to its own extravagant narrative ends. On the other hand, formalism is a quest for spareness which icon-making forever threatens to overwhelm in the pursuit of amazement, awe and thrills but never quite does so: the pursuit of formalism keeps reasserting itself.

The truth is that while the cinema can be shown to be highly sophisticated technically and artistically, its showground quality means it is commonly perceived as crude, as lacking refinement. In the Ancient World, literature was already considered to consist of various branches: among the Nine Muses are those for epic (Calliope), history (Clio), tragedy (Melpomene), comedy (Thalia). Nowadays we have a still greater sense of the diverse forms of literature: prose narrative, poetry (sub-divided into epic, lyrical, satirical etc), drama (sub-divided also), history, biography, philosophy and so on. Yet, although film can now manifest itself in several different ways, for most people film consumption is in watching fictional narrative, in ignorance of or indifference to other ways of appreciating films such as non-fictional narrative, documentary, short narratives, experimental cinema, animated films and so on. There may be a parallel here to the way modern poetry in English, despite its remarkable vigour, sits at the margins of popular consumption of literature.

Although we may be going through a period marked by a cinema of hyperbole, one promising development that will test and change people's perceptions is the erosion of the norm of the feature-length film from the standard two hours, a change brought about as much as anything by the advent of television and then the videotape followed by the dvd. David Lean's *Great Expectations* (1946) and *Oliver Twist* (1948) are 118 and 116 minutes respectively. Both are remarkably successful versions of Dickens's novels, but their narrative spread has been shoe-horned into the feature-length format. More satisfying have been the television adaptations of the novels in which the trickle of Dickens' adaptations has now become a flood - and heritage film-making now embraces several other nineteenth-century authors as well – in order to let the characters breathe, so to speak, since character quite as much as plot is the great strength of Dickens's writing. In this history of adapting Dickens to the screen the most remarkable achievement has been Edzard's *Little Dorrit* (1988), which did three particular things. As with the television adaptations, the characters are paramount. In preparing the script, Edzard even dropped some of the characters (so no Mr Blandois) in order to give proper time to those that were left. Secondly, and again in common with the television adaptations, she paid particular attention to costume, hairstyle and to both exteriors and interiors to give an authentic sense of the 1850s. Thirdly, and here she did something significantly different to her original, she divided the story into two three-hour versions of it, one told through Arthur Clennam's eyes and one through Amy Dorrit's. The two films become one interlocking jigsaw, with the audience making connections for themselves between them, with the second in particular illuminating and enlarging the first. The two films did well in the cinema, but they seem even more ready-made for the dvd era, to be watched from a sofa, to be played back in order to repeat the pleasure of a performance, to go back in order to compare the two versions of the story.

Soap operas were first popular in radio form in 1930s America (and so-called because they were largely sponsored by soap manufacturers), and have been very popular on television for some time. Their episodic nature is very suited to the telling of an extended family story, and the genre was given superlative form in Edgar Reitz's *Heimat* series, a narrative of a German family covering the whole of the twentieth century (see chapter 4). The principal vehicle for screening has been television. *Heimat 1*, covering the life of the central figure, Maria Simon, was conventional enough in form, and elegant, crisp and supple enough in execution to capture the imagination of audiences across Europe: Germany's history, to be handled with care, became our history. *Heimat 3* covering the fall of the Berlin Wall up to the millennium was also straightforward in its approach. These parts were respectively 15 ½ hours and 11 ½ hours. But it was the middle series, *Die Zweite Heimat / Second Heimat*, that really enlarged the sense of what film narrative could achieve: 13 episodes of almost two hours each made 25½ hours of film and the whole constitutes a film equivalent of Proust's 'In Search of Lost Time', as Reitz re-encounters his own student days from the vantage point of maturity. This narrow focus meant audiences who had warmed to *Heimat 1* quickly switched off, but it is *Die Zweite Heimat* that will be studied as an artistic pinnacle of the latter half of the twentieth century. Putting on one side its weaving of the different stories, in its vivid wrestling with Germany's recent history without ever resorting to flashback, in continually finding fresh visual perspectives on the multiple incidents that make up the film, and in the contribution of the composer Nikos Mamangakis who created arguably the most original score of any film in history, its immediate importance will be in having shown future generations how the boundaries of narrative can be extended.

The core of the *Heimat* series is a family saga, even if *Die Zweite Heimat* constitutes an extraordinary digression in this story. Another remarkable television phenomenon has been *The Wire*, consisting of five series, each of twelve 55-minute episodes, which capitalised both on audience fascination with character – the essence of Dickens, and the essence of the soap opera – and on plotting of extraordinary intricacy. The latter is nothing new to film, but the extended narrative of *The Wire* has given plotting a new dimension. Feuillade's *Les Vampires* is one story in ten episodes, but its episodes are largely self-contained. The different episodes of *The Wire* made a virtue of not being self-contained: developments are incomprehensible without an understanding of what has happened earlier, not just within a series, but from series to series giving the whole fifty-five hours particular cumulative power. It could even be said that *The Wire* is a triumph for the screenwriter, so long reduced to playing second fiddle to the director, or even more cruelly, to the producer. The series is the brainchild of David Simon, ex-reporter and writer, and Ed Burns, an ex-police officer. Their credits remain unchanged from episode to episode, but there is a pool of directors who take it in turns to direct episodes, as if for once the script was king. The same comment applies to *Band of Brothers* (2001), an earlier production from HBO to *The Wire* (2002-8). The series was the result of an immense collaborative effort: Stephen Ambrose's original book, the work of Tom Hanks and Eric Jendresen as hands-on producers, a battery of directors and script-writers, Angus Bickerton as Visual Effects Supervisor, Joss Williams as Special Effects Supervisor, Anna Sheppard as costume designer, and a host of others including an army of set constructors and decorators, and even a snow-creating team (for the 'Bastogne' episode). The result leaves little room for auteur-ship, the idea of a single begetter. The largeness of the effort correlates with the length of the final product, which at 705 minutes allows the film narrative to stretch its legs, even if it is constrained not only by the episode format but also by the allowance for appropriate advertisement breaks.

Another hopeful development is in the vehicles for showing short films. For much of the twentieth century, the short film fitted awkwardly into cinemas. Only the short animated cartoon found a regular place in the commercial cinema, and before television performed the function so much better, the short documentary. Otherwise serious short film-making remained at the margins. Artistically, it could flourish in some places, for example in France where it was consciously developed by the state so that the system produced a film like *Night and Fog* [see chapter 4]. In America, the market-driven cinema conquering the world dragged in its wake a vibrant alternative film culture of experimentation, aided by American affluence that allowed professional equipment to be available to people outside the system in a way not conceivable in other countries. This produced an honourable tradition of personal film-making [as revealed in the extraordinary box set *Treasures of the American avant-garde*, distributed by the National Film Preservation Foundation, San Francisco] but it was not until the 1950s, when Stan Brakhage working outside the commercial system jettisoned all norms about length that the potential of personal film-making began to be realised [see chapter 8]. But the accessibility of these films, admittedly in the most niche of markets, remained very difficult. Brakhage even tried to market his films in celluloid form for sale, an experiment rescued from failure by the advent of the dvd, so that the issue of a tiny selection of his vast output in that format in 2003 marks an important moment in preserving his work from oblivion. This is important for a number of other short film-makers as well, for example Norman McLaren, who was able to benefit from the patronage of the National Film Board of Canada, the Scot Margaret Tait who made thirty-three highly personal and original films over almost fifty years, the Czech animator Jan Svankmayer who preceded his career as a feature-length film-maker (*Alice, Little Otik, Faust*) with that as a short film-maker, an apprenticeship in which he became a master, and Robert Breer, the American experimental animator who stuck to the short-film format throughout his career (none of his films is over twelve minutes) despite the difficulties that posed over distribution and even in achieving recognition for his wit and his originality. Encouragingly, computer downloads are particularly apt for the short film; and furthermore the screening of shorts on plasma screens allows them to be shown in a museum setting.

Indeed, changes in how we watch films is bound to have an impact on existing formats, and open up considerable new possibilities in the way films are consumed and appreciated. While the commercial cinema will continue to operate at the spectacular end of the spectrum, offering all-enveloping sound and, in IMAX cinemas, all-enveloping images, this is merely a continuation of the traditional means of conceiving and making films. A much more radical impact on viewing habits, underpinned by the development of home cinema by means of large flat screens, has come from dvds, where we can stop and start them at will, or select particular sections for re-viewing, and from films downloaded on computers, films on laptops or other portable devices including mobile phones (which considerably extends the choice of where to watch). Even that development has now been superseded by the appearance of innumerable film clips on YouTube and other websites, allowing you to refresh your memory of how a particular scene went, an experience that even though imperfect is revelatory. For example, if you want to recall the precise nature of the conversation in the back of a taxi-cab between Terry Malloy (Marlon Brando) and his elder brother, Charlie (Rod Steiger), in *On the Waterfront*, look no further than YouTube where it has been posted by several people revealing a popular obsession with Brando's enunciation of 'I coulda been a contender'. Last but perhaps not least, to these developments can be added the creation of interactive film-watching as exemplified by the popularity of the PlayStation.

Will these new formats lead to a new film grammar or new structures? Not on their own, but they will help. On the other hand, more important than new formats is a new generation of creative film-makers: what countries will they come from? These days it could be anywhere. What will be their cultural background and education? It may be very different from one's own. How far will they be 'cine-literate', first in the history of the cinema then in its possibilities? That poets are born and not made is true of film-makers too, but as with all artists there is a technique to be mastered, and since film-making is so often collaborative, they have to learn how to work with others. Film is old enough too for the idea of 'tradition' to be a relevant one, and new film-makers have to choose between respecting and extending it, or subverting it – which is another way of extending it.

While much has been realised in the first hundred years of cinema, much more remains to be realised in the future: if we think of the history of music as a history of the sequencing and relationship of musical sounds, then the history of the cinema, both past and future, should be a history of the sequencing and relationship of images. Up to now we have only had glimpses of a golden age of the image; we need cine-literate film-makers and audiences who can sustain it.

HISTORY IN TRIADS

And what might this golden age look like? The future is opaque, yet we may still peer into it. Consider a brief history of painting and of music over a period of their history. If we regard sixteenth-century painting – artists such as Leonardo, Raphael and Titian – as exemplifying a classical ideal of the highest-quality draughtsmanship and painterliness, coupled with a mature understanding of perspective and the virtues of harmony and proportion inseparable from the humanist ideals being portrayed, then the Quattrocento period preceding it has an experimental quality – for example, with perspective, with rules of proportion – that creates a different effect, although in the monumentality of Piero della Francesca, for example, one equally profound. Secondly the period following Leonardo's generation – in artists such as Michelangelo, Tintoretto, Veronese, Caravaggio – virtuosic draughtsmanship inherited from their predecessors leads to a stretching of form, to an exaggeration of limbs, to the making of the drama more manifest, to a Mannerist style. Each of these three styles, which we can call pre-classical, classical and post-classical, have validity as art because they respond to different understandings of the world, even if they are closely linked by the fact that the painters of each generation learned from their predecessors and from each other. This triadic pattern can also be traced in musical history. The perfection of classical form in the work of Haydn, Mozart and Beethoven, characterized as the profound exploration of the human perception of musical sounds and their relation to one another and the perfection of the structures of sonata form that is complex yet satisfying, is preceded by a necessary composer like JS Bach, creating music within specific contexts such as church and court, and undertaking the most searching unravelling of the harmonic possibilities of music, that produces its own glories yet which opens the way to rich development. And after Beethoven, the development of symphonic music in composers like Wagner and Mahler took Western classical forms and harmonic language to limits where the musical edifice teeters over. But this teetering over, in both painting and music, does not result in ruin, but in a rebuilding of the edifice. Just as under the impact of photography painting reinvented itself, in the twentieth century music similarly uncovered entirely new directions in which to go.

While this triadic structure may seem tendentious and insufficient to take full account of the complexity of artistic development in painting and music, it does offer some way of structuring artistic history. In like vein, I propose that the first century of cinema can be interpreted in a similar way, not as an absolute master account of what has taken place in time but as offering a structure. So what might a pre-classical/classical/post-classical framework for the cinema looked like?

The pre-classical period can be much more starkly defined than in painting and music. As soon as the cinema was invented, film-makers, even as they had their main eye firmly fixed on turning film-making into a sound business proposition, found themselves experimenting with pictorial and narrative strategies, with the essential creative questions: where do I place the camera in order to take a shot? How do I splice together these shots in coherent, and in compelling sequences? The invention of the talkies in Hollywood and their spread to Europe and Japan accelerated a codification of a grammar of film that developed in the next three or four decades as a classical style, a marriage of strong narrative within the creative potential of camerawork, editing, film music etc. If the initial pre-classical period is a process of excitement at discovering what film can do, the classical period, having formulated a grammar that mass audiences could accept, subordinated that discovery to narrative, or rather harmonised the formal elements with the dictates of narrative, made them invisible as it were, a willingness to work within the bounds set by the commercial system. In Hollywood, the masters of this classical period are film-makers like Ford, Hawks, Huston, Ophuls, Preminger, and outside America film-makers like Dreyer, Carné and Prévert, Renoir, Mizoguchi, Ozu, Powell and Pressburger, Buñuel, Rossellini and so on. However, this mainstreaming of a style did not prevent expressionistic, anti-classical directors like Eisenstein, Hitchcock or Kurosawa flourishing as well, or the austere version of classicism, assembled according to his own rules, of Bresson.

When François Truffaut, writing in 'Cahiers du Cinéma' in the 1950s, attacked the *cinéma de papa* and the tradition of the well-made film, one of the first nails was being driven into the coffin of the classical film. One of the impacts of the Nouvelle Vague was the possibilities it revealed in breaking classical norms. By the early 1960s Antonioni had become a standard-bearer for decelerating narrative while preserving formal rigour, a process taken to new levels by Andrey Tarkovsky. Slow-motion photography exaggerates movement and time, to awe-inspiring effect or, if you prefer, gratuitously and superfluously, and the musical score begins to drown films. An egregious moment occurred when the Swedish *Elvira Madigan* (1967) could not refrain from linking slow-motion photography to the strains of Mozart's Piano Concerto no. 21 to make a cinematic sludge that was to become the norm in the cinema of hyperbole. Underscoring became overscoring. On the other hand narratives are liberated and made much more interesting by the manipulation of cinematic time, as explained in chapter 7. Film-makers expressed their consciousness of film history, and at the margins film historians and experimental film-makers (Andy Warhol, Ken Jacobs, for example) returned to the strategies of the cinema at its dawn in order to analyse them and reveal the quality and nuances of that history.

All this is at the formal level. At the subject level, one can trace a second triadic trajectory going from innocence to cynicism; one might label this triad prelapsarian, lapsarian, and postlapsarian. In the first phase, there is a rejoicing in the new morning of a new art form coinciding with a popular innocence at the portrayal of the physical world on film. The period following the First World War, marked by rapid social change and shifts in global power, leads into classical narrative and, after the Second World War, the emergence of a global industry in which films cross boundaries more easily than any other art form: for example, Western cultural engagement with the Orient is more fruitfully fostered by the revelation of Japanese and other East Asian films than by any other medium. This period from the 1950s to the 1960s is the golden age of genre film-making: Westerns/ samurai films, epics, gangster/yakuza/private eye movies, horror, comedy romantic, comedy satirical and comedy screwball, and so on. Genre film-making is durable because it capitalises on an audience's grasp of the conventions, how they should be played out, what variations are permissible. In calling this period 'lapsarian' I am referring to the way these narratives contain the seeds of their own overthrow, not just in the way genre elements are bent and stretched to disproportionate shapes, but also in the way the cinema rubs against censorship. In its quest for thrilling and provocative subject matter, no subject remains unsuitable for telling. Ultimately this lapsarian phase has led to a postlapsarian one: heroism is deconstructed, cinematic sex and violence are obsessively replayed, cinematic in-jokes are in, innocence is out, cynicism and irony rule. In specific terms, Ford has to give way to Peckinpah: the clinical shootout of *My Darling Clementine* becomes the orgy of blood in *The Wild Bunch*, a film in which the affecting strains of Ford's musical leitmotif, 'Come let us gather at the river', become irrelevancies, hypocrisies even. The heroic Kurosawa of *Seven Samurai* becomes the disordered Kurosawa of *Ran*: samurai battle becomes trapped in epic sweep, endless clash. Digital imagery permits the fantastic: when in *The Lord of the Rings*, Gandalf and his party travel through the Mines of Moriah, they are attacked by orcs, not in handfuls but in thousands. *Reservoir Dogs* reinvents the gangster film as an ironic and knowing narrative; the film noir ends up as satire in *The Big Lebowski*, or as an elegant student exercise in *Brick*. Even Antonioni's cool dissections of human isolation, already extended in *L'Avventura, La Notte, L'Eclisse* and *Red Desert* become the yet more extended alienations of Belá Tarr's *Satantango* or of Angelopoulos.

This postlapsarian, post-classical phase is now four or five decades old, which is a long time in the history of the cinema. Are we ready for something new? A lot depends on the political, social and cultural context throwing up individuals capable of expressing that context creatively. Film-makers are no more the 'unacknowledged legislators of the world' than poets are, but like poets and other writers, composers, painters and all the other artists, film-makers articulate what is happening in the world. Possibly they do this even more than those working in other art forms, since film-making is such a collaborative medium: where the pooling of ideas takes place just as much as the individual assertion of a single vision, the results more readily reflect a consensus on social and cultural values. Secondly, it is such a commercial art form that to survive it has to be in tune with what its audience is thinking, both the domestic mass audience and now the global one. Social history in those countries with major film industries cannot be written now without some reference to the products of its film studios, even the mediocre ones. It is fascinating to look at the history of the Oscars to discover how often the Oscar arbiters chose films of less artistic significance and less durable quality. The winners won because they reflect current notions of artistic quality, but also because they reflect the mores of the times, which may prove ephemeral.

The sense of uncertainty about the future revolves around how a globalised economy will or will not develop, how new technology will or will not shake the world, how far a new hostility between superpowers will or will not develop, whether the existing distrust between Western and Muslim cultures will or will not be resolved. Then there is uncertainty about social and religious values: is a belief in God going to wither away? How will the contemporary fashion for spirituality evolve? Will the institutions of marriage and the family change even further? Will major economic recession change powerfully how people think about the way they are governed? The answers to these questions will be reflected to intense degree in the works of art that society produces. But will they be compellingly reflected? Will the formal opportunities that any art form offers be taken in new utterly unanticipated directions?

A SHAKESPEARE FOR THE CINEMA?

The cinema is yet to produce its Vergil or Shakespeare, its Mozart or Beethoven, its Leonardo or Rembrandt. There is no *a priori* reason why it should not do so, and if it has not, it is only because it needs more time, maybe even several centuries of time. But is the present moment propitious for such a thing to happen?

Writers like Vergil and Shakespeare are singled out as special, because they not only articulated reflections on individual tragedy and mortality, but also portrayed these concerns in the context of political and institutional power. Shakespeare's greatness in part stems from an understanding of power and authority in which the powerful are not a separate demonised or even distrusted class, but tragic victims in the public eye. Even though Hamlet is so preoccupied with himself that his tragedy seems individual and private, which is one reason that this play has a special status in our own times, he is potentially a wielder of authority ("like to have proved most royal," we are told by Horatio), which connects him with the sane and humdrum world. Then there is the range of Shakespeare's work, from tragedy through history to comedy both broad and subtle. To crown all this, his gifts in employing the English language have not been equalled.

Any potential Shakespeare for the cinema now has a considerable body of films and of styles and techniques to draw inspiration from. He or she will be born but not without some process of making; innate gifts are a necessary pre-condition of artistic greatness, but for film-makers there has to be a process of 'making': any individual who is going to change the face of cinema is likely to have to come through film school in order to master the possibilities of the different equipment available, to explore the possibilities of film language, to learn the strengths and pitfalls of film narrative in order to get a sense of how films need not confine themselves to narrative, to realize that other formats than the feature film await them, and perhaps above all to learn the practice of thinking in images.

Will he or she support themselves in the marketplace, or as a result of public patronage? This is as great a conundrum as any. Take the case of Andrey Tarkovsky who, of all the twentieth-century film-makers, thought of his film-making as a mission to create a body of work that would be worthy of comparison with his predecessors such as Pushkin, Dostoevsky, Tolstoy, writers whom the Russian people felt were specially chosen as a source of authority, whom they acknowledged as 'legislators of the world'. Tarkovsky's career is especially vivid because it flourished, if that is the right word, under the auspices of the VGIK, the All-Union State Institute of Cinematography, the state apparatus for Soviet cinema, determining what films should and should not get made. It is in this unpromising context that Tarkovsky is able to make his great epic, *Andrey Roublev*, the size of which derives from the substantial resources put at his disposal, which allowed him to reshoot large sections of the film, and the universality of which was not choked off by Soviet control: out of falsehood came forth truth. It is in this system that Tarkovsky is able to follow *Andrey Roublev* with other projects that pursued private truths of universal import, most notably the sublime meditations of *Mirror*. So, state patronage can be fruitful and several distinguished national cinemas have been created through it in communist countries such as Poland, Czechoslovakia and the Soviet Union. Yet it is also fundamentally true that Tarkovsky's battles with authority over his various projects meant that fewer got made than should have been. More contentiously it could be argued that the emotional difficulties involved with those struggles and then with exile from Russia brought him to an early death at the age of fifty -four, depriving us of 'late Tarkovsky' and a final masterpiece.

Outside the communist bloc, America, Japan and India have relied virtually solely on commercial funding for their industries, the same being true in Britain to a lesser extent since there has been a greater readiness to use public money as seedcorn and the tax-funded BBC has been an important patron. France is more complex still, combining a vibrant commercial system with public support such as quotas to ensure that the distribution of non-French films does not overwhelm the home-grown ones. The achievements of the French cinema cannot be divorced from the role the state has played in creating a framework for it. In Sweden, the Svensk Filmindustri founded in 1919 is much closer to the statist model in terms of the support it gives and in the example of Ingmar Bergman shows how state patronage can create benign conditions for creativity to flourish. So, can the marketplace boast of doing things better than the state model? Not necessarily. Many film-makers have failed to find backing for promising projects. (Bresson conceived his *Lancelot du Lac* in the 1950s yet was only able to make it in 1973; Carl Dreyer wrote a script for a film on Jesus in the late 1940s but despite his best efforts was unable to get funding to make it.) The satirical edge of Altman's *The Player* revolves round the cruel dictates of the market place: Griffin Mill's job at the studio is to hear pitches from writers that could be made into films that will do well at the box office, i.e. their commercial potential is the sole criterion on which his decisions are based. A proposal is made to him for a film called *Habeas Corpus* about a man on death row who only confesses to his role in a case of rape and murder just before his execution, so that his execution takes place against the grain of his confession and request for forgiveness. Mill thinks this an absurd idea for a film, but the studio's internal politics and a threat to his job means he gives the go-ahead to the project and hands it to his rival. It then becomes Mill's role to offer an upbeat ending involving the killer being saved from execution by the last-minute arrival of a reprieve in the form of Bruce Willis. This farrago of ideas both saves the project and saves Mill's position, while showing how the marketplace operates to destroy good projects. Yet *The Player* is only a clever story, Altman's revenge on all those studio bigwigs who had either refused him or interfered. Five years after the film was made, Tim Robbins, who had played the lead role of Griffin Mill in Altman's film, directed a serious and moving version of the *Habeas Corpus* idea as *Dead Man Walking*, downbeat ending and all. The market can be broad: there is a market for cynicism, and a market for compassion. And this breadth can occur in a culture that fully sets forth its multiple ideas in a reflection of the multiple facets of human activity. Despite social constraints and censorship, just such a culture surrounded the Elizabethan dramatists: the plays pleased their audiences, whether they came for serious drama or for comedy or (one hopes) just to hear the poetry, newly minted. In the same way, the studio systems of the twentieth century have allowed creative genius to flourish.

So, what is the nearest the cinema has come to producing its Shakespeare? One characteristic of his genius is an ability to make us understand the motives and mindsets of his characters, even the morally dubious ones. To invent sympathetic fictional figures of authority in the twenty-first century one must steer a course between the whirlpools of despair in the face of the terrifying history of the last century and the rapids of cynicism about the social organisation of humanity, whether by religion or by government. However, there have been possible contenders in the persons of film-makers like Rossellini, Ford, Dreyer. But to look at each of these directors in more detail is to understand the obstacles they faced to the fullest realisation of their genius. Rossellini's humanism, Italian in the first half of his career, of European scope in the second half in the great project he undertook for television (starting with *L'età del ferro* in 1964 through to *Il Messia* in 1975, and including works such as *La Prise de Pouvoir par Louis XIV, Atti degli apostoli, Socrate, Blaise Pascal, Agostino d'Ippona* and so on), has an immense sweep of understanding but there is at present a significant obstacle to a true appreciation of his achievement: while the earlier neo-realist phase is well understood, and while in recent years it has become possible to see – and admire – his work for television from the 1960s and 1970s, the middle decade from around 1954 to ten years or so later remains largely unknown and underassessed.

John Ford having learned his craft before the advent of sound so that the non-verbal (gesture, look, the organization of space, and above all action) became second nature, throughout the rest of his long career did as much as anyone to create a classical conception of how to make films; in addition, he managed to imagine a history of America from the late eighteenth to the twentieth century, and Peter Bogdanovich has remarked: "It would be instructive (in fact schools might do well in making it a regular course) to run Ford's films about the United States in historical chronology [Bogdanovich p.22]." When considered as a whole the sequence reveals a warm understanding of people both in power and at the margins, as well as the dark complexity of that history, and he had the Shakespeare touch in the way he injected colour and humanity into the host of minor characters who appear in his films. All this was done within the constraints of a system requiring constant commercial success, a success that he delivered throughout his career. And yet one feels that the final quality of the highest achievement has been sacrificed for quantity, and because a collaborative system is flawed: Ford was not able to control every element, for example who edited his films or how the musical soundtrack was added. Finally, there is Carl Theodor Dreyer: he simply did not, could not make enough films. His films of the silent era are consistently remarkable but one senses Dreyer is an apprentice, learning not just how to make his own films, but how the grammar of film, less than thirty years old, is drafted. *The Passion of Joan of Arc* is a culmination of this process, but then five sound films over almost forty years, four of which are admittedly superlative – *Vampyr, Day of Wrath, Ordet* and *Gertrud* – are not enough for us to doff our hats to a companion worthy of Shakespeare.

There are other contenders for the crown. What about Jean Renoir? Perhaps forty years ago, he would be a natural candidate for this list because of the warmth and understanding he gives to his characters, but his postwar work has not worn well. What then about Yasujiro Ozu? A long career with several masterpieces on the list, including with *Tokyo Story* one that contains fascinating (even if unconscious) echoes of 'King Lear', but at present their difference from Western culture makes a barrier, albeit a self-imposed Western one. Time and understanding may well change this for the better: the well of sympathy he draws on in creating his characters reveals him as a humanist film-maker of the profoundest kind, and the growing availability of his films (fifty-three feature films in all, of which thirty-one survive) will reinforce an already stellar reputation. And what about present-day directors? The Coen Brothers for example, now with a considerable list of films to their credit, which include both comedies and dramas of excruciating individual dilemmas, a remarkable visual flair, and that rare ability to inject a weighty or 'tragic' element into comic situations, notably in the recent *A Serious Man* and *The Ballad of Buster Scruggs*. Their careers are not over, so it is too early to draw conclusions.

That leaves the director who many may consider to be the strongest contender for the Shakespearean crown, judging by the books and articles that have started to fill the shelves in film-study libraries: Alfred Hitchcock. Although he only died in 1980, the books pour out. In a few centuries' time, will there be enough secondary literature on Hitchcock to found a university department, as is now emphatically the case with Shakespeare? His career spanned six decades; there are almost sixty feature films to his credit, not to mention his work for television. They can be satisfyingly divided into early, middle and late Hitchcock, and at the height of his powers between 1956 and 1964, he directed an outstanding sequence of films: *The Wrong Man, Vertigo, North by North West, Psycho, The Birds* and *Marnie*. He is the supreme chronicler of twentieth-century anxiety. And yet to describe him thus is to give away the reason why he misses the cut: Shakespearean genius requires a humanist foundation, something that has made his plays speak across cultures and across the ages. Do Hitchcock's films do that? Certainly as a master of suspense he could arouse audiences anywhere. He had a remarkable gift, worthy of Shakespeare, for the vivid characterisation of cameo roles. But his heroes, whether English or American, have a brittle quality, and his heroines a heart of ice. It is true on the other hand that no director has made their villains more fascinating. No one does these types better but his sympathies, if that is the right word, were narrow: sensuousness, for example did not interest him. His is not a survey of mankind in all its manifold variety, more an obsession with our neuroses. This speaks powerfully to us now, but will it continue to do so in the following centuries?

So, assuming our Shakespeare of film is yet to be born, what cinematic landscape awaits them? I have tried to indicate in this book some of the riches of style that 120 years of cinema have been able to create, so that there is now a tradition to learn from and to draw upon. Secondly, one can be optimistic for the future that technological change will make it easier to find funding opportunities, whether public or private, and outlets for original work. In terms of production, equipment has become more flexible to use and digital technology increases flexibility still further; in terms of distribution, while films will still be consumed collectively whether in cinemas or through scheduling on television, that form of consumption can now be backed up by making the resultant work as readily available as a novel or a book of poems. Furthermore, the advent of streaming films on a private screen enhances these possibilities enormously Finally, Shakespeare's fame is closely allied to the rise of national consciousness in England as a result of the religious and political upheavals in sixteenth-century Europe. Those conditions won't repeat themselves exactly, but genius will express itself in alliance with some country or grouping or element of society, even if we cannot even guess which these might be.

CONCLUSION

Judgements on the most creative film-makers are by definition premature, since to achieve true greatness their creativity has to last several generations. Will there be a book in the twenty-fifth century entitled 'John Ford Our Contemporary'? We cannot tell. It is the case that the twentieth century has fostered a melancholic view of the artist unappreciated in his or her lifetime dying in obscurity, partial or total, to enjoy a resurrection of reputation only a good while after their death. Vermeer is a case in point: his contemporaries would surely be taken aback by the stellar reputation he enjoys today. Or take JS Bach: his prodigious talents were worked to the full, witness over 250 church cantatas composed for St Thomas's in Leipzig, but it has taken the centuries since his death in 1750 to come to grips with the riches of his music. When Wagner called him "the most stupendous miracle in all music", the miracles of his cello and violin sonatas (for example) were yet to be uncovered. On the other hand, exceptional artistic gifts can be recognized by an artist's contemporaries. When Beethoven died, a significant number of Viennese attended his funeral, the same people no doubt who had been challenged throughout Beethoven's career, perplexed by his latest chamber music, but uplifted and aroused by the way he expanded the possibilities of symphonic music, and dimly aware that in his passing, a person of truly exceptional gifts was gone from the living.

As outlined earlier in this chapter, the notions of pre-classicism, classicism and post-classicism might be applied to the first century of the cinema's history, and the post-classical phase we are now drifting in might create the conditions for new talent to emerge with a fresh approach to using the language of images. But there is an impertinence in this line of thought: to the question, 'What has been the impact of the invention of cinema?' the proper answer is that it is far too early to tell. Under the long view, a century or so is an eye-blink in human history, and much longer than that is needed for cinema's pre-classical phase. In effect, we are still at the beginning of cinema, at the period of inventing and exploring what might be possible, and we must not be pinched in too narrow a timescale. Shakespeare was lucky in a way, coming just as English was renewing itself as a supple, expressive language mixing the hard monosyllables of its Anglo-Saxon origins with the smoothness, softness and *gravitas* of Latinate speech. Buoyed up by a culture of competitiveness between the many gifted playwrights of the Elizabethan era, he moulded his words and his line to his dramatic sense in breathtaking ways. Shakespeare arrived at an understanding of the possibilities of modern English and gave it an inspiration that has so far lasted five centuries. Ben Jonson's poem 'To the Memory of my Beloved, the Author, Mr William Shakespeare', published in 1623, only seven years after Shakespeare's death, indicates how far he was appreciated in his own time: "Soul of the age! . . . not of an age, but for all time!" Intriguingly, Jonson indicates too that the gifts of nature are insufficient on their own, but that the poet must work harder to "write a living line", and concludes: "For a good poet's made as well as born."

So, good film-makers like poets are both made and born. An awareness of, and response to film past is necessary, but it is not sufficient. They need to understand where film future might take us, so that being shaped by the works of the past and trained in the craft of film-making will be the necessary keys to unlocking innate creative gifts. This book has endeavoured to range widely over what the cinema has already achieved, and to pierce the fog of the future to discern the outlines of what great films to come might look like. As new formats are created, as the cinema of excess begins to strangle itself, and as new cultural conditions are created, does the opportunity then exist for a giant step to be taken into the future that will transform the way we perceive and understand stories in images, to turn the showground created yesterday on the wasteland into a sublime palace, built long ago and deeply pleasing to the eye?

AFTERWORD AND THANKS

In 2004, I published 'The Filmgoer's Guide to God', about how the cinema has treated Christian themes and narratives. If it had any merit it was because it sought to value the films concerned through the way the film-makers conceived and realized their stories for the screen. Bresson, Dreyer, Rossellini and Tarkovsky headed my list of film-makers that had tackled Christian themes in a profound, affecting and cinematic way. It was well received in theological magazines and journals but unfortunately was quite ignored by the film press. But the subject continued to fascinate me so that in 2014 I self-published (through Troubador Press) an updated version entitled 'The New Filmgoer's Guide to God'.

In January 2006, suddenly having more leisure, I embarked on a second book, this time concentrating on film aesthetics or, if that is too grand, how films are perceived and received into the imagination. 'Film Past Film Future' has been the result. I have been particularly driven by seeing – and then seeing again – films in the cinema, on dvd, and streamed on the internet, and on thinking about the cinema in relation to drama, literature, painting and music, especially opera. While I did try to read some of the critical and theoretical literature, I am conscious that in doing so I have only peeled back one or two layers of the onion, while remaining aware that there are many more underneath. At the back of my mind has been William Carlos Williams's dictum, "No ideas but in things", and I translate that as including, "No ideas but in the films themselves". Since 2011 a digital version has been available through Amazon, but in view of the reluctance among many people, as I have discovered, to read books digitally, I have self-published this paperback version, which has allowed me to refine the text in places and even to update it – although keeping up with the pace of technological change in the cinema and cultural change in viewing habits and attitudes continues to present a challenge.

I am a freelance writer on film, and do not hold a teaching position at a university. This may be construed as a weakness in this respect, namely that the presentation and defence of my ideas before the discerning young and teaching colleagues would certainly have benefited the book. However, I have had valuable help from several friends whom I thank for their encouragement and advice: Stephen Adamson, Jonathan Hourigan and Professor Janet Montefiore. I have also been stimulated by numerous conversations with my wife, Maggie, about the many films we have watched together, the way they tell stories and what effect they have on the viewer. Another person to thank is my niece, Emma Roebuck, who has helped me with the design of a cover page.

Writing a book like this has been singularly rewarding to me as the author, but I hope that the reader will have derived stimulus and insight as well.

May 2019

BIBLIOGRAPHY

Arthur, Paul 'Stan Brakhage: Four Films' in 'Artforum' (January 1973)

Attwell, Lee 'GW Pabst' (Boston: Twayne Publishing 1977).

Bacon, Francis 'Francis Bacon interviewed by David Sylvester' (London: Thames and Hudson / New York: Pantheon Books 1975)

Barr, Charles 'English Hitchcock' (Moffat, Scotland: Cameron and Hollis 1999)

Barr, Charles and Alain **Kerzoncuf** 'Hitchcock Lost and Found' (Lexington: UP of Kentucky 2015)

Bergman, Ingmar 'Bergman on Bergman: interviews with IB' by Stig Björkman, Torsten Manns, Jonas Sima (London: Secker & Warburg 1973)

Bergman, Ingmar 'Images: my life in film' (London: Faber & Faber 1995)

Bergman, Ingmar 'The Magic Lantern' (London: Hamish Hamilton 1987)

Bershen, Wanda 'Zorns Lemma' in 'Artforum' (September 1971)

Bogdanovich, Peter 'John Ford' (London: Studio Vista 1968)

Bordwell, David and Kristin **Thompson** 'Film Art', fifth international edition (McGraw-Hill 1997)

Bordwell, David 'Film Style' (Cambridge, Mass. and London: Harvard UP 1997)

Bordwell, David 'Narrative in the Fiction Film' (Wisconsin: U of Wisconsin Press 1985)

Bordwell, Staiger and Thompson 'The Classical Hollywood Cinema: film style and mode of production to 1960' (New York: Columbia UP 1985 and London: Routledge 1988)

Boxwell, David 'Anthony Mann' in 'Senses of Cinema' January 2003: http://archive.sensesofcinema.com/contents/directors/03/mann_anthony.html, paragraph headed 'Pain'

Brakhage to Kelly: letter to Robert Kelly, 22 August 1963, in 'Metaphors'

Brakhage to Sitney: letter to P. Adams Sitney, 19 June 1963, in 'Metaphors'

Brakhage, Stan '**Metaphors** on Vision', published in 'Film Culture' no. 30, Fall 1963 (pages unnumbered)

Brakhage, Stan 'Seen' (San Francisco: Pasteurize Press 1975)

Brakhage, Stan '**The Brakhage Lectures**' (Chicago: The Goodlion Press, 1972)

Brakhage/Frampton in 'Stan and Jane Talking' in 'Artforum' (January 1973)

Breivold, Scott 'Howard Hawks Interviews' (Jackson: UP of Mississippi 2006)

Bresson, Robert 'Notes sur le cinématographe'(Paris: Gallimard in 1975) translated as 'Notes on the Cinematographer' (London: Quartet Books 1986)

Bresson, Robert interviewed by Jean-Luc Godard and Michel Delahaye 'La Question' in 'Cahiers du cinéma' no. 178 (May 1966)

Buscombe, Edward in 'The BFI Companion to the Western' (London: André Deutsch/BFI Publishing 1988) s.v. *The Furies* and *The Man from Laramie*

'Cassell's Encyclopaedia of World Literature' vol. 1 second edition (London: Cassell & Co. Ltd 1973) s.v. 'Supernatural story' entry by PJ Stead.

Cawkwell, Tim 'The New Filmgoer's Guide to God' (Kibworth Beauchamp, Leicester: Troubador Press 2014)

Christie, Ian in '"History is now and England": *A Canterbury Tale* in its contexts,' in 'The Cinema of Michael Powell', ed. Ian Christie and Andrew Moor (London: BFI Publishing 2005)

Cooke, Mervyn 'A History of Film Music' (Cambridge,UK: Cambridge UP 2008)

Deleuze, Gilles 'Cinéma I: L'image-mouvement' and 'Cinéma II: L'image-temps' (Paris: Éditions de minuit 1983 and 1985), translated as 'Cinema 1: The Movement Image' and 'Cinema 2: The Time Image' (Minneapolis: U of Minnesota Press 1986 and 1989)

Doane, Mary Ann 'The Voice in the Cinema: the articulation of body and space' in 'Yale French Studies' no. 60 (1980)

Drury, John 'Painting the Word' (New Haven and London: Yale University Press 1999)

Eisenstein, Sergei **'Film Form'**(New York: Meridian Books 1957)

Eisenstein, Sergei **'Film Sense'** (New York: Meridian Books 1957)

Fleishman, Avrom 'Narrated Films: storytelling situations in cinema history' (Baltimore and London: Johns Hopkins UP, 1992)

Frampton, Hollis **'Eadward Muybridge**: Fragments of a Tesseract' in 'Artforum' (March 1973)

Frampton, Hollis **'Meditations** around Paul Strand' in 'Artforum' (February 1972)

Frampton, Hollis entry in **Wikipedia**, http://en.wikipedia.org/wiki/ Hollis_Frampton (June 2007)

Frampton, Hollis interview with Simon Field and Peter Sainsbury in 'Afterimage' (Autumn 1972)

Geister, Michael 'The Battleground of Modernity: Westfront 1918' in 'The Films of GW Pabst' ed. Eric Rentschler (Rutgers UP, New Brunswick and London 1990)

Gidal, Peter 'Andy Warhol: films and paintings' (London: Studio Vista and New York: EP Dutton & Co. 1971)

Gunning, Thomas 'DW Griffith and the Narrator-System: narrative structure and industry organization in Biograph Films 1908-1909' (New York University PhD 1986)

Haggith, Toby and Joanna **Newman** 'Holocaust and the Moving Image' (London and New York: Wallflower Press 2005)

Harrison, Martin 'In Camera: Francis Bacon' (London: Thames and Hudson 2005)

Hedren, Tippi interviewed by Tim Teeman in 'The Times' (London), 11 September 2008

Insdorf, Annette 'Indelible Shadows: Film and the Holocaust' (New York: Random House 1983; the second edition has a foreword by Elie Wiesel (Cambridge UK: Cambridge UP 1989)

James, Clive 'Chamber Music of Horrors' in 'Times Literary Supplement' (31 January 2003)

Kaurismaki, Aki and others 'On Bresson' in 'Sight and Sound' (November 2007)

Keegan, John 'The Face of Battle' (London: Jonathan Cape and New York: Viking Press 1976; Penguin Books 1978)

Kitses, Jim 'Horizons West' (London: BFI Publishing 2004)

Levi, Primo **'The Drowned and the Saved'** (London: Michael Joseph 1988)

Levi, Primo **'The Story of a Coin'** in 'Moments of Reprieve' (London: Michael Joseph 1986)

Levi, Primo **'The Truce'**, translated by Stuart Woolf (London: Everyman's Library 2000)

Lewis, CS 'Of This and Other Worlds' ed. Walter Hooper (London: Collins Fount Books 1984)

Loshitzky, Yosefa (editor) 'Spielberg's Holocaust: critical perspectives on *Schindler's List*' (Bloomington and Indianapolis: Indiana UP 1997)

Milne, Tom 'Time Out Film Guide' (Harmondsworth: Penguin Books, published annually, now discontinued) s.v. '*The Big Parade*'

Montefiore, Janet 'Rudyard Kipling' (Devon: Northcote House 2007)

'Oxford Classical Dictionary' third edition ed. Hornblower & Spawforth (Oxford & New York: Oxford University Press 1996), s.v. 'Erinyes'

Perkins, VF 'Film as Film' in 1972 (Harmondsworth: Penguin Books 1972)

Reader, Keith *Robert Bresson* (Manchester: Manchester UP 2000)

Richie, Donald in 'Cinema: a critical dictionary' vol. 2, ed. Richard Roud (London: Secker & Warburg 1980) s.v. 'Mizoguchi'

Sadoul, Georges 'Dictionnaire des Films' (Paris: Editions du Seuil 1965) s.v. '*Quai des brumes*' and '*Feuillets du livre de Satan*'

Sands, Philippe 'East-West Street' (Harmondsworth: Penguin Books 2016)

Scruton, Roger 'Flesh from the Butcher: how to distinguish eroticism from pornography' in 'Times Literary Supplement' (15 April 2005)

Scruton, Roger 'Photography and Representation' originally published in 'The Aesthetic Understanding' (1983) and reprinted in 'Philosophy of Film and Motion Pictures' ed. Noel Carroll and Jin Lee Choi (Oxford: Blackwell Publishing 2006)

Sebald, WG 'Austerlitz' (Harmondsworth: Penguin Books 2001)

Studlar, Gaylin and Matthew **Bernstein** (ed.) 'John Ford Made Westerns' (Bloomington and Indianapolis: Indiana UP 2001)

Synessios, Natasha 'Mirror' (London: IB Tauris 2001)

Tarkovsky, Andrey 'Sculpting in Time' (Austin: University of Texas Press 1989)

Thompson, David 'Altman on Altman' (London: Faber & Faber 2006)

Ure, Peter 'Arden Shakespeare: King Richard II' (London: Methuen & Co., and Cambridge, Mass.: Harvard UP 1956)

van der Knaap, Ewout (editor) 'Uncovering the Holocaust: the international reception of *Night and Fog*' (London and New York: Wallflower Press 2006)

Vardac, Nicholas 'From Stage to Screen: theatrical method from Garrick to Griffith' (Cambridge Mass.: Harvard UP 1949)

Wieseltier, Leon in 'Yosl Rakover talks to God' by Zvi Kolitz (London: Jonathan Cape 1999)

INDICES

of films: p. 210; of non-film works: p. 213; of names: p. 214; of genres etc. p. 218

INDEX OF FILMS

Bold digits indicate that the film receives more than a passing mention in the text.

INDEX OF NON-FILM WORKS

INDEX OF NAMES

INDEX OF GENRES ETC.

ABOUT THE AUTHOR

Tim Cawkwell is a freelance writer on film and other subjects, having launched in 2008 his own website for writing about the cinema, www.timcawkwell.co.uk, later adding to it a Wordpress blog, www.cawkwell200.com. Sforzinda Books is the name of his self-publishing venture.

From 1968 to the 1980s he was a film-maker working initially in 8mm and then in 16mm. His dvd LIGHT YEARS – THE FILM DIARIES OF TIM CAWKWELL 1968 TO 1987 was released in 2018.

He is the author of several books on film, travel and cricket:

- *The World Encyclopaedia of Film* (co-editor, 1972)
- *Temenos 2012*, a diary about the Temenos film festival in Greece in 2012 (digital only)
- *From Neuralgistan to the Elated Kingdom: a personal journey inside Sicily* (2013, digital only)
- *Between Wee Free and Wi Fi: Scotland and the UK belong surely?* (2013, digital only)
- *The New Filmgoer's Guide to God* (2014, Troubador Press)
- *A Tivoli Companion* (2015, Sforzinda Books)
- *Cricket's Pure Pleasure: the story of an extraordinary match – Middlesex v. Yorkshire, September 2015* (2016, Sforzinda Books)
- *The Tale of Two Terriers and the Somerset Cat: the County Championship 2016* (2017, Sforzinda Books)
- *Belaboured. Bats Broken. Britain Shaken – a personal account of the 2017 General Election* (2017, Sforzinda Books)
- *Compleat Cricket: eight days in September* (2018, Sforzinda Books).
- *Bittering, Norfolk, Lost and Found* (2019, Sforzinda Books)

He was born in 1948 and lives in Norwich in the United Kingdom.

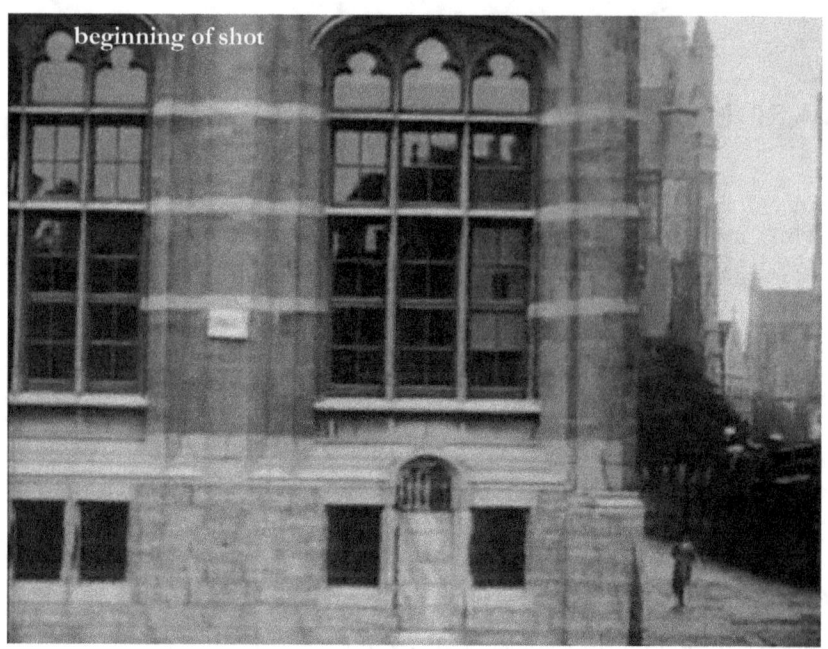

beginning of shot

Visual grace: the drama of André Antoine's *L'Hirondelle et le mésange* (1922) has a background on the canals between France and Belgium. It includes a 160-second 'Passage through Ghent' which takes pleasure in the floating quality of the solid buildings traversed by the film camera located on a barge.

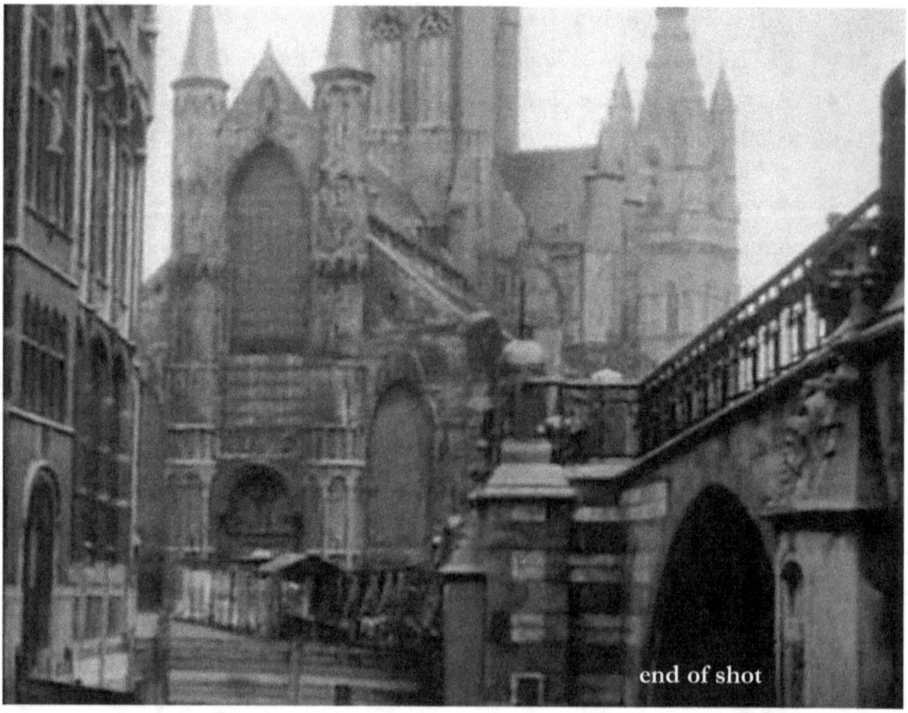

end of shot

www.ingramcontent.com/pod-product-compliance
Lightning Source LLC
Chambersburg PA
CBHW071256220526
45468CB00001B/157